Public Policy Values

Also by Jenny Stewart

THE DECLINE OF THE TEALADY: Management for Dissidents

THE LIE OF THE LEVEL PLAYING FIELD: Industry Policy and Australia's Future

RENEGOTIATING THE ENVIRONMENT: The Power of Politics
(*co-author with Grant Jones*)

Public Policy Values

Jenny Stewart
Australian Defence Force Academy
Professor of Public Policy
University of New South Wales, Australia

© Jenny Stewart 2009

All rights reserved. No reproduction, copy or transmission of this publication may be made without written permission.

No portion of this publication may be reproduced, copied or transmitted save with written permission or in accordance with the provisions of the Copyright, Designs and Patents Act 1988, or under the terms of any licence permitting limited copying issued by the Copyright Licensing Agency, Saffron House, 6-10 Kirby Street, London EC1N 8TS.

Any person who does any unauthorized act in relation to this publication may be liable to criminal prosecution and civil claims for damages.

The author has asserted her right to be identified as the author of this work in accordance with the Copyright, Designs and Patents Act 1988.

First published 2009 by
PALGRAVE MACMILLAN

Palgrave Macmillan in the UK is an imprint of Macmillan Publishers Limited, registered in England, company number 785998, of Houndmills, Basingstoke, Hampshire RG21 6XS.

Palgrave Macmillan in the US is a division of St Martin's Press LLC, 175 Fifth Avenue, New York, NY 10010.

Palgrave Macmillan is the global academic imprint of the above companies and has companies and representatives throughout the world.

Palgrave® and Macmillan® are registered trademarks in the United States, the United Kingdom, Europe and other countries.

ISBN-13: 978-0-230-55400-9   hardback
ISBN-10: 0-230-55400-8   hardback

This book is printed on paper suitable for recycling and made from fully managed and sustained forest sources. Logging, pulping and manufacturing processes are expected to conform to the environmental regulations of the country of origin.

A catalogue record for this book is available from the British Library.

Library of Congress Cataloging-in-Publication Data
Stewart, Jenny.
　Public policy values / Jenny Stewart.
　　p. cm.
　Includes bibliographical references and index.
　ISBN-13: 978-0-230-55400-9 (alk. paper)
　ISBN-10: 0-230-55400-8
　1. Policy sciences—Moral and ethical aspects.   I. Title.
　H97.S77 2009
　172—dc22   2009013643

10 9 8 7 6 5 4 3 2 1
18 17 16 15 14 13 12 11 10 09

Printed and bound in Great Britain by
CPI Antony Rowe, Chippenham and Eastbourne

For Timoshenko

Contents

Acknowledgements	viii
Introduction	1
1 What Are Policy Values?	14
2 Value Conflict and Policy Change	33
3 Implementing Fairness	47
4 The Impact of Efficiency	68
5 Values and Policy Instruments	87
6 Where Policy Meets the Personal	108
7 Values and Public Management	124
8 Greenness and Growth	146
9 Universality and Choice in Health and Education	170
10 Conclusion	186
Notes	207
References	208
Index	226

Acknowledgements

Thanks are due to the University of Canberra for supporting the research upon which this book is based. I am grateful to Bob Goodin, John Dryzek, Alex Millmow, John Braithwaite, John Halligan and Alison Stewart for reading and commenting upon various chapters in draft form. Christine Nam provided useful research assistance.

Chapter 2 is a revised and extended version of my paper 'Value conflict and policy change', which appeared in the *Review of Policy Research* for January, 2006.

Jenny Stewart
Canberra

Introduction

The belief that governments should make a positive difference to our lives remains as strong as ever, even if there is a veritable industry of books about how they are getting it wrong. Governments (we are told) are the captives of large corporations; they are enslaved by simplistic ideologies about market forces; they subvert true democracy; they are not to be trusted; their bureaucracies are incompetent. Every day, even (or perhaps especially) in countries that are blessed with relatively stable and competent governments, the media bring out stories of regulators that did not do their jobs properly, of services poorly delivered, of the weak and vulnerable left unprotected.

If citizens did not believe that governments should do better, they would simply accept these shortcomings as inevitable. The fact that the public face of government is about trying to do better suggests that for many, perhaps most of us, governance is a values-based activity. If public policy is, as Thomas Dye defined it, what governments choose to do or not to do (Dye, 2005, p. 1), it is of enormous importance whether they choose to do good things or bad things. For a political scientist, however, to write a book about the place of values in public policy is to argue uphill. Political scientists wonder about what governments actually do, as distinct from what they ought to do, or even what they say they do. While most observers would agree that values – principled goals – come into the picture, the concept has not previously been accorded explicit attention by policy analysts.

The reasons are not far to seek. Values are tricky to capture, changeable and much less robust than the more familiar forces of self-interest. Rather than seeing values as playing an independent or even quasi-independent role, most commentators have preferred to view the language of values as a device for the prosecution of self-interest.

Scratch a protestation of 'security' or 'freedom' or 'family values' and underneath it, according to this view, we find something much grubbier. If politics is about who gets what when and how, and public policy is the delivery mechanism, there would seem to be little to be gained by worrying about a values dimension in public policy.

This book is an attempt to correct that assumption, not by arguing that a values-based approach should supplant others, but by showing how a values perspective helps us understand more fully what public policy does and the way it does it. Interests can (and do) push and pull governments in different directions, but once the decision is made – the dam is built, the road goes through, the troops are despatched to war – a choice between values has also been made. This is the key point to observe. Whatever forces go into the production of public policy, the result is always a compromise between different value positions.

Sometimes the compromise is seen explicitly in values terms, as when the war on terror obliges policymakers to trade off personal freedom against security. But whether they are explicit or implicit, in every policy field, we find conflicts between powerful values that structure the kinds of decisions that can be taken. These values run so deep that we are often not conscious of them – indeed many of our administrative practices and routines are de facto devices for avoiding value conflicts that would otherwise paralyse us. This book is an attempt to give these values a cogent reality and to suggest ways that the 'values analysis' of public policy might be taken forward.

My awareness of the importance of policy values developed gradually during the course of my teaching and research, so it will be useful to describe how each influenced the other. When I began to teach students about public policy in the early 1990s, I introduced them, as such courses traditionally do, to the many theories about the nature, purposes and origins of public policy. We discussed the way policies were structured, or biased, by the operations of power in general and of self-interest in particular.

Oddly, though, I found that interest-based theories of policy (such as public choice theory) went over like a lead balloon. It was not that students could not see that self-interest explained a good deal of political behaviour. Australians are all too ready to see politicians as charlatans. But whether they were school leavers or more mature students with public service jobs, there was considerable resistance when we went through the basic theorems of rational choice politics. Indeed most theories of public policy, whether of the rational choice variety or more interpretivist in character, left them cold. Students wanted to engage with the subject matter of public policy in ways that made sense to them in terms of their own values and interests. They also wanted to know more about the political and policy history of their own country.

As the course developed, I did not give up on the theoretical understanding of public policy, but I emphasised more strongly what public policy was for – what those who discussed, or advocated, about public policy were actually trying to achieve, and what had happened as their hopes were turned into practice. As a former public servant with a good deal of programme administration experience, I paid a good deal of attention to the problems of implementation, that mysterious yet crucial set of activities where the hopes of activists were so often dashed.

Increasingly, I found myself discussing values as a way of connecting public policy with the political process. This was not precisely Fischer and Forester's 'argumentative turn', which stresses the role of language itself in framing problems in political ways (Fischer and Forester, 1993), but a strategy for delivering signposts, for mapping the terrain of action and thought. We can readily see that a particular public policy – for example, giving public support to non-government schools – benefits some group or interest. It would be a rare public policy that did no one any good, although I can certainly think of some (ironically, some of the most idealistic) that have come close.

But (to revert to the education example) 'telling the story' of the financing of education simply as a kind of interest-based vector analysis would tell us very little about educational administration in a country of which we knew little. To understand this policy, we would need to understand the context in which it was applied, the way in which education was socially constructed in that society. We would need to know something of the politics in the sense of the way the interests had lined up, the battles that had been fought and the words that the combatants had used to press their case.

To be sure, the arts of analysis had then to be applied to these understandings. When policy stories were told, it was necessary to draw on many themes to make sense of what had happened. To use one notable definition of public policy, it was necessary to discuss relationships between institutions, values, interests and resources (Davis, Wanna, Warhurst and Weller, 1993). But somewhat to my surprise, I found the values element coming increasingly to the fore. I could see that when governments did their policy choosing, it was overwhelmingly value choices that they made.

If values were as important as I thought they were, it seemed to me that it ought to be possible to use values analytically. I began to use values as a type of heuristic, as a way of interrogating policy in new ways. As time went on, I came to see how what I initially called policy 'tropes' could be used as a way of structuring policy problems. In most policy fields we could see evidence of these struggles, which could be metaphorised as tensions between values pairs. Some of the pairs I used for teaching in the 1990s included multiculturalism versus integration; globalisation versus autonomy; conservation versus development; obligation versus entitlement; public versus private; centralisation versus devolution; accountability versus responsiveness; secular versus religious values.

These 'deep structures' could be used analytically as a way of illuminating change and identifying significant friction points. But there was also a language of values, an overt use of values to describe favoured directions. President George Bush, for example, was fond of using the word 'freedom' as a way of justifying his policies. When politicians started using the language of values in order to justify a particular course of action, they were almost certainly up to something. But this, in turn, was a good way of describing one of the classic tactics of agenda management – the use of potent symbols to harness attention and entrench support.

Australian Prime Minister John Howard was particularly adept at this form of symbolic politics. In June 2004, for example, his government announced a new educational policy: as a condition (among a number) for the payment of direct Commonwealth funding, all Australian schools would be required to acquire a flagpole and to fly the Australian flag (ABC, 2004). The proposal made sound political sense, as it appealed to Howard's constituency, those who wanted schools to reinforce traditional Australian values. The flag stood for many things, among them an antipathy to the multiculturalism that Howard had successfully opposed since his election in 1996.

Here was a policy about values. But its outcome, a flagpole outside a school, belonged in the realm of symbolism, rather than improved educational practice. In any case, as many commentators pointed out at the time, most schools already had their flag and flagpole. They did not need the Commonwealth government to bully them in this way. In this case, values were being used in the way a public choice theorist would expect them to be used – as a means for defining and harnessing political support.

But it would be difficult to argue that the government invented the values concerned. Rather, Howard was responding to public sentiment, widely held at the time, about the importance of traditional values in schools (Lewis, 2007). The politics (and undoubtedly his own personal views) made that concern a government concern. From the point of view of the policy-attentive public, it was another salvo in the ongoing culture wars, in Australia less a matter of courting the religious right as of attacking left-leaning practice and opinion. The purely symbolic policy reflected back to the PM's supporters a version of their own patriotism, in contrast to the (supposedly) wishy-washy views of the policy elites. The gesture worked, precisely because it was divisive.

On the other hand, it was undeniable that the pursuit of more idealistic values was no guarantee of success. In Aboriginal affairs, policies intended to promote equality had led to little practical improvement in the lives of many Aboriginal Australians. For example, the 1966 policy of the Australian government to award equal pay to Aboriginal stockmen working in the Northern Territory arguably began a disastrous era of welfare dependency for many remote communities, because employers were not prepared to pay them the new wage. It appeared that new values, inserted into complex and changing societies with their own values and traditions, had little chance of realisation in their own terms.[1]

In teaching students about public policy, the question of personal values inevitably came up. Many of my students came from country towns, and their views about most policy issues, once they realised they were allowed to express them, were very conservative. We had to address the question as to whether policies founded on their values would be likely to work. Then there was the question of my own values as an academic policy analyst. What was I trying to achieve? Having worked for many years as a public servant, I was keen to show ways in which policy might be made better. But 'better' was clearly a subjective term, impossible to divorce from one's personal orientation towards policy and habitual ways of making sense of the world.

My introduction to research in the field of policy analysis came through industry (industrial) policy, now a much less important subject for study than it was in the 1980s, when the governments of nation states were attempting to come up with policy responses to the rapid post-war industrial growth of Japan, and subsequently, of other Asian states, such as Taiwan, South Korea and Hong Kong. Industrial policy encompassed so much – the role of the state in the economy, the nature of the evidence about public support for private business, the pressing concerns of intensifying global competition. For most economists, the verdict was clear-cut – free trade was best. For political scientists, it was a more difficult question. Political scientists study the state – it was only natural that we should want to prove the effectiveness of states in more areas than simply the redistributive.

My own background was unusual in that my father ran a manufacturing company. Public choice theory had it that he was a 'rent-seeker', a man who lived off the fruits of tariff protection. Indeed, I was astonished to learn that the entire family was sustained in this illicit way. This was a thrilling but also a somewhat unsatisfactory description of the true situation. Far from exhibiting a rent-seeking mentality, my father was passionate about what he did, keen to develop and employ new engineers and always looking for new business opportunities.

It was almost impossible to reconcile the often bitterly competitive world my father described, with the way manufacturing was viewed from Canberra, my home since the mid-1970s and the seat of economic rationalism in Australia. From being national heroes, as they had been seen in the 1960s, manufacturers were now social pariahs. By the 1980s, the tide was running out for Australian manufacturing industry. Production patterns were changing as low-cost competitors emerged in Asia. The dominant values were also changing, away from supporting a manufacturing presence to an embrace of globalisation and international competitiveness.

As industry moved, particularly to the giant manufacturing house of China, interest in industrial policy waned. Tariff battles (except for a few remaining areas) receded into the past. Flexible exchange rates (the dollar was floated in 1984) seemed a more effective answer to the problem and certainly one that involved much less work from governments. In Australia, a late and unusual industrialiser, the structural shift in the economy was rapid. The pull of resource-based industries became relatively even stronger, and a growing population with an avid demand for houses and gadgets to put in them kept services-based employment buoyant.

I came to see that my own interest in Australian-based production, the encouragement of science-based industry and the use of public purchasing to promote industry, were themselves based on my own values. I argued that much had been lost in the pursuit of an abstract efficiency. Bowing to the dictates of something called 'the market' seemed to be to give up our sense of agency to an abstraction. 'The market' seemed to me then (and still does) to be a good servant, but a bad master (see Stewart, 1994). Subsequently, I became interested in public action in many fields – in relation to environmental questions and, later, education. The more I looked at these fields, the more it seemed to me that finding ways of bringing interests together to solve problems meant talking about values. But there was not much scope to bring this aspect out into the open.

One of the main problems, I found, was the schizophrenic character of policy studies: the split between policy analysis as a form of normative social action and policy analysis as a mode of positivist explanation. From the point of view of those who 'do' policy, public policy is about values (although those same people may well decry the short-termism and expediency of political decision-making). Harold Lasswell, the founder of policy analysis as a distinctive intellectual process, was always clear about the importance of values. In his view, public policy existed to improve the world, so that as a rational and principled activity, it could scarcely avoid the task of values clarification (Lasswell, 1948, p. 122). But policy studies did not follow this lead, preferring to move in more positivist directions. Within this approach, public policy was considered as a dependent variable – the main empirical studies of the 1970s and 1980s considered what were the key factors, in terms of the known categories of political science, that produced particular outcomes – the relative strengths of parties of the left, for example, in determining the salience of welfare policies (see, for example, Castles, 1982, 1989).

In the final decades of the twentieth century, positivism beat something of a retreat. We started to be more wide-ranging in our thinking about the nature of public policy – it was clearly not a thing but a kind of activity or perhaps many different kinds of activity. As Colebatch put it, public policy could be regarded as authoritative choice, as structured interaction or as the construction of meaning (Colebatch, 2002). With these more nuanced approaches, we came to see that the theories that we used were not alternatives that could be proved or disproved, but were perspectives or lenses, which brought some things into focus, while leaving others blurry.

A particularly useful lens focused on public policy as itself being part of a process involved in the creation of meaning. Yanow opened up an interpretivist way of looking at policymaking and policy implementation that understood the policy process as 'a struggle for the determination of meanings' (Yanow, 1996, p. 19) and a policy itself as an expression of the meanings communicated in 'interpretive communities' of policymakers, implementers and their wider (potential) publics (Grin and Loeber, 2007). Values are more obviously involved in this way of seeing policy, because our cognitive maps are themselves predicated in complex ways on what we believe about the state of the world and what we would like it to be. From an interpretivist perspective, values are part of the currency of communication that enables action to be taken.

Institutionalist theory, too, gave a role to values, particularly in relation to organisational cultures. Schneider and Ingram gave prominence to this aspect of policy design, when they described the processes through which institutions perpetuated themselves by recruiting, indoctrinating and rewarding members who will reflect the dominant culture. Public policies themselves 'construct' their clients in ways that reflect a certain social framing of the issues (Schneider and Ingram, 1993, p. 76–77). This kind of work raised fresh questions about the nature of policy implementation. For decades, scholars had grappled with this infuriatingly vague, yet vital, activity through which policy plans were carried out in the real world. Yet there was a disconnect between the way public administrationists (and public managers) thought about implementation and the value-laden world that Schneider and Ingram had opened up. Government is not a post-modern activity, and public servants are rational beings who are required to achieve designated outcomes. But at the same time, the choice-making of implementation raises as many value questions as does policy design itself.

Meanwhile, the study of public administration was emerging from a long period of stasis, with interesting consequences for the link with public policy. It had long been known that administration as a form of rational order simply cannot operate on an ad hoc basis. In order to carry out their work, public agencies required operating instructions – public policies had to be turned into regularised decision-making. New techniques in public management enlarged the implementation choices that had to be made. Do we outsource, or do we keep the work in-house? What kinds of criteria do we employ for selecting contractors? Inside its bland and technical camouflage, public administration was values all the way down.

As I grappled with these issues, it became clear that what I was doing was finding a way of joining the 'inside' of public policy (the way practitioners saw it) to the 'outside' (the way academics saw it), in a way that the more I experimented with it, the more it seemed to offer rich possibilities for discovery. The individual chapters of *Public Policy Values* record this process of discovery across a number of fields. The technique that emerges from this process – values analysis – is less a proposition about the nature of public policy than it is a methodology for understanding it better.

Structure of the book

Using values analytically means choosing values to write about. The potential list is enormous. Identifying dominant societal values at any point in time narrows the field, but societal values are difficult to pin down.

The very act of trying to clarify them seems to cause them to change their contours. At the level of public policy, however, the task of identifying values is a good deal easier because public policies often tell us the values with which they are concerned. The familiar categories of 'adjectival' public policy – environmental policy, health policy, education policy – yield a rich harvest of values, expressed through debates, commentaries and, often, legislation itself.

Choosing which values to write about from among these possibilities is a somewhat arbitrary exercise. Some policy values, such as efficiency or equity are too ubiquitous in the sense that they are too prominent in discussions about policy to leave out. Similarly, the choice of 'greenness' and 'growth' reflects a policy debate too prominent to overlook. The choice in other cases was determined by the 'reach' of the values concerned, that is, the extent to which they illuminated significant areas of policy and/or demonstrated common themes across different areas of policy. I am not, of course, suggesting that the values I have dealt with are in any sense definitive or even representative of the range that might be covered. My hope is that other scholars, working in many different contexts, will identify and utilise values that suit their purposes.

My job was not to evaluate policy, rather, it was to develop and describe a convincing schema for the analytical use of values. They had, in a sense, to be 'inside' the policies, in the sense that they were evident in the actual intent. But to see them I had to be 'outside' the realm of application, which meant taking a comparative perspective. The extent to which the exercise became comparative was something of a surprise. Looking only within the one system seemed to blur the picture because, although I had started with working definitions of the values I was interested in, their contours in practice were not always sharp-edged. The values became clearer when I examined the ways in which other polities had either chosen to effect a different values balance or had achieved a similar values outcome in a different way.

Each of the chapters is self-contained, but it will be necessary for the reader to read Chapters 1 and 2 fully to understand the theoretical approach. Chapter 1 sets out the schema for values, drawing a connection between political and policy values and 'naming' policy values in a straightforward way. It is here that the dichotomous nature of many policy value pairs is first drawn out. Often, a value is only truly identifiable through its opposite. Searching for a strongly contrasting values pair is often a good way for 'seeding' an analysis.

Chapter 2 makes a contribution to the theory of policy change. Just as Berlin had argued for the incommensurability of values

(Berlin, 1998, p. 241), so it seemed that many structures were created for the purpose of avoiding the value conflict that this incommensurability entailed. Public policy is not often given to the grand gesture: it works because the deeper questions with which it deals overall are avoided when it comes to making administrative decisions. The key understanding developed through Chapter 2 is what Rose has called the 'heritage effect' (Rose, 1990). Policymakers, those sitting at the top of the policy tree, think that they are making zero-based policy. In fact, their initiatives are piled into a system that is rigid with the effects of previous decisions. These effects continue to exert significant motivating power.

Using values analytically means coming up with specific, working definitions. Chapter 3 considers 'equity', the principle of justice or non-discrimination and 'fairness', the principle of just deserts or legitimate equivalence. These values are ubiquitous in policymaking, with numerous possible sites for considering them. In this case, I have chosen the conventional context of modern welfare states, where policy is confronted with the task of maintaining an equal society when global competitiveness is demolishing older accommodations. But asking whether welfare states achieve equity or not does not tell us anything new – welfare states have been extensively evaluated from this perspective. Looking at value conflicts, however, yields a different perspective. Chapter 3 highlights the motive power of fairness, an equally powerful value, in stimulating change.

Efficiency (Chapter 4) was another obvious value to choose. Efficiency prioritises the relationship between costs and benefits. In the post-1980s period, the concept of efficiency guided policy-framing and decision-making in an obvious way in every advanced industrial society. But considering efficiency as a value – as a goal that is not self-evidently correct but can be chosen (or sacrificed) in relation to others – provided a useful link between the 'inside' and the 'outside' and between the paradigm of economic analysis and the politics of economic management. Other chapters cover specific policy fields from a values perspective. Chapter 5 extends the approach to the analysis of policy instruments, using the ordering values pair of toughness versus tenderness. 'Toughness' – the insistence on self-reliance – is contrasted with 'tenderness' – the view that help and support are required to overcome disadvantage. This contrast enabled me to bring together discussion of drugs policy, unemployment benefits and (an area often overlooked in policy analysis) criminal justice.

One of the most revealing explorations is in Chapter 6, 'Where policy meets the personal', in which I look specifically at areas of public policy where human relations are mediated most extensively by the state, such as marriage and the family. It is territory where social and economic change has had a huge impact. Attitudes towards marriage, work and the family have undergone a revolution since the middle of the twentieth century. But the way public policy reflects new ways of thinking and provides rationales and means for new kinds of decisions is often partial, oblique and contested. So many spheres of action have been created that it is almost inevitable that there will be interference effects. Family law, for example, has changed not solely because of the women's movement, but because of intersections between values expressed in one sphere (for example, the provision of benefits for single parents) and the institution of marriage. Helping single parents may mean letting their former partners off the child-support hook. These friction points come to government attention when they affect interests large enough to weigh on public budgets.

Public administration, in contrast to its somewhat dusty image, is a field replete with values. In Chapter 7, I discuss some of the key trade-offs that shape both the trajectories of public organisations and the debates about them. Values such as 'responsiveness' (doing what ministers want) and 'independence' or 'autonomy' (reserving a public interest role to public servants) animate continuing tension and debate. Chapter 8 explores what is undoubtedly the most significant value conflict humanity currently faces: that between 'green-ness' and 'growth'. 'Green-ness' is broadly defined as the embodiment of environmental concern in policy. 'Growth' is the familiar emphasis on expansion (in employment and output). In this chapter, I show both the effects of implementing these two values and use the analysis to explore the likely future of these attempts.

Health and education are similarly values rich. The challenge here is to choose a values pair sufficiently broad to illuminate policy dynamics in a number of states. Two values – those of universality and choice – are significant motivators of policy in both fields. Universality describes the objective of common provision for all and choice the objective of competitive provision. The trade-off between universality and choice structures the kinds of choices that are available and establishes contrasting value positions between different states. Interestingly, this comparative perspective suggests that rigidity in implementing certain kinds of values may work against their achievement.

Writing about public policy in this way may seem somewhat impressionistic. The reality is that an enormous amount of detailed knowledge is required in order to 'get right' the complex values balances that appear in the policy ledgers of individual countries. Consequently, the reader will find that the country with which I am most familiar – Australia – appears more frequently in my examples than any other. I have leavened this emphasis with a wide range of instances and examples from other countries (principally New Zealand, the United Kingdom and the United States) because understanding values stances must involve comparison across space, as well as across time. But I make no apology for the Australian emphasis.

To do otherwise would have required the assignment of individual authors to specific countries, the usual approach when comparative public policy is attempted. There have been many excellent studies using this approach, but the present exercise required the use of comparison within each chapter. Moreover, the book had to be anchored in a specific way. A good part of the point of the values-based approach is that it requires the practitioner of it to interrogate and develop his/her own sensibility as a tool of analysis. It is my hope that others will be inspired to develop accounts of public policy in their own countries and societies, using the concepts developed here.

As with any methodology, the measure of its worth will be its utility. The concluding chapter reflects on the nature of this utility. After reviewing the nature of the contribution made by each of the chapters, I bring together a number of implications for the understanding of policy process. These relate to the importance of administrative realities and the need to address deeper levels of structure in comparative work. I also argue, more ambitiously, that an appreciation of values allows analysts to find ways of joining the 'inside' to the 'outside' of public policy, that is, to come up with arguments for change based on a deeper understanding of the ways values are allocated.

To see how this works, it must be accepted that *Public Policy Values* is an exploration rather than a journey. The world that the book explores is in many ways a paradoxical one. Values matter profoundly in public policy, but their influence is deep-seated rather than obvious. Despite the many complexities, our attempts to improve a particular circumstance or solve a problem reverberate through a complex world of administration and negotiation to emerge in the production of effects that will invariably disappoint the idealist. In short, 'something happens' to our cherished goals when we attempt to enact them through policy. To understand what this 'something' is we need to step from the inside of public policy to the outside.

Taking this step shows us a world in which valued goals are refracted through multiple administrative realities. But paradoxically, the key to understanding these realities is found within the original values, rather than in the elaboration of process, or the changing parameters of technical issues. These things are important, but they take their cue from and are structured by different value positions. Public policy values are not the big ideas of truth, freedom and justice. Rather they are a welter of valued orientations – conservation, privacy, equality of access and so on. Nevertheless, their sum total will represent what a society has achieved in these directions.

These value positions are often linked to interests, but to describe them as ideologies puts the cart before the horse. An ideology is a value with hardening of the arteries. Interests can never be separated from values – both motivate our political activity. But the space we allocate to values should be a larger one than is customary in political science. It is almost as if, over time, the original interests wash out, and what we are left with is an elaborate array of settings, instructions and requirements, a kind of moral architecture that is given life by the people who interpret and inhabit the edifice. Exploring the edifice is a rewarding activity. Ultimately, though, the worth of any approach is its usefulness. The technique, further elaborated in the concluding chapter, is a rich and exciting one. Intuit the values from your understanding of a policy field, then trace them onwards and outwards: this is policy analysis for the broad scope and the long term.

1
What Are Policy Values?

Our values, to use Berlin's words, are 'what we think good and bad, important and trivial, right and wrong, noble and contemptible' (Berlin, 1998, p. 127). By extension, policy values are the valued ends embodied in, and implemented through, the collective choices we make through policy processes. Values are also functional. From a psychological perspective, they can be 'thought of as priorities, internal compasses or springboards for action' (Rezsohazy, 2001). A policy value, therefore, can be defined as the informing principle of collective action: it is both motivator and object. A public policy constructs a sense of reality by orientating both observers and participants in a kind of emotional space. The values it represents are the mechanisms of this orientation – sometimes explicit, sometimes implicit.

Policy values are related to political values, but they are conceptually distinct from each other. Political values – such as freedom, democracy, equality – underpin the broad design principles of the governments of nation states and change very little over time. Policy values manifest themselves in particular areas of government action – such as in the design of health systems, or in the support given to regions – and change over time, usually slowly, but sometimes quite quickly.

Why worry about policy values? There are a number of important reasons. Firstly, many policy problems are values based in an explicit way, for example, whether to ban the wearing of the hijab, whether to liberalise (or tighten) drug laws, whether to permit the harvesting of foetal stem cells to treat certain diseases, whether to preserve a heritage site against development. Secondly, in a deeper sense, all policy questions are values-based. David Easton called politics 'the authoritative allocation of value' (Easton, 1965). Public policy is the process through which this happens.

Giving values their place

Despite their omnipresence, values tend to be under-acknowledged when public policy is dissected or explained. They are 'leached out' of positive policy analysis in favour of interest-based and institutionalist approaches. This is not to say that values are forgotten, but they are subsumed within accounts of the policy process itself – manifested 'in action' through the activities of interest groups and implicit in the way institutions are designed. This emphasis is understandable, because while values are clearly important, they are difficult to detect and almost impossible to measure. Interests, institutions and even ideologies are much more tangible. Moreover, if we want to explain why a particular policy change has occurred, or how a new policy has come about, our policy 'story', at least in the qualitative traditions of post-behavioural political science, will draw on the tools of agenda analysis, the depiction of political and deliberative action and the responses of interests to events.

Interests are thought of as 'vectors' or carriers of value. But this approach is unsatisfactory for a full understanding of public policy because, in the analytical sense, a value is quite different from an interest. We can negotiate, more or less rationally, about our interests, assuming we can define them sufficiently clearly. On the other hand, because values relate to beliefs about what is right or wrong, good or bad, desirable or undesirable, we find it almost impossible to negotiate about them. If, for example, I have a strongly held belief in individual freedom, I will find it difficult to negotiate about policies requiring the wearing of school uniforms. If I believe that all life is sacred, I will not wish to compromise with those who advocate legalised abortion.

Values trump interests. If I am a farmer who has set aside a piece of uncleared woodland on my property because of the wildlife it protects, I will not clear it, even if it is in my financial interests to do so. If I am a dedicated evangelical Christian, I will not vote for a party that favours gay marriage, even if in every material respect that party offers me more than its conservative competitors. Moreover, policy itself, whether it is public or not, performs a function which is quite clearly values-based. To construct a policy about anything is to try to make sense of the world. 'Every citizen over the age of 65 is eligible to receive an age-pension' may appear to be a purely administrative policy, but it is one of many that constitute the values web of the welfare state, which promotes some version of social equity.

Even policies with an obviously economic focus – 'New businesses receive a start-up grant of $20,000' – reflect some version of a desired future. So we have something of a conundrum – public policy in its enacted sense, allocates values. Yet at the same time, we find it difficult to give convincing labels to the values that are so enacted, because we lack the tools, indeed the language, to conceptualise what is going on. In their long journey from politics to policy, values enter a much more ambiguous terrain in which they are refracted, combined, modified or, simply, lost.

Positioning the analysis

I have contrasted the emphasis on values with interest-based and institutionalist analyses. There is, however, a broad sweep of policy-related writing that focuses explicitly on the ways in which policy is defined by the problems with which it deals and on the activities of interests that are, in turn, shaped by changing understandings of what is at stake. How does the values-based approach differ from these?

Policy as meaning-making is clearly inseparable from values: indeed values are themselves as much the subject of meaning-making as they are its object. The 'argumentative turn' uses the methodological tools of discourse analysis to demonstrate the importance of narrative in constructing policy realities (Fischer, 2003). Values are also intimately involved in social constructivist theories of policy (a point I return to in the discussion on policy instruments in Chapter 5).

Other analyses stress forms of issue construction, drawing on Rochefort and Cobb's insight that 'policymaking is a struggle over alternative realities' (Rochefort and Cobb, 1994, p. 9). These analyses, many of them based in America, include studies on the work of Congressional committees in relation to work, gender and the family (see Burstein and Bricher, 1997) and on struggles between different interests to define problems in their favour (see, for example, Cobb and Coughlin's work on efforts to define elderly drivers as a road hazard: Cobb and Coughlin, 1998).

The Advocacy Coalition Framework (ACF) pioneered by Sabatier and Jenkins-Smith placed values and beliefs at the core of coalition formation (Sabatier and Jenkins-Smith, 1993). Case studies explored by Sabatier and others emphasise social learning, as groups grapple with the job of exercising influence in changing milieux (Sabatier, 1999). Kubler's excellent study of change in drug policy in Switzerland showed how well the ACF illuminated the ideas component of the activities of contending groups (Kubler, 1999). Contests over the policy agenda, as Cobb and Ross's work showed, combine strategic factors with choices between competing worldviews (Cobb and Ross, 1997).

While a role for values is explicit (or at least implied) in all these accounts, the research reported here sees values somewhat differently: as broad principles of commonality and difference that operate as a kind of deep structure in public policy. It is the choice-making of enacted policy, rather than the interactions of policy contest, that assume centre stage. We are showing, not how policy comes to be, but how the past of policy structures its future. This may sound like a rather grand claim, but it must be emphasised that the approach is a heuristic or a tool, rather than a framework or a theory.

It is not possible to 'test' the approach developed in this book. My claim is, simply, that there is much in public policy that is not only difficult to track in the discursive realm but is also difficult to ascribe to particular actors, or groups of actors. In particular, patterns of stability and change seem to fall into this category, perhaps because of the recursive elements in public policy (that is, the tendency, over time, for public policy to be a cause of itself). This dimension, oddly enough, comes most vividly to life when we take values seriously.

The values bridge between politics and policy

If politics is the ultimate source of policy values, we can detect three subdisciplines that help us to conceptualise the nature of the bridge between politics and policy. They are political philosophy, political sociology and policy sciences. Political psychology is clearly important in understanding the relationship between individual values and their political expression. I cross this particular bridge later in the chapter.

Political philosophy

In essence, the task of political philosophy, where it has considered questions of public policy, has been to develop tools for understanding the moral agency of the state. Scholars in this tradition may ask questions such as 'What is liberalism?' or 'What is conservatism?', but they are not primarily interested in the ideological function of such positions. Rather, they are concerned with engaging in forms of reasoning that provide ethical justification for particular kinds of collective choices. The literature in this tradition is vast, but some examples will illustrate the approach.

Scholars such as Goodin, Nozick and Dryzek, from different perspectives, describe value parameters for the state, that is, how we might arrive at compelling arguments for what the state ought to be, and ought to do. Thus Goodin has developed a rationale for the welfare state that relies precisely on the basis that collective compassion is not intrinsically differentiable from individual compassion (Goodin, 1988). Nozick, from a libertarian perspective, derives a theory of justice that explicitly repudiates the redistributive ethos of the welfare state (Nozick, 1974). From a systems-design perspective, Dryzek constructs a framework for defining the values and practices of ecological rationality (Dryzek, 1987). This kind of work helps us to answer questions: 'If we wanted a state that embodies certain kinds of values, what would it look like, and how might it be justified?' But, to use a homely analogy, political philosophy deals with the architecture of the building, whereas we are concerned with the design and uses of specific rooms.

Political sociology

The second way to build the bridge is to search empirically for evidence about relationships between the values held by individuals and groups and those manifested in politics. This approach sees politics as a social mirror. As social values change, so will politics, and also policy. Streams within this tradition vary in the extent to which the structure and actions of the state are viewed as emanations of deeper power structures. Pluralist accounts stress the normative and practical benefits of multiple, well-organised interests (Dahl, 1997). Others point to the importance of ideology in focusing the power of elites and the related role of institutions in 'organizing out' particular interests, needs and values as well as organising them in (Bachrach and Baratz, 1962).

A broadly structuralist tradition explains the phenomena of late capitalism in terms of the class interests of managers and information brokers, operating in a self-described globalising world. In this vein, Pusey has shown how important economic rationalism has been to the construction of public policy in Australia (Pusey, 1991). In a more general way, many writers have construed a rightwards shift in public policy in all the English-speaking countries as a manifestation of 'neo-liberalism' – an updated version of the classical liberal ideology of nineteenth-century Britain (Dean and Hindess, 1998).

Political sociology can tell us a good deal about where policy values come from, in the direct, flesh-and-blood sense. Working-class politics of the nineteenth century and the first half of the twentieth century stressed equality of opportunity for all and the redress of material injustice. More recently, political sociologists have detected a change, at least in the richer Western countries, in the relationship between interests and political action. As Inglehart pointed out in 1977, values had been shifting from an emphasis on material well being, towards a greater emphasis on quality of life (Inglehart, 1977, p. 3).

The great social movements of the 1970s and 1980s – feminism, environmentalism, gay liberation – appealed, not simply to equality (although in the case of feminism, this was obviously crucial) but also to questions of human rights and the needs of the non-human environment. The bridge to policy for these values-based movements is explicit in terms of equal pay for equal work, anti-discrimination legislation and specific forms of environmental protection (see Sawer, 1990). Similarly (although from a different segment of the political spectrum), the rise of the religious right in the United States in the latter part of the twentieth century connects with explicit policy demands. The focus provided by political sociology tells us a good deal about the ways in which values inform policy in a number of key areas, although as we shall see, the connections are inevitably much less direct than a simple model would suggest.

Policy sciences

The third way of building the bridge is the one adopted by those writing in the policy sciences tradition, in which values are seen primarily not as ideological emanations but in relation to their role in the policy process. Harold Lasswell, in many ways the founding father of policy sciences, argued that 'human beings pursue values through institutions so as to shape and share values to effect resources' (Parsons, 1995, p. 447). It followed, therefore, that a policy science designed for application in the real world, should stress the importance of the normative dimension in approaches to decision-making. If policy science were to improve the world, it had to give those involved a way of using 'the best of what is known' (Cunningham in Parsons, 1995, p. 448).

Yehezkel Dror, one of Lasswell's successors in the policy sciences tradition, pinpointed the difficulties posed by values in policy analysis. Not only were there the well-known theoretical problems posed by interpersonal comparisons of utility, but often the presence of 'compact ideologies' (groups of tightly held beliefs) prevented even small-scale trade-offs. In addition, there were latent values, beliefs and motives which could not – indeed should not – be explicated by analysis because they were dealt with by the ritualistic and symbolic, even cathartic, functions of policymaking (Dror, 1971, p. 57).

Subsequent analysis found ways of moving beyond these constraints while retaining a broadly rationalistic approach to values. One example of this approach was to identify values as the basis for 'framing' policy problems, essentially in the 'real-time' process of policy discussion and policymaking (Schon and Rein, 1994). More recently, Thacher and Rein have pointed to a variety of devices employed, more or less unconsciously, by administrative systems for bypassing or sidelining the values conflict (Thacher and Rein, 2004).

Policy values reflect both dominant modes of thinking and dominant interests. Neoconservative policies, for example, construct wealthy business interests favourably, while viewing single mothers much less favourably. Bureaucracies, too, provide 'scripts' for their clients that determine how much or how little they are able to participate in the decisions that concern them (Soss, 1999). Generally, though, policy science has not concerned itself with a values vocabulary that might link with the broader values of political theory. Indeed, insofar as policy science has a theoretical 'take' on values, it is to see the values-hunt a little like chasing a chameleon. As Lindblom has observed, values-based choices are made simultaneously with the alternatives – in other words, questions of principle are left unresolved, while decision-makers concentrate on specific proposals they may be able to agree upon (Lindblom, 1995, pp. 146–7).

This is not to say that the implications of choices for particular values cannot be analysed. While welfare economics tends to be fixated on Pareto optimality as the criterion for policy choice, there is no inherent reason why distributional equity cannot also be considered (Stilwell, 1975). Amartya Sen's classic lectures on economic inequality, in which he demonstrated the importance of the philosophical underpinnings of measurements of inequality, highlighted the limitations of welfare economics in this respect (Sen, 1973). But achieving improvements in particular values can rarely be done unambiguously. As Abelson points out, the real world already embodies, however roughly, conceptions of what is fair, and rule-changes that do not acknowledge the existing state of affairs, may well make matters worse (Abelson, 1987).

Deborah Stone's *Policy Paradox* shows that too uncritical an acceptance of values as virtuous may have the same effect. While Stone does not view policies themselves as values artefacts, she shows how particular values are pressed into service in political debates about public policy and how 'policy' values reflect the perspectives and interests that put them forward (Stone, 1997). Concepts such as 'equity' and 'fairness' do not have unequivocal meanings in policy contexts, because they depend very much on 'where you are coming from'. Thus, values do not enter the policy process already formed. Often, they emerge as policy meanings are 'constructed' by participants in the policy process, as they struggle to arrive at a practical framework for compromise (Steinberger, 1980), or label opponents in ways that are politically convenient (Chanley and Alozie, 2001). The huge apparatus of 'spin' – the deliberate slanting of information so as to secure political advantage – manipulates the language of values (for example through repeated references to the value of freedom), so as to produce a vague penumbra of favourability around specific actions.

'Grand values' and public policy analysis

Many of the values we like to think of as somehow immutable owe their resonance to the particularities of time, place and economic fortune. In the 1970s and 1980s, across a broad range of states (both developed and developing), the value of economic nationalism was important as a policy goal. This was the view (distinct from a belief in the broad-based value of growth) that the structure of the economies of nation states mattered and that it was important to secure the development of a strong manufacturing sector.

Globalisation or, to be more accurate in the current context, globalism changed the way most people saw the relationship between place and production. Goods (and increasingly services) were being produced in countries with low wages but also high levels of investment in plant and machinery. It mattered less that one's own country was involved than that financial tools were available to finance the purchase of the latest consumer goods. The policy sciences literature has reflected these changes, both implicitly in the sense that the major works on industry policy date from the 1970s and 1980s (Johnson, 1982; Zysman, 1983) and explicitly in the sense that commentary and analysis in the 2000s focus on the implications for the policy of globalising markets (see for example Braithwaite and Drahos, 2000; Bell, 2002).

Values-balances also change. Almost 40 years ago, Daniel Bell announced a new kind of values to accompany the end of traditional industrial society (Bell, 1973). For a while it seemed as though the new left, with its emphasis on individual empowerment, and what we would now call 'identity politics', might produce a new kind of society. But the new left was overpowered by the new right. Far from being a post-materialist era, the final decades of the twentieth century were, in the countries of the West, a time of an even more triumphalist materialism than the post-war decades had been.

It was easy to believe, at least before September 11, that the whole world was united in its celebration of, or at least fervent pursuit of, material goods: capitalism had emerged victorious from the Cold War (see, for example, Fukuyama, 1992). For the modern, secular West, the realisation that puritanical, misogynistic and profoundly medieval forms of Islam could command the attention, the loyalty and ultimately the lives of some of Islam's best-educated and most idealistic sons came as a profound shock.

Even so, as Bob Dylan put it, 'money doesn't talk, it swears'. And money swore its head off as the swelling tides of finance capitalism washed in and out of the Western democracies and the eager industrial states of Japan and south-east Asia during the 1990s and into the new millennium. A concern for the environment might manifest itself in stronger anti-pollution measures. But a green consciousness, in the sense of a desire to preserve and protect more of the natural world for its own sake, remained a rhetorical hope rather than a policy reality. Green values promised new kinds of policies, but found it difficult to compete with the siren song of economic growth even when, or perhaps especially when, the siren song lured the global economy onto the rocks. Only if the earth itself threatened to strike back, as it seemed to be about to do in relation to climate change, rightly called 'humanity's giant, uncontrolled experiment with the atmosphere', would its plight succeed in attracting the attention of significant sections of the populace.

But it is not primarily with what Dror has called 'grand policy' (the policy of major institution building) that this book is concerned (Dror, 2006). Rather it is about more mundane forms of policy, the everyday actions of governments everywhere that help to create the kind of society we live in. And this is why the policy sciences approach is so important. It is not because it has more to say than other modes of inquiry about policy values, but because the kinds of questions that it asks, and the reasons it asks them, are of the right kind, and at the right level, given my motivation for investigating policy values. Policymaking – and an interest in it – is about what 'ought to be done'. It is this orientation that distinguishes policy studies from other sorts of political science. As Goodin, Rein and Moran put it, policy studies are 'explicitly normative', characterised both by a desire for relevance and an action orientation (Goodin, Rein and Moran, 2006, pp. 5–6). It is impossible to be interested in the policy world without caring about what is happening within it.

The quest for values is important, firstly because so many members of policy communities need to find ways of making policies that reflect particular values. This means not only contributing to Lasswell's project of understanding and contributing to the values contexts of public policymaking but also finding out why it is that the real world of implemented policy seems to dilute, and even to fracture, the values that inform policy change. Secondly, I want to find out what a values-based perspective tells us about public policy that we did not know before. To make values more explicit in the policy science tradition, we need to find ways of measuring, or at least, characterising them. In turn, this means developing an approach for tracking what we might call enacted values.

What do policy values do?

Two key functions are identifiable: values as motivators and values as the basis for choice. Values as motivators help to orientate political action and catalyse change; as the basis for choice, they provide a structure for both means and ends. From the standpoint of practical policy analysis, values constitute the framework for evaluation – the very word (beyond its purely technical camouflage) denotes the significance of valued goals. These goals may not be clearly specified (or even specifiable), but they orientate the flow of both thinking and practice.

Values as motivators

The tools and orientations of psychologists have been used to illuminate significant aspects of public policy, particularly international relations and foreign policy (see Levy, 2003; Herman, 2003). Political psychologists have also invested much effort in identifying connections between personality types and political behaviour. The deployment of values as an intermediate concept (between the individual's psychology and political behaviour) has also attracted considerable attention. At the individual level, values help us to navigate our way through the world, by telling us what is acceptable and what is not (Reich and Adcock, 1976). Although values are powerful, they cannot (unlike behaviours or actions) be directly observed. They provide a kind of standard of which we are aware, even if we cannot invoke it precisely.

As Rokeach, one of the most-cited researchers in the field puts it, 'Values operate as constituents of dynamic systems of social action because of their interconnectedness, their informational or directive effects, and their capacities to serve as "carriers" of psychological energy' (Rokeach, 1979, p. 21). Rokeach was also one of the first researchers actually to name values. He came up with a list of 36 values – 18 were what he called self-directed and another 18 were society-directed (Rokeach, 1973). Rokeach was able to make some headway in proposing connections between value-rankings and the party-choices of political activists. Those working for then Democrat presidential candidate McCarthy ranked 'equality' much more highly among the list of values than did those working for the conservative candidate, Wallace.

Despite many efforts, no one has been able to come up with a clear-cut theory of a relationship between personal values and political ideologies.

Nevertheless political attitudes (beliefs about particular situations or problems) are known to be deeply structured by values (Feldman, 2003). Since the 1960s, studies of the determinants of voting behaviour across Western countries have identified a waning of the influence of class (see, for example, Franklin, Mackie and Valen, 1992), although there has been considerable controversy over the influence of 'issues' (relative, for example, to ideology or party identification) in determining choice. Even if issues are held to be the more significant determinant, however, they do not occlude values, either in their origins or their presentation.

The declining influence of class has been noted in many country-based studies. Work by Kemp in the 1970s pointed to the embourgeoisement and homogenisation of Australian politics. Values, he stated, were increasingly important in explaining party/political choice in this context, because structural trends were altering the bases on which perceptions of political interests were formed (Kemp, 1978, p. 348). While later work showed that the trend was less clear than Kemp and others had identified, the general direction of change was confirmed (Charnock, 2005). Following Kemp's line of reasoning, it is probable that, as class cleavages decline, values have become more important in explaining policy change, both as conduits between policy effects and political pressure and as sources of mobilisation for the politically astute. The policies put forward by political parties at election time must obviously be tuned to the perceived interests of voters, but with the aid of focus groups and constant opinion-polling, their packaging and grounds for attack on opponents are more likely to be tuned to perception, emotion and aspiration than to ideology.

Values as the basis for choice

Public policy is not a 'thing' but a series of processes (Colebatch, 2002). Some of these processes have to do with thinking about what is possible (policy formulation), and others have to do with translating thoughts into action (policy implementation). Together, these processes create value for the public, that is, they produce measured or at least measurable increases in desirable outcomes. These gains or losses are what we try to measure when we evaluate policies. Putting cameras alongside roads, or at traffic lights, improves safety by reducing speeding and red-light running (and the resulting fines are also welcome sources of revenue). Other kinds of outcome (for example, improved trust) are much harder to measure, but are still clearly values-based.

Values choices are made about means as well as ends (although these are less frequently evaluated). For example, when we install cameras in an attempt to reduce crime, we substitute surveillance for other forms of policing – again, a values choice. Finance might dictate the choice, but in naming what we might have lost, we become more aware of the implications of our choices. It is through these processes that values are (to extend Easton's phrase) 'allocated' by policy. In making a policy choice, we are also choosing the values balance that will prevail at any point in time. This is not to argue that powerful interests do not shape outcomes, or that electoral considerations do not frequently hold sway over policymakers. These factors are clearly highly significant. But once the choice is made (for example, the nuclear plant is put where it will be least politically damaging, rather than most environmentally safe), a polity has traded one value (safety) for another (political expediency).

Allocating values

How does public policy 'allocate value' in a given society? The most obvious example of policy working in this way is the budgetary process. When dollars are attached to programmes, we implicitly reveal what is important to us – a dollar more on defence is a dollar less for education, and vice versa. Further, our preferences can be made explicit in relative terms by comparing expenditures across nations. If relative to the size of our economy, we consistently spend more on education, or overseas aid, than the average, that tells us something about our enacted values. But budgets are not very reliable indicators of policy values. If we spend relatively highly on education, it could be that we have more powerful teachers' unions than other countries, rather than that we value education more. Then again, it might be that we value education as highly as another country with more generous levels of expenditure but are more efficient in the way we go about achieving that objective.

Another way of identifying expressed values would be to assess their effects in the physical world in which citizens live. We might visit particular countries, or regions within them, and observe how cities are laid out, the kinds of housing that are available to rich and poor, and the general level of social amenity expressed through town planning and the built environment. While we would clearly need to know a great deal about the history of each country to explain what we see, the built environment tells the observer the relative weight that particular societies accord to private rights as against public utility; the value that is placed on heritage; and the effectiveness or otherwise of controls on industrial pollution, car use and the heights and appearance of private buildings.

Clearly, though, if we are to cover the gamut of public policy, we need a way of detecting value-positions within the fabric of policy itself. The operative assumption made in this book is that in any kind of collective activity we construct a relationship between the individual, group or organisation and the resources of the state. Policy values, therefore, operationalise these relationships. Once we have a feel for the relationships, we can name the values. The four categories of values described below – outcomes, design, instrument-related and administrative – represent a rough hierarchy of choices that are made whenever a policy is produced and implemented. They do not correspond to a policy 'cycle', but rather to the scale of consideration involved. We can think of each type of choice, and the relationship it governs, as representing an aspect of policy design.

As articulated by Parsons, a policy design is both a means for understanding reality and a means for acting upon it. Implicitly, policymakers choose designs that enable goals to be achieved, in much the same way as an architect or engineer might design a house or a bridge, although the process in the case of policymaking is more chaotic and rarely results in an articulated plan (Parsons, 1995, p. 564). The design of a policy is intensely evaluative, involving the linking together of values, models of causation and instrument choice (Linder and Peters, 1987, p. 468). To illustrate, the prime objective of social policy is as a means for improving social equity, that is, it is customary to see the value as the social outcome. But this traditional way of understanding social policy overlooks the overall value structure, which relates the individual to the state, through the policy – in other words, many kinds of value choices are made, relating to process and design, as well as to outcome.

It is also possible to see social policy as a process of action and reaction, a pendulum moving between the twin poles of obligation and entitlement. Thus the Australian idea of 'mutual obligation' is an attempt to rebalance policy between these two poles. How and to whom we pay a pension, and how it is financed embody a relationship between the individual and the state. To take the story further, whether we choose to be tough or tender in our choice of policy instruments to get people back to work is also a values-based choice.

A values vocabulary

Using this insight as a starting point, we can now begin to develop a values vocabulary – a way of naming values in policy-relevant ways. It is evident that we can classify values according to the role they perform, and we can also use these roles to generate values labels. The list given below is clearly not exhaustive, but it indicates the range of desirable attributes that are selected in (or selected out) when policy choices are made. In constructing these lists, I have taken my lead from Rokeach's 'society-centred' values (both those relating to means and those relating to ends), with some additions and deletions to reflect the kinds of resonances that public policies have sought to create over the past several decades, largely in the English-speaking countries with which I am most familiar.

Outcomes values (the desired end-point in values terms)

Outcomes values may be expressed in a variety of ways. The Beveridge Report, for example, that established the template for the post-war British welfare state did not announce that its goal was to enhance equality of opportunity for all Britons. Rather, Beveridge identified five freedoms that he claimed his policies in social security, national health, education, housing and employment would deliver: Freedom from Want, Freedom from Disease, Freedom from Ignorance, Freedom from Squalor and Freedom from Idleness (Beveridge, 1942; Pilkington, 1998). These freedoms were the basis of the positive forms of liberty that, Beveridge believed, informed true citizenship.

Nevertheless, we might think of 'equity' as the meta-value subtended by Beveridge's mighty principles of policy design. As a policy value, equity denotes a particular relationship between the individual and the state, one based on a pervasive principle of justice based on equality of opportunity. Equity is often equated with fairness. In policy terms, however, it is useful to distinguish between the two because (as I shall argue in Chapter 2) fairness has a somewhat narrower relationship to justice than does equity. The following list of outcomes values is drawn from a review of major policy initiatives and developments across the five English-speaking democracies in the post-war period:

- Fairness (minimum wage legislation; non risk-rated health insurance; compensation for forced structural change)
- Equity (equality of opportunity in education; redistributive tax and pension systems)
- Efficiency (micro-economic reform; structural adjustment; performance enhancement; market regulation)
- Growth (interest-rate management; business support)
- Diversity (multiculturalism)
- Green-ness (anti-pollution; environmental protection; sustainability)

- Self-determination (political autonomy for aboriginal peoples)
- Security (war against terror; counterterrorism legislation)
- Responsibility (increasing obligations in return for state benefits)
- Choice (opening previously regulated areas to competition)

Many of these values have a 'shadow' outcomes value that is sacrificed when they are chosen (for example green-ness may be chosen at the expense of growth, security at the expense of privacy).

Design values

Design values govern the institutional choices through which policy will be implemented. More so than outcomes values, they lend themselves to presentation as 'dyads', because, within a given system, there is a tension between each nominated value and its antithesis. These tensions arise because of the symmetrical nature of the costs and benefits that particular choices imply. For example, when decision-making is centralised, we gain some benefits (for example, better coordination), but this is at the expense of other benefits (for example responsiveness). The costs of one choice are the benefits of the other. Design values include:

- Cooperation/competition/coordination (choices between networks, markets and hierarchies)
- Centralisation/decentralisation (who decides what, where)
- Closed/open (how much participation in policy-making and implementation)
- Top down/bottom up (control versus responsiveness)
- Obligation/entitlement (the balance between what we give and what we get across broad areas of social policy)
- 'Publicness' (universality versus choice)
- Accountability (trust versus control)

Instrument-related values

This category derives from Schneider and Ingram's work on the behavioural theories that are implicit in policy-makers' choice of policy instruments (Schneider and Ingram, 1990). Policy instruments are the means through which policy seeks to change behaviour in desired directions, and Schneider and Ingram detect five main types – penalties, incentives, persuasion, encouragement and learning. Many factors are involved in the choice of one instrument over another – cost, state capacity and the appropriateness of the measure. But there is also a political, or value-based element, relating to beliefs about the motivations and attitudes of target groups. For example, a programme designed to get the unemployed back into work may employ sanctions (such as removal of public benefits if insufficient effort is put into searching for a job); incentives (such as encouraging employers to take on the long-term unemployed); and/or education-based programmes that address deficits in literacy, numeracy and other skills. Of course, most programmes employ a number of instruments. But the balance between them reflects assumptions about the behaviour of the unemployed. If they are seen as shirkers, then they will be handed penalties, rather than incentives or education. A balance between toughness and tenderness is determined by these kinds of choices (that is, the extent to which penalties rather than incentives or other types of actions are used to induce compliance).

Administrative values

The Canadian public administration theorist, Kenneth Kernaghan, identified, from a range of prescriptive documents, 25 'core values' held by Canadian public servants (Kernaghan, 2003). The Australian Public Service Act is more parsimonious – nevertheless, if we define a value simply as a 'desirable property' of someone's behaviour, the potential list is indeed extensive. However, from the relational perspective I have identified that the relevant values are those that define the behaviour of public servants (and others) as implementers of or, more precisely, deliverers of policy. They include the following:

- Consistency (equivalent decisions in equivalent circumstances)
- Customer service (satisfying clients)
- Efficiency (minimising waste)
- Neutrality (avoiding politicisation)
- Responsiveness (reacting appropriately to the needs of clients and customers)

Again, there are (depending upon institutional structures) trade-offs between these (and other) values. True consistency, for example, may be difficult to rationalise in terms of administrative rigour – decision-making 'by the book'.

What the values-based approach explains

Naming values is one thing. We need a way of getting at what difference a values perspective makes to our understanding of public policy. By putting values centre stage, we see that that inevitably, there will be an incompatibility between values (inherently non-negotiable) and the necessarily compromise-based, incremental nature of policy decisions. We see this incompatibility most clearly when values conflict in an outright sense, raising political temperatures and straining the capacity of legal and political systems. Richardson has described this values plethora as the defining characteristic, the 'deep pluralism', of modern political systems (Richardson, 1997, p. 238).

This insight suggests another perspective on policy values: precisely because they are so destabilising, a large component of policy systems is devoted to the control and management of values. Just as nature abhors a vacuum, so do policy systems abhor outright value conflict. Thacher and Rein propose three mechanisms through which policy-makers deal with obvious forms of value conflict: cycling (in which conflicting values are attended to sequentially, firewalls (in which they are separated organisationally) and casuistry (forms of reasoning that allow value conflicts to be transcended) (Thacher and Rein, 2004). In Chapter 2, I suggest three additional techniques for addressing value conflict: structural separation, hybridisation and technicisation. Note that I am not suggesting that decision-makers consciously use these techniques – simply that when we think about how to organise ourselves in public contexts, we are faced with the task of giving administrative form to many kinds of purposes. Indeed a major part of the art of administration is to routinise what would otherwise be a series of difficult, or even agonising choices.

I have found, too, that the values perspective is of enormous value as an analytic heuristic in the development of comparative methodologies. It will be useful to go over some of the issues in comparative writing here. When policies are compared across countries (welfare policies in particular), each country is seen as a set of observations on the problem which the policy is seen to address. For example, Esping-Andersen's well-known work on welfare states finds patterns of difference and similarity, which leads to the identification of groups of countries with key characteristics in common (Esping-Andersen, 1990). Other types of comparative work focus on inter-country differences (as when, for example, two countries with very different policy structures are compared), or (as in the case of much comparative writing in public management) analysts ask whether and how a particular set of practices has (or has not) been implemented in each nation state.

When identifying values and using them heuristically, an interesting phenomenon occurs. Searching for common values obviously will not do, as it is precisely in the differences in their interpretation of values, such as social equality, that countries most obviously differ. But another approach is possible, and that is to use tensions within and between different values (trade-offs) as a way of exploring difference. This is the way I use 'fairness' in Chapter 3. I ask how different polities enact fairness, viewed from the perspective of the balances that are struck between obligation and entitlement. This gives a perspective on welfare states that stresses the connection between the implied contract that underpins all states (expressed as obligation and entitlement) and its practical realisation in policy. I am not arguing that this is the only basis on which countries might be compared nor that the values I have chosen to structure the analysis are necessarily definitive. The test is how intuitively plausible the work is and how useful or illuminating its results seem to be. Bear in mind that 'values' are not a hypothesis to be tested, but a lens to be employed.

I have suggested that the values lens is pre-eminently suited to comparison. But does using it explain anything about how policy works? I argue that the values approach is particularly suited to the analysis of change (discussed further in Chapter 2). The field of policy dynamics has highlighted the importance of 'policy as its own cause', that is, the effects on future policies of past decisions (Bardach, 2006). The values-based approach directs our attention as analysts to points of conflict – to places where March and Olsen's 'logic of appropriateness' starts to break down (March and Olsen, 2006). Present can more readily be compared with past, because, in identifying these critical junctures, we have a periodisation that is more immediate than instituitionalism's long term, without losing sight of underlying relationships.

Separating values and interests in the practical world of policy debate, argument and decision is neither practical nor desirable. But there are many areas of public policy that are under-analysed precisely because the role of interests is less significant or less obvious than the norm. How do public policies deal with (for example) religious values in relation to issues such as abortion, or the wearing of religious symbols? What about drugs policies? Again, changing values priorities are both markers and precipitators of change.

In addition, there is a deep structure of policy that the values perspective gets at, which other approaches do not. The reason we remain so distrustful of values is that the legacy of neo-Marxist structural analysis lives on, in the sense that political science always looks for interests, because interests are pre-eminently economic. And the primacy of the economic engine is always with us. As political scientists, we are trained to see values as epi-phenomena, lodged somewhere between interests and ideologies. If, at a seminar, you argue that something happened because it is in someone's interests for it to happen, there is always agreement. To argue that espoused values might also be real is to risk being labelled naïve. In this way, an easy cynicism is substituted for explanation.

But when we consider public policy, unless we are complete reductionists, we are dealing with a rational platform for dealing with the world, with a state that is, at least up to a point, well-intentioned enough to want to look after its citizens. Or to put it differently, a state that has been brought to heel by its citizens. At election time, new policies may appear to be no more than grab-bags of promises concocted to buy votes, but politicians must still devise a values story to justify them. And at implementation time, the apparatus of accountability, due process and pluralist commentary imposes at least some pressure for improvement and learning.

Making policy means trying to find a way of ordering reality. It is often a very disorderly, messy and contingent process. The values (in the sense of the desired states of the world) that are poured into developing or changing it are mangled out of all recognition by the impact of multiple practicalities and the awesome simplifications imposed by the upper reaches of the bureaucratic and political executives. But they do not disappear – indeed as each chapter in this book shows, they resurface when the ideals and good intentions (for that is how even the most self-serving policies are framed) are turned into actions during the implementation process. If values become more real during implementation, it is because (as many policy scientists have pointed out) public policy does not stop at the point of enunciation, it is only just starting.

Conclusion

By looking at the ways in which policy systems deal with values, we can understand a good deal more than before about how they are structured and also how they change. Policy systems both defuse values, so as to enhance stability and tractability, and highlight them in ways that release tension and also, when the conditions are right, support creativity and change. Moreover, by developing techniques for naming values, we can see that the familiar left–right spectrum is only a small part of the multiple dimensions in which policy values operate. By understanding the role that values play, it becomes possible to understand the paradox of values: it is because of their overwhelming importance that it is necessary to tame them through processes that minimise conflict.

2
Value Conflict and Policy Change

In what ways can a values-based perspective on policy be used to gain a better understanding of policy change? In an obvious sense, when policy changes, it is the enacted values that change, and where there has been associated controversy, the role of values can be very visible. But there is an invisible role as well. We know, from the work of Arrow and others, that under most assumptions there can be no non-arbitrary way of making a choice between values (considered as preference orderings), which suggests the overall importance of institutional structures in managing value conflicts.

While the nature of these processes is implicitly addressed in many accounts of the policy process, it is rare to find them explicitly delineated. Following the lead established by Thacher and Rein (2004), this chapter examines ways in which patterns of policy change reflect the power of the political and bureaucratic executive to manage value conflicts. I argue that this power is partly situational and partly deliberate. In its situational forms, it manifests itself through the processes and structures of budgetary and other forms of decision-making. In its deliberate forms, it assumes the character of dominant policy paradigms, which cement the pre-eminence of central agencies and, with political support, provide a firm platform for change. Under certain conditions, however, conflict-management escapes from 'insider' channels, and policy values themselves become an axis or dynamic of change.

The chapter proceeds in three stages. Firstly, I review contemporary theories of policy change, describing the ways in which they conceptualise value conflict. I conclude from this examination that all the extant theories have deficiencies in this respect, particularly when it comes to the analysis of change in Westminster-based policy systems. Secondly, I consider ways in which institutionalist accounts of change can be modified to include bureaucratic and political processes for separating, concentrating and routinising values choice. These processes allow for significant degrees of change without overloading processing capacities. Thirdly, I suggest that certain kinds of rapid and marked policy change can be explained by the overwhelming of these capacities by the political effects of values trade-offs.

Theories of policy change

Understanding why, when and how policy does (or does not) change is one of the key problems of the policy sciences. Although precision has been difficult to achieve (empirical studies tend to assume, rather than to define 'policy change'), the study of change focuses attention not only on processes over time but also on significant broad-scale relationships within policy systems (Pierson, 2000). *Policy* change, however, (as distinct from broader social or political change) denotes a perspective that is more fine-grained, in that it describes changing patterns in choice-making, and shorter-term, in that it focuses on decades rather than centuries. When change occurs at this level and in this way, the dynamics of knowledge and power that underpin all policy are exposed in a way that is often not apparent in times of stability. Thus change is used as a method of interrogation, rather than (as in analyses that focus on pathways of change) as an object of analysis in its own right.

Peter John has identified a grouping of theories of policy change which operate within the broader frameworks put forward by political science, but which take into account the influence of policymaking structures on outcomes, particularly those that identify interpersonal and inter-organisational linkages (John, 2003). In a useful categorisation, Zahariadis has identified three distinct (although in some ways overlapping) conceptual lenses evident in this literature: rational choice, the advocacy coalition framework (ACF) and the multiple streams approach (Zahariadis, 1995). (Note that all three models are in a sense agnostic on the question of exogenous versus endogenous policy change. In the discussion that follows, I will concentrate on comparing the models on the basis of endogenous change).

Rational choice models in the policy sciences take the form of theories of bounded, rather than comprehensive rationality. In its institutionalist guise (which seems most appropriate for the current inquiry), the theory of bounded rationality proposes that choices are satisfied under institutional conditions that push decision-making in particular directions (March and Olsen, 1984; Jones, 1994). For the outcomes of the choice process to change, therefore, requires that preferences change and/or that the institutional structures that condition choices change. Although there is an element of circularity in rational choice models of policy change (institutions are themselves policy-influenced structures), they do direct analytical attention towards the workings of bureaucracies and legislatures and the interactions between them in a way that is particularly useful in the analysis of Westminster-based systems, where the political executive and the legislature are fused.

Whether or not they explicitly employ an institutionalist framework, many studies point to the powerful role of bureaucratic factors in either frustrating or promoting change (see, for example, Rose and Davies, 1994; Mathieson, 2000; Eisner and Meier, 1990). With some refinement, essentially rational choice models also proved applicable to the analysis of Congressional decision-making in US policymaking. By adding a process of attention allocation to the study of the behaviour of political organisations, Jones, for example, was able to explain 'punctuated equilibria' in budgetary decision-making (Jones, 2001).

Sabatier and Jenkins-Smith's ACF was initially advanced as a corrective to staged models of policy development (Sabatier and Jenkins-Smith, 1993). The model has proved attractive, because it links change with the activities of interest groups, allowing for a learning dimension and a specific role for the development of knowledge, as well as the practical imperatives of exercising political influence. Because of these factors, the ACF has proved useful (although not entirely successful) in explaining change in environmental decision-making (see, for example, Kamieniecki, 2000).

Illuminating policy change through the concept of agenda (how governments focus their attention) has proved fruitful in a number of policy fields. In this conceptualisation, policy activity takes place in multiple streams, which, when particular opportunities arise, can be linked to produce shifts in the attention of policymakers. Multiple streams direct attention towards issue-framing, as well as to the often contingent and opportunistic processes by which particular agendas are transported to the centre of the political stage (Kingdon, 1984). Baumgartner and Jones showed how these processes could be aligned with decision theory to form a satisfying account of the very complex activities of Congressional committees. They point to problem definition, the links between knowledge and power and how these may shift in response to a number of factors, including the presence of negative feedback, which damps down potential change, and positive feedback, which allows certain issues to 'take off', in terms of public and policy attention (Baumgartner and Jones, 1993).

Of the three models, the ACF assigns the most explicit role to values in policy change. Values form part of the core beliefs of advocacy coalitions, and their persistence, according to the theory, reflects the dominance of one coalition over another. Value conflict, under certain conditions, produces policy learning. Empirical studies covering a wide range of policy problems have drawn on the framework to show groups competing with each other on the basis of the belief systems that structure the groups' priorities, approaches and causal theories (Sabatier and Jenkins-Smith, 1993, p. 41).

Issue definition (usually associated with the multiple streams approach) has a values component (for example, when disability is defined as a rights issue rather than a medical issue), but does not emphasise values as such. Rational choice (as an explanation of what happens, rather than a prescription for decision) sees values as filtering devices, allowing some policy options through while blocking others. Within organisations, rational choice depicts values as informing organisational behaviour through their incorporation in rules and incentives.

While the ACF deals explicitly with value conflict (and indeed, makes it central to the analysis of change), it does so in a way that is less relevant to the analysis of policymaking in Westminster and in European systems than in the United States. The reason seems to lie in the fact that in non-presidential systems there is much less openness and contact between actors in different institutions (Parsons, 1995, p. 200). Indeed, Sabatier and Jenkins-Smith have acknowledged limitations in the extent to which the theory may generalise to parliamentary systems (Sabatier and Jenkins-Smith, 1999, p. 151). In addition, the implicit pluralism of the ACF allows little scope for the exercise of systemic or other forms of power in policymaking.

There is a further deficiency, which results from the fact that the ACF covers only a very small part of the value conflicts relating to public policy. Value conflict arises not just because interests are competing for policy power but also because public policies represent enacted values (i.e. they embody values), and because of this fact, they conflict with each other. Once policy has taken institutionalised forms, the problem of actual or potential value conflict is extreme. These conflicts arise for a number of reasons: at a fundamental level, they are inevitable, because within any given social order, we cannot simultaneously achieve every value. Some necessarily trade-off against each other. For example, we cannot increase risk (for example, by removing social welfare supports) without at the same time decreasing security. The implied conflict at the development stage will re-emerge after the policy has been implemented.

More obviously, when a new government takes the reins of power, it will be faced with a considerable weight of policy, hard-wired into the institutions of the state, and bearing the ideological imprimatur of its predecessor. Public policy, like the iceberg, is nine-tenths submerged. Ultimately, a determined government may alter the entire mindset of the state, but before that point is reached, it will be laying new strata of decisions on top of the old. Forms must be found to give effect to these new or revived values, or existing organisations must adapt to carry them out, giving rise to multiple and often conflicting values at these sites. Unless these kinds of value conflicts are managed in some way, governments would find it almost impossible to operate. Thacher and Rein's important study suggests a number of ways in which this management occurs, from the perspective of individual decision-makers within government agencies. Following their lead, I argue that similar forces are at work in structuring relations between agencies and in privileging certain kinds of decision-making procedures. Further, I suggest that these mechanisms have complex but clear relationships with patterns of change.

Bureaucratic decision-making and values choice

Thacher and Rein put forward three mechanisms through which, at the level of individual decision-makers within agencies, they see value conflict being managed. They are cycling (in which conflicting values are attended to sequentially; firewalls (in which they are separated organisationally) and casuistry (forms of reasoning that allow value conflicts to be transcended). To what extent do these forms of conflict management translate into the analysis of policy change?

Of the three, cycling is the most obviously relevant to the issue of change. Thacher and Rein give the example of Australian pensions policy, in which oscillation between two value positions – means-testing and citizens' rights to a retirement income – shapes the trajectory of policy over time. As the authors point out, this phenomenon occurs because of the trade-offs that are implicit in this particular policy. Thacher and Rein's remaining two mechanisms – firewalls, and casuistry – are less clearly related to change because they tend to bypass a value conflict, rather than confront it directly. In each case, however, they enable change to occur (or to be accommodated) without undue disruption. Examples in the next section will suggest how this happens. Three additional mechanisms should, however, be added to the list to produce a more comprehensive theory of value conflict and policy change. These additional mechanisms include hybridisation and incrementalism, which can be thought of as structural, and bias, which reflects the conscious exercise of power.

Six responses to value conflict

Thus, by extending the Thacher and Rein framework, we can see that policy systems handle values choice through six kinds of processes, each with its own relationship to change. The six are:

- Structural separation
- Hybridisation
- Casuistry
- Incrementalism
- Bias
- Cycling

Structural separation

'Firewalls' are forms of structural separation that enable new or different policies to be accommodated within the one entity without exposing officials to the problems of incessant values choice. Similar formations are apparent in the broader structure of government as well. Conventional government works by dividing up its complex systemic reality into functional chunks, the familiar departments of health, education, industry and so on. In this way, policy systems determine 'who gets what' by separating differently valued policy objectives into separate spheres.

Structural separation allows value conflict to be accommodated, but it also produces stresses and tensions elsewhere in the system. The example of environmental policy is particularly apposite. Most governments handle the value questions posed by sustainability by creating separate departments dealing with 'green' issues, while production-related departments and agencies continue much as before. Coordination is effected, if at all, at much lower levels of decision-making (for example, when forest management bodies are required to determine management regimes that provide for sustainability). Occasionally, pre-existing separations or firewalls allow significant change to be achieved because value conflicts are displaced, frustrating possibilities for policy learning. Australian educational policy provides a good example of this phenomenon. Asymmetrical governance structures derail productive debate, because funding and accountability for government and non-government schools are separated by federal 'firewalls' (Stewart, 2005).

Structural separation works well enough when there are clearly defined jobs to be done, and stable professional paradigms to accompany them. However, difficulties arise when governments need to act consistently across a broad range of functions. New values can be accommodated by creating new agencies to carry them forward, but in these cases, the stress of values adjustment can fall on the targets of policy – for example, individuals in the case of welfare and employment policies whose values often conflict with each other. Calls for 'whole-of-government' responses to these and other problems reflect the impact of these unresolved conflicts.

Hybridisation

Values separation does not always occur. In particular policy fields, we observe hybridisation, that is the co-existence of two policies or practices with different values bases. Hybridisation can be seen as a manifestation of the 'inheritance' effect explored by Rose and Davies, whereby an incoming government inherits the policy choices of its predecessors, and then adds further layers of its own (Rose and Davies, 1994). A good example of hybridisation is the values mixture that constitutes new public management, as a result of which public servants are meant simultaneously to be professional, efficient, neutral and responsive. The market-oriented values have been overlaid on top of the more traditional public service ethos, to form a hybridised result. Hybrids such as this satisfy the need for an all-embracing rhetoric, although as the practical level, they give little real guidance for dealing with conflict (Langford, 2004).

Work by Pratchett and Wingfield in British local government showed that institutional change allowed the traditional Public Service ethos to co-exist, if not always happily, with the newer values. For example, they found that contractors operating in purchaser–provider relationships had introduced new values as the basis of their professional ethos, such as commitment to efficiency and flexibility in service delivery, and the importance of measuring performance (Pratchett and Wingfield, 1996). Another type of hybridisation results from incremental amendments to legislation, as new values are articulated, or the unexpected results of old ones, dealt with. As a result of these processes Tax Acts, for example, embody attempts simultaneously to promote multiple and often conflicting values (industry promotion; redistribution; consistency and efficiency). The cycle continues as legislators deal with undesired interaction effects by adding yet more amendments.

Casuistry

Thacher and Rein define values-oriented casuistry as a form of moral taxonomy that aids in values-balancing. They give as an example the way in which police departments, required to give their officers guidance in how to handle criminals effectively without using undue violence, often come up with case-by-case approaches on how to respond to particular situations (Thacher and Rein, 2004). In a similar way, many forms of decision-making in government can be seen as casuistic responses to the problems of value choice. This is not to argue that this is their only purpose, rather that the values component of bounded rationality contains an element of values choice that affects inter-organisational, as well as intra-organisational, decision-making in policy systems. This casuistic component can be clearly seen in the making of budgets.

As Wildavsky (and others) have pointed out, there can be no normative theory of budgeting, because the fundamental budgetary problem is one of values choice (Wildavsky, 1984, p. 128–9). In concrete terms, how do we compare the marginal utility of one extra hospital or community health network against the marginal utility of an extra frigate for the navy? Governments know what each of these things will cost, but it is much harder to work out the benefits. Even if they could do so, a simple dollar metric would not capture the fact that individual citizens' valuations of the benefits would differ. Politically, governments do not wish to be seen to be robbing Peter to pay Paul, even if this is what they are doing. Far easier to bypass these problems by making decisions through budgetary processes which keep major categories of expenditure strictly segregated, and which employ a mixture of rule-based methods and strategic behaviours to cross values divides.

Empirical work on budget making (as distinct from managerialist accounts stressing overarching rational norms) testifies to the ubiquity both of the rule-based methods, and the strategies. In their pathbreaking work on the UK budgetary process, Heclo and Wildavsky found a bewildering range of stratagems employed by civil servants to get their way in interagency budgetary negotiations (Heclo and Wildavsky, 1981), as did Donald Savoie in his study of the Canadian budgetary process (Savoie, 1990). While Wanna, Kelly and Forster found evidence of much stronger control by 'guardian' agencies in Australia as compared with Canada, expenditure reductions were imposed across the board, rather than by comparing program benefits – an example, in terms of the current discussion, of the continuing importance of rule-based casuistry in budget processes (Wanna, Kelly and Forster, 2000, Chapter 12).

Casuistry does not always imply incrementalism. Jones's study of Congressional budget-making found that the complexity of the process required that decision-makers focus their attention in ways that often produced non-incremental change (Jones, 2001). Kelly found that while there was evidence of incrementalism in some parts of the British social security budget, shares could change dramatically, reflecting the impact of new priorities (Kelly, 1989). In general, however, while some areas might be dramatically increased or reduced, most expenditures were determined incrementally because they represented entitlements that were 'hard-wired' into legislation.

Incrementalism

As a decision-making strategy, incrementalism is generally thought of as a response to there being a lack of sufficient information to make fully rational decisions, or where the technical complexity of non-incremental change is overwhelming (see, for example, Lindblom, 1995; Simonsen, Johnson and Barnet, 1996). But it may also represent a way forward when non-incremental change is likely to arouse value conflicts that are difficult to manage. Incrementalism, or stepped change, eases systems and dampens opposition, while signalling longer-run intentions. As an analytical device, incrementalism generates a short-term response to a perceived need for change, while avoiding the need to engage in more deep-seated analysis.

Incrementalism may, however, run into limits when the relationship between the values of the implementing bureaucracy, and those embodied in new policy are at odds. In these situations, entrenched and relatively autonomous bureaucracies may resist even small moves in a direction they consider undesirable. Indirect evidence for this proposition comes from the fact that steady and unflinching political will (or other forms of external pressure) is required to bring about change in powerful public bureaucracies, precisely because of the institutional values that are 'locked-in' to their outlook and practices. As Weissert and Goggin showed in their analysis of the move to managed health care in Michigan, strong leadership and political support are needed to remove the old guard, and bring in new people and fresh ideas (Weissert and Goggin, 2002).

Bias

Schattschneider famously defined organisation as the 'mobilisation of bias' (Schattschneider, 1960). Political contests were less pluralist than supposed, because conflict was managed through the exclusion of alternatives. Since that early work, analysis of the policy process has shown the importance of knowledge in underpinning the exercise of power in policy communities, by forcing those who wish to take part, to 'speak the language' of the dominant discourse (Hajer, 1993). Values, as well as ideas, are 'organised in' and 'organised out' through these processes. Drawing on these perceptions, the value conflict perspective suggests that alternatives (that is, alternative values) are excluded through two power-related techniques: firstly, the development of dominant policy paradigms; and secondly, through what I call technicisation.

Policy paradigms have been defined as sets of ideas that make sense of the world, and, along with power, organisation and policy itself, one of the four constitutive dimensions of governing arrangements in a specific issue area (Wison, 2000). Paradigms can change in response to many factors – being overtaken by events (Hall, 1993) or as a result of complex processes of knowledge-brokering (Howlett, 1994). Paradigms can also alter as a result of advocacy coalition formation (Wallis and Dollery, 2001). In the present context, we are interested, not in paradigm change as such, but in the relationship between paradigms, value conflict and policy change.

Much policy-advising and decision-making takes place within an assumed set of values or paradigms. These paradigms permeate established practice, and orientate the thinking of professionals within particular policy communities. When paradigms clash (as they often do in professional bureaucracies such as hospitals or educational institutions) the response is often to separate them into distinct spheres of action (medical staff and administrators; academics and general staff). But paradigms, by their very pervasiveness, can do their work by subverting or overwhelming dissident ways of thinking. The supremacy in Australia and New Zealand of policy-advising based on economic rationalism has been extensively noted by commentators (see, for example, Pusey, 1991; Kelsey, 1997). Even Vickers's 'appreciative judgment' (an experience-based assessment of what is possible and what is not), applied in the context of an elitist civil service, eliminates alternatives even before they are considered (Vickers, 1965).

In this way, the dominant values orientation can seem truly invisible from the 'inside', because it is totally taken for granted. It is worth noting that, within a bureaucratic system, a dominant coalition does not (as hypothesised by Sabatier and Jenkins-Smith) always produce programmatic stability (Sabatier and Jenkins-Smith, 1993, p. 34). A dominant coalition favouring change (as seen in the market-oriented policies of the 1980s and 1990s in New Zealand, Australia and the United Kingdom) is able to bring about substantial institutional change by marginalising alternative approaches. In the context of bureaucratic politics, a dominant paradigm underpins organisational power by forcing policy discourse into a particular frame, which privileges some values over others, and forces participants to 'speak the same language'.

By 'technicisation', I mean the tendency, partly inevitable, partly chosen, for value conflicts or even differences, to be dealt with by technical means – the 'instrumental rationality' Max Weber saw as one of the hallmarks of bureaucratic governance. In some situations, technicisation works by 'crowding out' other values. Over the past 20 years, the values and language of management has had an enormous impact on the public sector in most OECD countries and in the English-speaking countries in particular. Despite the talk of values pluralism discussed earlier, the use of performance measures based on efficiency and effectiveness tends to drive out less quantifiable values such as trust and professionalism. A similar narrowing occurs where decisions must be made in situations of value conflict, such as we observe in disputes about the environment. Much to the chagrin of activists, values must ultimately be turned into management regimes 'on the ground', that represent multiple compromises in terms of action (for example, forestry authorities are required to observe particular set-back provisions when logging near streams).

In setting up these regimes (more usefully described as forms of governance), techniques can be developed to use the energy represented by strongly held value positions to forge better (more enduring) solutions (Stewart and Jones, 2003). But in negotiating the details, values must be translated into specific demands (this piece of land for a national park; that quota for a particular species of fish), so that their relative impacts can be assessed. The application of technical decision-making tools makes problems more manageable by giving them a quantitative form, but removes from the debate those unable, or unwilling, to speak the language of managerial engagement.

Only those on the 'outside' can see what has been lost. Witness this assessment by Tim Doyle of the consequences of co-optation for the 'professional elite' of the environmental movement:

> The professional elite speaks the language, utilises the same arguments and is beginning to think in the same way as the governors of our society. No more arguments about wilderness; no more talk of scientific diversity; instead the game is mainstream politics: deals, bargaining, pragmatism and money.
>
> (Doyle, 1990)

Technicisation produces a pragmatic kind of change without major values-related disruption, a source of major disappointment to many environmentalists, but arguably a necessary foundation for compromise in highly conflicted situations.

Cycling

Cycling is a form of sequential attention-giving within organisations. In the broader context discussed here, this type of change occurs when value conflicts can no longer be accommodated through the mechanisms discussed earlier, and policies themselves oscillate between value pairs, cycling from one value to the other in a process of flip-flops and backlashes. Flip-flops are repeated, usually low-key patterns of alternation, whereas backlashes are more dramatic in character.

While explicit values trade-offs are usually avoided, in the longer run, policy values do 'trade off' against each other, although the extent to which they do so, and the way they do so, depends on the particular system that we desire to change. To take two examples: more flexibility may mean less consistency; more diversity poorer coordination; more efficiency less equity and so on. Certain types of policies exacerbate these effects. For example, in means-tested welfare systems, very high marginal tax rates are inflicted on welfare recipients when they find a job. Self-reliance (finding a job) conflicts with the fairness ethic of welfare rationing. Over time, policies flip-flop between generosity (allowing welfare recipients to keep more of their pension when they find part-time work) and harshness (forcing recipients into full-time work).

Organisational change, particularly, moves between more or less devolved structures, and often involves a series of flip-flops. Centralisation produces more control, but detracts from responsiveness, and so on. The changes may have strong elements of symbolism about them, suggesting the importance of action and reaction at the level of rhetoric. Writing about local government reform in a range of European countries in the 1970s, Jack Brand commented on the cyclical nature of many of the changes, noting that public institutions 'appear to move between periods of emphasising the symbols of administrative efficiency and those of democracy and public participation. An over-emphasis in one seems to lead to a balancing emphasis in the other' (Brand, 1976, p. 54). In the years since (to take one example), many local governments have flip-flopped between outsourcing services (on the one hand) and bringing them back in-house (on the other), as tensions between efficiency and control are played out.

The backlash phenomenon reflects, not just trade-off effects, but a full-blown, conscious rejection of the status quo. Barak Obama's victory in the 2008 US Presidential election might be seen in this light. A backlash occurs precisely because of the salience of a set of policy values which are, or have become, unacceptable to a sufficient number of voters to make it politically worthwhile for a party or political figure to champion the cause. That voters think in values-based terms about policy issues has been noted by a number of commentators, particularly in fields such as criminal justice and welfare policy, where 'deservingness' figures prominently (Aaron, Mann and Taylor, 1994).

Writing in 1975, Heidenheimer, Heclo and Adams could see little prospect of dramatic change in welfare states, including the somewhat tenuous American variant, because of the complexity of the issues involved and the fact that so many citizens' lives were intertwined with the welfare system (Heidenheimer, Heclo and Adams, 1975). Heidenheimer was clearly right about the political disincentives in substantially reducing pension benefits. But public disapproval of those seen as the 'undeserving poor' was of sufficient strength that even a relatively progressive politician like Bill Clinton eventually authorised massive reductions in federal government support for single parents (Chanley and Alozie, 2001).

The political success of former Australian Prime Minister John Howard is testimony to the power of backlash. Backlash can derive from voter reaction to unpopular policies (witness the electoral annihilation in 1993 of Canada's Conservative Party, in part as a result of the introduction of a widely detested Goods and Services Tax). But it can also reflect a reaction to the perceived values of particular regimes. Australian voters wanted to punish Prime Minister Paul Keating for the recession of the early 1990s, but they were also heartily sick of the political correctness that was perceived to characterise federal Labor in its later years. The brief political career of the populist Pauline Hanson, who denounced multiculturalism and Aboriginal reconciliation and questioned high levels of Asian immigration, demonstrated the depth of feeling in many parts of the community.

Howard was far too shrewd to discuss these issues explicitly in the 1996 election campaign. But when he talked about being 'comfortable' being Australian, voters knew what he meant. In his first term in office, Howard effectively demolished the apparatus of multiculturalism, refused to apologise to Aborigines for the white settlement of Australia, and reduced the family reunion components of the immigration intake. Australian refugee policy, which requires the mandatory detention of all asylum seekers, is among the toughest in the world. The importance of backlash should certainly not be overstated: any government that attempts to harness it, while neglecting the basic economic interests of its constituents is in dire trouble. But in a media-dominated age, political leaders must project a sense of themselves that is pleasing to the electorate, and if they are identified with policies that the electorate has tired of, or which are seen as having served their purpose, they will have difficulty in hanging on to power.

Conclusion

Focusing on value conflict gives us new tools for analysing public policy. Using this method, we have seen how governments structure, control and condition values, in a variety of ways, so as to minimise their disruptive potential. Further, the nature of these processes helps to explain key aspects of the ways in which policies change. The value conflict approach can be thought of as supplementing existing institutionalist approaches to the analysis of change. It is particularly useful when Westminster-based systems are under consideration, because of the power of the political executive to impose its will (and hence its values preferences) on both parliament and bureaucracy.

But the method can be more widely applied by searching for key sources of tension within particular systems. We are concerned, not so much with struggles over problem definition or indeed agenda creation, but with the day-to-day work of mid-level policy analysis and adjustment. Understanding value conflict at the agency (or interagency) level, for example, illuminates both the sources and implications of broader-scale political change. The approach draws attention to the ways in which value conflict permeates bureaucratic structures and processes which must not only carry the imprints of all past policies, but must also accommodate new ones.

The approach gives additional insights into limiting factors on policy change. In bypassing or marginalising value conflict, responses such as values separation, hybridisation, casuistry and bias allow for a considerable degree of policy change over time, without the need for significant change in policy processes. However, this capacity for managing change has its limits. Forms of cycling occur when trade-offs that have been bypassed within subsystems resurface as value conflict in the broader political world.

3
Implementing Fairness

We tend to think of fairness primarily in connection with social policy, because it is through social policies (education, housing, health and social security) that societies attempt to improve the lives of their least-advantaged citizens. In the analytic sense though, the problem of fairness is at the heart of all public policy, precisely because it is through public policy that governments distribute our collective goods, and, when sacrifice is called for, our collective burdens as well (Vanderheiden, 2004). So responding to climate change ends up being about fairness as well as reducing emissions, because without attention to fairness, the costs of change will impact more heavily on the poor than on the rich.

In the political world of public policy, where leaders trade values for votes, the desire to be fair (to others) has varying degrees of resonance with the public. Altruism is real, up to a point. But there is another dimension to the fairness story, one that is much more closely aligned with self-interest. As with other policy areas, described in other chapters in this book, any given allocation of fairness establishes a reaction to itself, in a way that reflects the kinds of balances struck when the policy was created. Analysing these tensions is highly complex because of the entanglement between interests and values described in Chapter 1. I want to suggest that beyond the immediate language of fairness, it is possible to discern what we might term the structural meta-problem of fairness, the relationship, described through policy, between obligation and entitlement.

Public policies that assume institutional form (as in welfare states) are very stable over time, partly because they are so complex, and the influence of past decisions is so great (Pierson, 1994, p. 175). At the same time, the internal tensions of these large structures remain inherently unresolvable, which is why issues relating to fairness are always on the agenda for governments. It is commonplace, in political philosophy, to describe the relationship between citizen and state as having the characteristics of an implied bargain, or contract. I go a little further than this, and argue that tensions between the concepts of obligation and entitlement shape large parts of the landscape of public policy, with particular flash points (such as when welfare states come under attack) where we see the underlying dynamic at work.

When we apply the concept of fairness, as developed here, it is possible to see how values do indeed shape change. The analysis is developed in three sections:

Firstly, I consider how fairness is conceptualised analytically and instantiated in policy.

Secondly, I consider the values dynamic associated with fairness – the way in which ideas about fairness enter the political world.

Thirdly, I show how this values dynamic can be used to explore the recent evolution of welfare states of Europe and the English-speaking world.

Conceptualising fairness

There is no one theory of fairness. Indeed the normative literature about fairness stresses that fairness, while we might feel we know it when we see it, means different things to different people. We might argue that fairness involves the acknowledgment, preservation or even promotion of certain rights and that unfairness means disregarding these rights. Alternatively, we might rest our conception of fairness on the processes that are used to produce outcomes. If the process is fair, the outcome is fair. Or we might rely on an assessment of the outcomes themselves, using criteria such as the extent to which inequalities are rectified.

Economic theory has little to say about fairness per se. The criterion for distributive efficiency – Pareto optimality – favours any distribution of resources where no one can be made better off without someone else being made worse off. In practice, policy analysts rarely use Pareto optimality as a basis for deciding whether a particular outcome is fair or not. Rather, they employ rough and ready versions of cost–benefit analysis to determine whether or not there is a net gain. If the benefits outweigh the costs, the redistributive aspects are overlooked. It is enough that the winners could compensate the losers, rather than that they should do so. More generally, deciding whether or not the outcome of a particular policy is fair or not lies in the realm of value judgements, and for economists, values are considered to be exogenously given.

The terms fairness and equity are often used interchangeably. But from a policy values perspective, they serve different purposes. This is because, as I argued in Chapter 1, the values perspective brings out, from both a political and a policy point of view, the dynamic tension between policy intentions and policy outcomes. I shall reserve the term 'equity' for judgements about the final distributions that policy processes produce, whereas fairness, if we make full use of the English-language sense of the word, is a far more subjective concept.

We might regard fairness as the politics of equity. When we (metaphorically) stamp our feet and say 'that's not fair!' we are appealing to some standard of rightness that we feel has been violated. Invocations of fairness are often related to self-interest, but that does not mean that the value is therefore merely a fig leaf. I may consider that my pay is too low, but if I believe that it is unfairly low, I am seeking to persuade others of a quasi-moral case. If I believe that the wages of others are too low, for example because they are being exploited, my personal view of fairness starts to assume policy relevance: it can then be used to drive change.

Fairness is a ubiquitous policy value because of this dual character: partly self-seeking, partly other-regarding. But even if my concept of fairness embraces equity for others, there are limits to this degree of altruism. After all, I am much more likely to believe that my wage is too low, than I am to believe that the wages of others are too low. Then there is the reality of envious preferences. Social psychologists have long known (and economists seem to be just discovering) that people are not rational utility maximisers in their decision-making. Some would prefer a distribution in which they received less in absolute terms, if another group whom they regarded as unworthy, received less relative to themselves. Such groups adhere strongly to the principle of just deserts, even when doing so means that in absolute terms, their return is less than it would otherwise be. In politics, it is not so much self-interest which counts, but self-interest in relation to others that does. Many people would rather see a system that was less productive overall but forced others to do their 'fair' share.

Fairness in the policy world

In comparison to its more sober sister, equity, fairness can be unpredictable, even changeable. Being fair is not always easy, even if our intentions are good. We can see this in another way, by analysing the decisions involved. The traditional way of dividing a cake fairly is the 'cut and choose' approach, whereby one person cuts the cake in two, and the other chooses the piece he or she wants, leaving the remaining piece for the cutter. Obviously, the cutter will go for equal shares. But this leaves the matter of preferences unresolved. What if I have little liking for cake? What if I am on a diet? My utility will be enhanced by a smaller, rather than a larger, share.

Fairness in the policy world is a still more complex matter, because in the policy world, everything is up for grabs. In a well-known thought-experiment, Deborah Stone asked a group of students how the proverbial cake she had brought to class ought to be divided. The simple answer – that the cake should be divided equally – did not last long, because those who were not present (when they heard about the opportunity) realised that they had claims to make. Why should students in this class (rather than another) be entitled to receive a piece of cake? What about students who would have enrolled in the class had they known that a delicious piece of cake was on offer? The examples multiplied, until eight different 'takes' on fairness were arrived at (Stone, 1997).

Distribution (or even more so, redistribution) is an activity that cannot be imagined without some recourse to concepts of fairness. In her examination of equality in the polis, Stone divided these perceptions of fairness into three dimensions: recipients (who is included in the distribution, and how are they classified in terms of the outcome?), items (what is to be distributed: fresh air; scholarships) and processes (chance, competition or voting). We can see how useful Stone's analysis can be by looking at the fairness value as it comes into play in a case study that will resonate with many readers. Every year, at the start of the semester at my university, there is a shortage of parking. A strenuous debate develops. Who should have priority? Administrative staff? Academics? Possibly even students? Each of these groups has some claim to consideration. Then it is claimed that many of the spots are taken by interlopers who work downtown, but who evade the parking charges that would apply, by using the university's car park and then catching the bus to town.

This analysis attracts a considerable following, until someone points out that the car park in question is not in fact a private car park but is open to anyone to use. So claims based on membership of the university community are not a sufficient starting point. Fairness, even in private policy-making situations, connotes more than the principles of distribution – it relates to perceptions about where we draw boundaries, about the structuring of relationships, about who is regarded as worthy and who is not. Who will decide on what is fair is almost as important as how it is decided. We can also see that, whatever *solution* is adopted – whether we have first come first served, boom-gates and passes (allocated how?) – it leaves a residue in terms of perceived unfairness that may well cause the problem to be revisited. (Or there could be other changes that gradually cause the original solution to unravel).

Fairness and social construction: Who is deserving?

The sustainability of welfare states based on an assumed social homogeneity has been questioned by a number of commentators (see, for example, Baldwin, 1997). If citizens' entitlement to support is somehow called into question, the values basis of the welfare state moves into a state of flux. If the aged are 'us' a little further down the track, are the unemployed 'us' but for an unlucky break? And what about those who are obviously different, such as recent immigrants from different cultural and racial backgrounds? These are not issues that can be wished away. Citizens are actively aware of obligation and entitlement and quick to take exception to those who do not appear to be doing their fair share. The design of welfare states can either exacerbate these problems, or it can prevent them.

Our understanding of the value dimension of this problem has been considerably enhanced by the literature linking policy-making with social construction (Schneider and Ingram, 2005). Policies do not 'allocate fairness' in a vacuum. Fairness is itself based on ideas about deservingness. In constructing fairness, the aged are (generally) at the more deserving end of the spectrum. And as populations age, they represent a lot of votes. But deservingness has other dimensions, as well. In egalitarian societies, the super rich may be seen (certainly by the middle and working classes) as less deserving than themselves. At the same time, the middle class may be simultaneously envious and contemptuous of the poor. The very wealthy have the means, and the incentive, to remove themselves and their families, in whole or in part from the taxation burden. The very poor receive from the state what they are presumed to need. Where does that leave the group in the middle? It is here that most of the taxes are collected, and it is clearly this group whose interests and values will largely drive the future of obligation and entitlement.

Using values analysis to understand fairness

Can we use the concept of values analysis to illuminate the operation of fairness in relation to the functioning of welfare states? This might seem a rather unchallenging objective – after all, welfare states are supposed to be about fairness. They are usually evaluated according to the degree of social equality that they make possible. But welfare states, as an epic literature makes clear, have diverse origins, characters and structures. Classifying them in fully satisfactory ways, or even finding clear-cut ways of categorising the various types and combinations of policies they employ, has eluded many years of analysis (see Jones, 1997, p. 4).

Esping-Andersen's well-known three worlds of welfare correspond to the corporatist states of central Europe, the Scandinavian model, and the more limited American (or possibly Anglo-American) model (Esping-Andersen, 1990). Work by Castles proposes a fourth world, one embracing the UK, Australia and New Zealand (Castles and Mitchell, 1993). Jones (1997) emphasises policy design as a basis for classification: social insurance, in which premiums are effectively pooled and recipients receive benefits proportionate to their original salaries; universal systems of retirement provision, in which a prescribed pension is paid to all; occupational superannuation, in which individual accounts are maintained with superannuation funds; and means-tested systems, in which payments are made only to those in need.

But these classifications are essentially static. A growing literature on policy dynamics suggests a way of 'capturing' fairness (Bardach, 2006). We know that politics causes public policy. But, as Theodore Lowi was among the first to point out, public policy also creates politics. As public policies enact fairness, they create counter-reactions from those who perceive themselves as being treated unfairly, or who see their interests as being ill-served. We might simply describe this as interest politics, except that, as I argued in Chapter 1, the collective heart of public policy is not fully described by interest-based theory. Claims cannot be made on the basis of interest alone. And when policy is actually implemented, it becomes the starting point for the calculation of further claims.

I want to consider these interaction effects in relation to welfare policy in four English-speaking countries, two continental European countries (France and Germany) and one Asian country (Japan). In each case, I use the values analysis technique to explain aspects of policy change over time. As the design principles of welfare states (which enact obligation and entitlement in particular ways) both shape and interact with public perceptions of both these values, we see differing patterns of policy-based, and hence political, stress beginning to emerge. I argue that these factors shape the capacity of states to respond effectively to demographic change, and to the challenges (for many) posed by 'outsiders' who are difficult to place within the intersections of pre-existing circles of obligation and entitlement.

In each case, values tensions differ with each combination of obligation (defined as the extent to which citizens are required to contribute to the welfare of the collectivity) and entitlement (defined as the extent to which citizens receive, by virtue of their citizenship, benefits from – or via – the state.) In reconstructing their welfare states, governments are faced with the task of reconstructing fairness, an undertaking which requires political tact, some policy imagination and an ability subtly to alter expectations.

Trajectories of change

In developing these themes, I put forward vignettes of change in a wide range of welfare states in the period 1980–2005. The exercise is not comparative in the sense of attempting to explain welfare states by treating each state as a set of observations on key variables (see, for example, Castles, 1989). The *explanandum* is not the welfare state itself, but change. I use the values approach to demonstrate the closeness of the relationship between the way in which fairness was constructed and the pressures for change in each country.

Australia

In the 25 years from the early 1980s, the Australian welfare state and, in particular, the social security components of it underwent something of a revolution. In the 1980s, most of the elderly received a publicly funded pension. The unemployed received modest benefits for the time they were out of work. While some segments of the population (for example public servants and some managers in private industry) had access to occupational superannuation, in general, the expectation was that the government would look after you if you lost your job and in your old age. These benefits were paid for from general taxation, which at the time was heavily skewed towards taxes from income. Marginal tax rates were high, but impacted on a relatively small section of the population (Jones, 1996). In some respects, it was a highly egalitarian system in that those with resources were expected to provide for their own retirement, while those without received a pension paid for by the taxes of those still working. The pension was modest, and with a relatively young population, the system was financially viable.

It was not, however, a particularly fair system in that many of those receiving the pension could have provided for their own retirement had they been obliged to do so. It was a system that, because of its peculiar brand of particularism, emphasised entitlement rather than obligation (Jones, 1996). It has been a singular achievement of Australian federal governments since the 1980s to reduce entitlement, while still retaining an aged pension that is 'livable' for those forced to rely on it. How has this been done? Ironically, the residual nature of the Australian welfare state gave governments much freer scope in reshaping the system than was the case for the more universalist systems of Western Europe. The Hawke–Keating Labor government laid the groundwork by extending occupational superannuation to every employed person, by making employer contributions compulsory and privileging superannuation in terms of its tax treatment (Fenna, 2004). At the same time, means-testing of the public pension was made more stringent (through the inclusion of assets as well as income), as well as more generous (by indexing payments to average weekly earnings).

The use of compulsion, in the form of a superannuation tax paid by employers into the employee's fund, was crucial. Without it, many would have continued not to save and to rely on the public pension. By individualising retirement provision, however, and making benefits reflect, as far as possible, the earnings performance of superannuation funds, the government privileged 'super' as an attractive form of investment. Over time, more and more superannuants would have sufficient retirement income not to need 'topping up' from the public pension system. Necessarily, though, while more stable in the values sense, this type of system increases income dispersion among the aged. Those 'on the pension' are more likely to represent the genuinely deserving, but at the same time, they are more likely to be stigmatised than in the past. For those on the cusp of qualifying for pension benefits, whose personal calculus represents high obligation and low entitlement, the sense of unfairness is likely to be considerable.

The unemployed and mutual obligation

The spread of occupational superannuation, however, does little to address the values tensions resulting from an open-ended, non-means-tested system of unemployment relief. Indeed in some ways, by forcing a higher level of self-provision in relation to pensions, it highlights the situation of the unemployed (from the perspective of the average voter) as being 'undeserving', particularly during periods of relatively low unemployment, such as Australia enjoyed from the mid-1990s.

The government of John Howard, first elected in 1996, began to address this question (to considerable public acclaim) by bringing in a policy unambiguously entitled 'Work for the dole'. In return for receiving unemployment benefits, recipients would be required to submit to a regular work test. They would not be able to claim benefits unless they applied for a specified number of jobs referred to them by the employment agency. Alternatively, they could continue to receive benefits if they (a) engaged in full-time training or (b) joined a government-funded employment scheme, in which they would undertake socially and environmentally useful projects.

Later, this tougher line was extended to other beneficiaries, including single parents and the disabled, under the rubric of 'mutual obligation'. First brought to policy prominence by the work of the Reference Group on Welfare Reform chaired by Patrick McClure, mutual obligation required a reconstruction of both obligation and entitlement. The state's obligations were no longer encompassed simply by making payments, because payments induced welfare dependency. Rather the state's obligations would be couched in terms of training and re-training payment recipients so that they, too, could take their place in the workforce (Reference Group on Welfare Reform, 2000). While some 'third way' ideas about social exclusion found their way into the McClure report, the policies actually enacted by government between 2000 and 2005 were much more akin to the 'workfare' ideas that had characterised welfare changes in the United States than to those of the Blair government in the UK.

An astute reader of public opinion, Prime Minister Howard had divined that substantial sections of the electorate, many of them former Labor voters, were unhappy about their taxes supporting beneficiaries whom they regarded as undeserving. This version of fairness clashed with the version promulgated by many social policy professionals and academics, who saw the government's hardline treatment of the unemployed, single parents and the disabled as being the mark of a society that had lost all sense of fairness. In this kind of contest, however, and with a government determined to use the issue politically, the influence of public opinion upon policy would always outweigh that of the professionals.

New Zealand

Australia's neighbour, New Zealand, with a more universalist system of welfare provision, showed a quite different pattern of change during the 1990s. Although the management of the economy was totally rethought during the 1980s in a way that reflected deregulatory thinking at its most adamant, the fundamental contours of the welfare state remained fundamentally unaltered. In 2007, every New Zealander continued to be eligible to receive a non-means-tested pension at the age of 65. Although the financial sustainability of this arrangement had been widely questioned (Jones, 1997; Easton, 1999), its political popularity was undeniable.

From a values perspective, the New Zealand aged pension constructed obligation and entitlement in a way that stressed not the fairness of self-provision, but the fairness of collective provision. Unlike Australia, which (except for a brief period in the mid-1970s) means-tested its cash benefits, New Zealand aged pensions had no such limitations. Thus, the stability of the New Zealand system was guaranteed by its universalist qualities. There was little political support for change and (unlike in Australia) little scope for bringing in a compulsory system of occupational superannuation, except as a top-up for the pension.

The uniqueness (by the late 1990s) of New Zealand's largely pay-as-you-go universal pension cut both ways in terms of obligation and entitlement. New Zealand lacked a 'contract' between the individual and the state based on self-provision for retirement (Jones, 1997, p. 49). However, it would be equally possible to argue that the New Zealand system was based on a collectivist contract between the individual and the state, one which proved robust because it 'gave back' something to everyone. Treasury control over the terms of this contract was, moreover, absolute. Benefits to any category of recipient could be adjusted to suit the fiscal circumstances of the day. The unemployed and single parents could be (and were) kept on much lower payments than the aged. There has, however, been little evidence found of the kind of 'mutual obligation' policies towards single parents, the unemployed and the disabled in Australia. Why are New Zealanders much less likely to construe these groups as unfairly taking advantage of the state than Australians?

Part of the answer may lie in the complex relationship between Maori and non-Maori New Zealanders. While New Zealand Maori constitute a higher proportion of those on unemployment and single parent benefits than they do of the general population, Maori entitlement to social welfare benefits was recognised from the time of the establishment of the first aged pension in 1898. Maori were disadvantaged, but also sufficiently powerful to resist derogatory forms of social construction. To impose mutual obligation on a group that had successfully established its right to occupy the mainstream of New Zealand society, would be seen (not least by the Maori themselves) as highly discriminatory. While, during the 2000s, the Pakeha (white New Zealanders) were increasingly critical of benefits enjoyed by Maori by virtue of being so (for example, ownership of land and natural resources, see Kukutai, 2004), the basis for this sense of unfairness was not related to the social security system.

If the political stability of the New Zealand system is not in question, how does it (in contrast to other universalist systems) remain financially viable? Control is an important part of the answer: governments are able to adjust payments to keep the cost within bounds that are considered financially acceptable. Moreover, New Zealand has a readymade mechanism for releasing the build-up of financial pressures in that New Zealanders have free rights of entry to, and settlement in, Australia. When New Zealand economic performance falters relative to that of Australia, young New Zealanders have the option of moving across the Tasman in large numbers. This reduces pressure on the New Zealand unemployment benefits system and also, for those who stay away, on the retirement system, as there are residency requirements for claiming benefits.

United Kingdom

By the time Mrs Margaret Thatcher came to power in 1979, the UK was a full-fledged welfare state, with relatively high taxation of incomes and generous benefits for the unemployed, the sick and the aged. Retirement incomes were based on a two-tier system, with a universal flat-rate pension (the Basic State Pension), which reflected only years of contribution to the national system, supplemented (from 1975) by a second-tier publicly run scheme which provided earnings-related pensions (the State Earnings-related Pension Scheme). A partial exit option from the second tier was provided to those who wished to pursue private, occupational plans (Galasso, 2006, p. 164).

Why, if the UK was a fairly stable welfare state, did Mrs Thatcher's governments attempt, at least partially, to retrench it? The answer lies, not only in the political ideology of neo-liberalism, but also in the politics of values. Mrs Thatcher was a self-confessed adherent of Victorian values – the spirit of civic contribution and self-help and also of the Victorians' distinction between the deserving and the undeserving poor (Thatcher, 1993, p. 627). As a shrewd politician, she also understood the extent to which those in employment, particularly those not earning high incomes, resented the proliferating culture of dependency among those on benefits.

Her government reshaped the relationship between obligation and entitlement by reducing the top marginal income tax rate and by reducing by 5% benefits for sickness, unemployment, injury, maternity and invalidity. She also arranged for these payments to be indexed according to prices, rather than to wages – an important fiscal step, but also an important values-based step. She did not, for political reasons, touch the basic old-age pension. Later, the government of John Major required all unemployed people to enter a Jobseeker's Agreement committing them to a plan of action to seek work and means-testing benefits for those who had not made a specified number of National Insurance contributions (Wu, 2000).

The social inclusion policies of the Blair years represented a reaction against the harshness of many of these policies, applied at a time of massive industrial restructuring and social upheaval. Importantly, thinking about welfare had 'moved on' from ideas about equality (whether of ideas or of access) to ideas about the systemic causes and consequences of poverty and illness (Alcock and Craig, 2001). But social inclusion did not deny the importance of work – indeed, far from constructing work as the necessary price for social autonomy, work was constructed as the connecting, socialising experience that, for most people, it is. Tony Blair's political genius was that he was able to capitalise on the sense among many that Thatcherism had done as much good as it was going to do and that it was time for a change, without putting at risk the new construction of fairness. As Davies puts it 'club membership' (Blair-style) was governed by a substantive vision of the political good – personal entrepreneurialism and ethical communitarianism (Davies, 2005, p. 23).

In the crucial period of the 1980s, Mrs Thatcher had restructured obligation and entitlement in relation to social security in a way that was more sustainable for the British state, by reducing taxes on the one hand and qualifying access to benefits on the other. Clearly, the interests of her middle-class political constituency were involved in this. But many working-class people were also put out by a sense that others were getting benefits they were not entitled to. A welfare state that, in pursuing equity had come to violate fairness, was not one that, unaltered, could continue to command the support it had traditionally enjoyed.

United States

It is usual to think of the United States as an aberrant or unusual welfare state (Clarke and Fox Piven, 2001, p. 26). But in important respects, it subscribed to the same, collectivist employment-based social insurance schemes that characterised the British and European systems, albeit on a later and more fragmented basis. As Costa shows, the idea of retirement in the United States followed a path that was *sui generis*, but by the time of Roosevelt's new deal, the US system had started to look more like its exemplars elsewhere (Costa, 1998). There were, however, important differences, reflecting the diversity of the United States, the role of the South in frustrating welfare state legislation, the role of federalism and the antipathy of Americans to both big government and welfare (Peele, 2005).

In 1981 Ronald Reagan came to power promising a messianic war on communism and reduced government involvement in the lives of individuals. Like Thatcher, Reagan was a conviction politician whose political appeal rested on his ability to project and to dramatise his personal values. Henceforth, it would be what made America different from the social democracies of Western Europe that would structure policy. Reagan cut taxes for the rich and reduced benefits for the poor. But it was not a Republican but a Democrat (Bill Clinton) who introduced what Jones has called the 'employment-workfare' version of the welfare state (Jones, 1997). Popular frustration at the lack of success of welfare programmes for the poor and his own need to amass some political capital for his projected health care reforms, led Clinton in 1996 to bring in new social security policies that required single mothers to work in return for receiving public assistance (Peele, 2005). Not for the Americans the encouragement of Blair-ite social inclusion. Rather, it was to be the harshness of benefit restriction, aimed squarely at one particular group – lone mothers.

Why did this happen? The value placed on work in American culture is an obvious factor. But the relationship between this value and the institutions of the American welfare state provided additional impetus for change. The tax-funded programmes of assistance to the poor had never been as popular as the more broadly based 'New Deal' programmes that had delivered pension incomes to the retired. Moreover, the decentralised federal structure of the US welfare state brought home to those paying the benefits, their relationship with those receiving them. Indeed some states (such as Wisconsin) had been working actively to reduce their welfare rolls since the mid-1980s. A decade earlier, when Ronald Reagan, Governor of California, had famously excoriated welfare 'bums'. But this propinquity was associated with exclusion, rather than (as in Sweden) with forms of communitarianism that emphasised supervised inclusion. For many Americans, those on welfare were, by definition, outsiders.

Sweden

Sweden, as many studies have shown, is the *locus classicus* of the Scandinavian welfare state model, based on relatively high levels of taxation and widely dispersed benefits. We would expect such a system to be highly politically stable, because its fairness is of the universalist, rather than the particularist variety (that is, it is much less likely to arouse perceptions of unfairness from the perspective of particular groups). The architecture of the Swedish welfare state developed over a 50-year period of Social Democratic rule, lasting from the 1930s until the 1980s. Of particular importance was the introduction of a universal, earnings-related pension scheme in 1960 (Palmer and Wadensjo, 2004), which, coupled with wide-ranging schemes governing health and family needs, gave post-war Sweden one of the most comprehensive forms of social policy in the world (Olsson, 1990).

The stresses to which the Swedish state was subjected in the more volatile, post-1980s economic climate were fiscal, rather than values-based. The fact that the values basis held firm is a tribute to the power of universalism to resolve practical questions of fairness and also to the robustness, reinforced by a strong communitarianism at the local level, of the work ethic (Hort, 1997, p. 334).

Those changes that did occur to social security programmes were minor in character. Sickness insurance regulations were slightly changed in the 1990s, largely in response to employer complaints that they were too easy to access (Olsen, 2007). The retirement system was restructured in the 1990s to ensure greater financial sustainability, to ease the transition to retirement and to retain older adults in the workforce (Curl and Hokenstad, 2006).

While some studies suggest that Western Europeans have more interventionist attitudes towards social welfare than do Americans (Keman, 1998, p. 58), the broad consensus is that the underlying strength of the Swedish model rests, not upon Swedish preferences for equality, but upon Swedish universalism. The capacity of the Swedish state for this universal kind of fairness helped to bypass the kind of disaffection observed in the UK and in the United States in the 1980s and 1990s.

Germany

As the original Bismarckian welfare state, Germany was subject to the same forces that afflicted others in this mould. Its fundamentally corporatist architecture and moderately redistributive character ensured high levels of social stability, operating in tandem with a cooperative industrial relations system and a highly managed, yet market-oriented economy (Goodin, Headey, Muffels and Dirven, 1999, pp. 72–3). But the financial weight of the system was to prove more onerous with the passage of time. By the 1970s, the system (as with other social insurance models) had become effectively pay-as-you-go, rather than being fully funded (Esping-Andersen, 1996, p. 72). It also permitted, and even encouraged, early retirement.

Matters came to a head during the 1990s, when the worsening performance of the German economy was tied, by all but the political leadership of the left of the Social Democratic Party, to the excessive costs of employing workers. Policymakers responded by redefining obligation – initially forcing up contribution rates and slimming down benefits, and later, with the implementation of the Rurup reforms from 2002, a gradual increase in the retirement age and the consolidation of improved access to private pension plans (Galasso, 2006, p. 102).

During this period of 'mild retrenchment' of the social insurance system, German unemployment continued to worsen. Again, there seems to have been little of the resentment of the unemployed so conspicuous in Australia and the United States, and the UK. This may have had something to do with the fact that the very employment taxes that helped to fund social insurance were also implicated in worsening rates of unemployment (because they added to labour costs). The unemployed were in this state because there were no jobs, rather than because of a suspected disinclination to work. The very real challenges of the 1990s (population ageing, globalisation, the absorption of the former East Germany) could be addressed, at least in part, because of the solidity of the institutional structures of the German welfare state. These structures supported gradual change, without disturbing the prevailing ethos (Leisering, 2001).

France

The French case is one of the most interesting of all. Values analysis suggests that as a social insurance system, it should be politically sustainable, but subject to the same financial shortfalls and pressures as other systems of this type. We would expect, therefore, numerous efforts at reform, with (as in Italy and Germany), a tendency to buy reform by incremental increases in the retirement age. This strategy penalises younger workers relative to older ones (because the younger workers have to work longer), but has the advantage that it does not truncate the expectations of those nearing the current retirement age.

Successive French governments (beginning with the Juppe reforms of the 1970s) have indeed attempted to make changes to the social security system. Resistance to changing the contours of pension provision for the aged is among the strongest in Europe because of the tightness of the social coalitions underpinning the various social insurance schemes and in particular, the militancy of unions protecting the conditions of workers in the public sector (Palier, 2000). Workers who have contributed over many years to pension plans having (as they would see it) discharged their obligations already are reluctant to have their entitlements reduced. Moreover, there is a strong attachment by the French to their *sécurité sociale* as an integral part of their national identity (Childers, 2006).

As with all Bismarckian social insurance systems, participation depends upon employment, and those who miss out must rely on publicly provided social assistance, much of it means-tested. Nevertheless, the scale of benefits for those who have never worked is relatively generous. Unlike the Australian and US systems, however, where public sentiment and system design tend to accentuate resentment of the unemployed because they are unemployed, in France, there is little public sense that the unemployed should be more tightly bound by a sense of obligation to the state. Commentators write of the 'invisibility' (to the majority) of the suburbs of major cities containing the housing estates where many immigrants live (Caulcutt, 2007). As the riots of 2005 demonstrated, resentment works the other way – from those who are excluded to the majority of citizens who are comfortably provided for.

In the systemic sense, the French have become caught in a classic vicious circle. Excessive taxes on employment and considerable labour market rigidity result in more unemployment than there would otherwise be. And this unemployment falls disproportionately on the unskilled and in particular on recent immigrants. If these immigrants were constructed as insiders who had somehow fallen down on their responsibilities, we would expect the tighter policing that is characteristic of the Anglo-American democracies. Ironically, the psychological isolation of these immigrants and their physical seclusion in the *banlieus* of big cities like Paris, enabled them to be constructed as complete outsiders, beyond even the reach of fellow-citizens' notions of obligation.

Japan

Japan is usually described as a particularist welfare state on the basis of a social insurance model for those in employment, but at the same time, showing a strong reliance on the family (for which read women) as the site of social welfare and service delivery (Goodman and Peng, 1996, p. 193). The relationship between obligation and entitlement is intricately bound up with the productive structure of the country in a way that is usually held to be typical of the East Asian developmental state (Aspalter, 2006). Japanese policy places a heavy reliance on the 'lifetime employment' traditionally provided by large Japanese companies to their loyal workers (Peng, 2000).

Slower economic growth during the 1990s placed this social contract under increasing strain, while demographic factors have also played their part. The numbers of the elderly, considered particularly deserving in Japan, have been growing at an internationally unprecedented rate. The elderly have universal access to national health care, although care for the frail age is not well-developed. Aged pensions, although means-tested, are typically generous. The revenue design of the system (from the 1970s, fundamentally pay-as-you-go) meant a substantial intergenerational transfer from the working population to the elderly (Uzubashi, 2001).

The Japanese state was able to come to grips with pension reform by reshuffling costs and benefits within the system of social insurance. This task was made less onerous by the fact that, unlike in Western Europe, male workers were much less likely to be on pre-retirement disability benefits, and there was little, if any, trend towards early retirement. Despite slow economic growth during the 1990s, the Japanese 'welfare society', based on the provision by major Japanese companies of corporate welfare to their employees, remained largely intact into the twenty-first century (Uzubashi, 2001).

If there is a values tension within the Japanese welfare state, it would appear to arise from two sources, the young and women. Fushimi points to the extent of the transfers from young workers to the elderly and to the disillusionment of the young with the social insurance system (Fushimi, 1997, p. 90). The emphasis on the family is held to be a defining characteristic of east Asian welfare states. But this emphasis gives a gendered basis to obligation and entitlement that places a heavy reliance on women acting as caregivers to the young and the elderly, without adequate social support – a form of institutionalised unfairness that policymakers began to address in the mid-1990s with provisions for paid leave for carers. Nevertheless, much remained to be done, as the government acknowledged with its 1999 Framework for the Promotion of Gender Equality.[1]

Implications for policy analysis

The values analysis brings out the importance of the interrelationships between structures, policy design and social construction in explaining particular political features of welfare states. It does not address outcomes in the sense of measured levels of social equity. But in concentrating on the dynamics of fairness, as they played out over the last two decades of the twentieth century, it brings out similarities between two of the English-speaking countries – Australia and the United States – and also differences with two others, New Zealand and the UK. While in many respects not alike, Australia and the United States showed a kind of convergence in their policy values.

This perspective does not suggest a new way of classifying welfare states, but it does suggest the importance of policy design, as well as institutional structure, in explaining change. It also provides a way of linking the tax and welfare systems. In allocating fairness, states come up with differing balances between obligation and entitlement. No one system can be stable in the long, or even the medium term, because populations change in their composition, budgetary conditions alter and the global economy exacts its own competitive pressures. This comes out more clearly when we link the tax system with the welfare system.

In the political sense, taxation is usually thought of as the politics of self-interest, *tout court* (Peters, 1991). Yet what is 'fair' in taxation also affects national policy debates, and the pattern of taxation in every country is finely balanced between citizens' sense of solidarity with others and what they perceive as fairness (to themselves). We might expect that preferences for fairness in the design of tax systems would remain fairly constant over time. In practice, since the 1960s, high marginal taxes on incomes have been considerably reduced not only in the UK but also in the United States, Australia, and also in the several countries of the European Union.

When citizens are asked about their attitudes to tax, they reply that they are not really conscious of what they receive in exchange for their taxes. Rather, they are motivated by much more vague notions of social solidarity; in other words, by their sense of obligation. There is not a great deal of evidence that this sense of obligation has diminished over the past 50 years. But there is certainly ample evidence that tax rates on income, at the top end of the progressive scale, have fallen. Why? In part, the shift has been caused because it is simply too difficult to collect taxes at this level. High-income individuals have strong incentives to avoid or to evade tax, and a small army of tax professionals is only too willing to help them do it.

Globalisation, too, has had an impact. In open economies, taxes on employers or more broadly, taxes that raise the cost of employing people, may act as a disincentive to invest in (or to remain in) particular countries. Bracket creep puts middle class taxpayers on a par with the rich. And governments believe they can always buy popularity with tax cuts. But there has also been a shift in public perceptions as to what a given level of obligation means in practical terms. Conceptions of fairness have changed. As they have grown richer, societies have become more tolerant of wider disparities of wealth and income and less tolerant of redistributive levels of taxation. This values change is often portrayed in ideological terms as the result of a resurgent 'new right' undermining a previously dominant Keynesian welfare state. The perspective adopted here suggests that at least some of the story lies within the dynamics of the welfare state itself.

Values, ideas and the movement to the right

There are many accounts of the 'movement to the right' that took place in the politics of English-speaking countries in the 1980s, but discussion of the origins of the change is rather circumscribed. The conventional account tends to operate at the level of ideas, rather than of politics. It goes something like this: Keynesian paradigms broke down in the 1970s, as it began to be observed that traditional demand management was no longer as effective as it had once been in combating recessions. The 1970s witnessed both low growth and relatively high rates of inflation, causing governments, assisted by a growing body of international economic opinion, to rethink the role of government in the economy. Big-spending, deficit-producing governments came to be seen as being part of the problem, rather than part of the solution.

At the same time, the 'new Right', which taught a much narrower form of liberalism than had prevailed in the post-war period, was beginning to attack the welfare state, not simply (or even primarily) from an efficiency perspective, but from that of an individual rights-based, even libertarian, perspective. Taxing some so as to make redistributive payments to others was attacked as constituting an unwarranted interference with liberty. These two trends were combined, by many academic commentators, under the banner of 'neo-liberalism'.

By implication, according to the conventional account, the move to the right was a pastime of policy elites, rather than one that reflected any fundamental change in public opinion. To a degree this was true. Business played a strong role in moving the policy agenda to the right. But this agenda change reflected a new mood in the broader public which itself reflected disillusionment with a system that seemed to have led, by the 1980s, to a kind of economic and social sclerosis. Few scholars predicted this reaction, and few have commented upon it in these terms, largely because the values present in welfare state policies were assumed, rather than problematised. Pressures for change were seen to come overwhelmingly from outside influences (such as globalisation) and from the financial demands imposed by aging populations.

There was little space, in scholarly reasoning about policy, to understand the relationship between the values represented by policies and the reactions of those exposed to them. I suggest that, coupled with the institutional design features of policies, these relationships explain a good deal of the policy change that has been observed, particularly in relation to the welfare state, in the period since the 1980s. Concepts of 'undeservingness' (that is of unfairness) ran deeply in the English-speaking democracies, particularly in relation to the payment of social assistance. These problems were avoided in the Scandinavian and European welfare systems, because of the more universalistic qualities of their social insurance systems which, by extending benefits to groups who would otherwise receive little, tend to assuage concerns about 'undeserved' redistribution. At the same time, every country finds itself in the position of having to constrain or otherwise manage the expectations of retirees.

Conclusion: Improving equity

The conventional view is that improving equity means improving the reach or effectiveness of those policies whose objective is in some sense to do this. This is difficult enough to do. However, the reality of social policy, viewed from a values-analysis perspective, is both more complex and simpler than this. It is more complex because social policy is as much about fairness as it is about equity. As it is implemented in the real world, social policy invokes a set of intricate relationships between different perceptions of fairness. In particular, perceptions of unfairness (that is, feelings against those receiving more than they are entitled to) play a decisive role in shaping responses to the distributions of goods and services that existing policies make possible. The paradox of social policy is that, the more redistributive it is seen to be, the less stable it becomes, precisely because redistribution arouses perceptions of unfairness from those in the middle of the income distribution.

But social policy may also be simpler than is generally allowed, because, using the kind of values analysis I am arguing for here, it is possible to see beyond the distributive aspects of social policy to the broader relationships of obligation and entitlement that determine longer-term sustainability. Most citizens understand that whatever government spends must be paid for by taxpayers. There is no magic pudding. Public policies, whether explicitly or implicitly, express our sense of an appropriate balance between obligation and entitlement – who will pay and how, and who will receive and how?

Economists (and not only those of the right) have argued at length about the sapping effects of too much welfare. But politically, change becomes possible only when citizens start to believe that the calculus of obligation and entitlement has gone out of alignment. What was done in the name of fairness has become unfair – to them. The situation becomes more politically powerful when those on welfare come to be seen not as 'me' or 'potentially me' but 'the other'. Those who look different are more likely to fall into this category. But it applies equally to those who look the same, but are perceived to be acting unfairly.

Policy systems keep the lid on these problems by applying different combinations of universalism and particularism to them. Universalism is politically popular, because it retains middle-class allegiance. But the price is a high degree of fiscal strain, particularly in the case of the aged. Schemes that became entrenched in the post-war years assumed relatively large numbers of working age people and relatively small numbers of retirees. In other words, intergenerational transfers made the system sustainable.

In rebalancing the system, what is 'fair'? And how far does the ambit of fairness run? We expect more fairness of governments than we do of the private sector. If a big shot is shown to the best table in the restaurant, while we are placed beside the toilet entrance, we ruefully reflect that is the way of the world – or go to McDonalds. We are rightly angry when governments (metaphorically) do the same. The meta-problem here is that economic sustainability requires some form of targeting, while political sustainability requires some form of universality. States that best resolve the fairness problem, best resolve the issue of political sustainability.

4
The Impact of Efficiency

This chapter argues that efficiency is a policy value in the same way that (for example) equity is a value. As with the other public policy values, efficiency is allocated through choices made both explicitly and implicitly, as polities decide the extent to which social systems are to be characterised by efficient solutions.

The explicit part of the story is easy to see. Through market competition, the pursuit of efficiency comes to dominate ever-larger areas of public policy – not just those considered to be 'economic' in character, but penetrating areas of social policy as well. Ewen Michael puts this position well. 'Policy', he writes, 'must complement the driving forces of the market and mirror the framework of competition so that public resources are allocated where community demand dictates' (Michael, 2006, p. 213).

The implicit part of the story, that is, the way values choices are made through institutions and processes, is more difficult to conceptualise. Efficiency is a paradigmatic policy value, one that holds its sway as much by the courses of action it invalidates or excludes as by those it privileges. The paradigm of efficiency helps to conceal trade-offs; that is, the costs to other valued objectives that are occasioned by improvements in efficiency. If these costs are simply benefits enjoyed by the inefficient, they would not be considered significant. But some of these costs will correspond to other valued objectives such as work–life balance or job security. The pursuit of efficiency may jeopardise social equity, or (as is often the case in urban contexts) amenity. The pursuit of global efficiency through free trade may favour rich over poor nations and undermine environmental protection. Efficiency casts a large 'values shadow' in this sense.

Efficiency is also an asymmetric value in the sense that while an argument *for* efficiency is self-legitimating, it is difficult to argue *for* policy objectives that involve efficiency costs. But if efficiency is the same kind of 'thing' as any other valued objective, it means that it is possible to choose – explicitly – not to be efficient, that is, to privilege other values, even though that choice may detract from efficiency.

This kind of consideration brings us to a difficult intersection between economics, as undoubtedly the premier policy science and the broader world of policy reasoning. The usual response from economists to charges that their discipline is in danger of overreaching itself is that efficiency is not an end in itself but a means to an end. As Argy puts it, 'When economists seek market-based solutions, they are discussing better means to given ends' (Argy, 2003). Within this context, efficiency is privileged because it is, according to the economics paradigm, welfare-enhancing; that is, it adds to utility and saves resources.

But the power of the economic paradigm goes beyond this terrain because of the agenda-setting and policy-framing roles the mantra of efficiency exercises. The pursuit of efficiency tells us where to look for change, it helps us to drive change, and it constructs targets as 'inefficient' and therefore undesirable. The unleashing of competition through deregulation becomes a policy panacea. Paradoxically though, creating the competitive markets upon which efficiency relies involves concerted and comprehensive efforts from government. It is something of a myth that efficiency will implement itself once sufficient regulatory debris has been cleared away. If it is ever cleared, the debris is replaced by more regulatory mechanisms.

This chapter shows how, in the period between 1980 and 2000, the value of efficiency shaped public policy in both national and international contexts. These effects are considered both directly (that is, when governments take action in the name of efficiency) and through the oppositional or counter-trends that the pursuit of efficiency creates. I tell this story in three parts:

Firstly, I consider the role played by efficiency-based paradigms in setting policy agendas.

Secondly, I describe, in broad terms, the kinds of policy initiatives that represent the value of efficiency in action.

Thirdly, using values analysis techniques, I discuss the kinds of changes efficiency-based policies set in train, as values traded off or overlooked in the implementation of policy, resurface through politics.

Efficiency and agenda-setting

We know that economic analysis provides a useful way of understanding and structuring many policy problems. But this does not explain how the efficiency value shapes public policy. I argue that it exercises its power through a paradigm; that is, a way of seeing the world that not only structures specific problems, but (perhaps more significantly) also marginalises other approaches (Hall, 1993). The structuring role of efficiency highlights resource allocation and cost. An efficient solution to an emergent problem (such as how to cut back on greenhouse gas emissions) is one that brings about a desired result at the least cost.

Economists have traditionally recognised two main varieties of efficiency: productive (or technical) efficiency and allocative efficiency. Productive efficiency is the form most familiar to the layperson. It is usually invoked at the level of the firm or organisation and describes the way that a firm or industry uses resources to achieve its outputs. Improving productive efficiency, therefore, means getting more out of your resources: either achieving more outputs with the same inputs; or achieving the same outputs with fewer inputs. Many managerial policies (such as outsourcing) aim to increase the efficiency of the organisation in this sense.

Allocative efficiency, by contrast, refers to the way resource inputs are distributed within an entity or, more broadly, in a society as a whole. Allocative efficiency in an economy is enhanced when resources are redistributed between uses in such a way that a higher level of consumer surplus is achieved. The idea behind allocative efficiency is that competitive markets do the best job of aligning resource use with personal preferences. Together, these two kinds of efficiency constitute cost efficiency (Productivity Commission, 1997).

In theory, improving productive efficiency means finding sources and locations of inefficiency and removing them. In practice, unless the problem is very obvious, it is difficult to know without comparing yourself with others whether you are inefficient. As Deborah Stone puts it, 'Trying to measure efficiency is like trying to pull oneself out of quicksand without a rope' (Stone, 1997, p. 65). While in the private sector competition (at least in theory) winnows out the less efficient, in the public sector there are fewer messages from the marketplace and ways must be found to mimic them. Surrogates for competition include compulsory competitive tendering, which requires that providers within an agency compete for work against those outside, usually (although not exclusively) on the basis of cost-competitiveness.

Thus (according to the theory) the public sector, when it awards the contract, imports the cost-efficiencies of the marketplace into its operations. Comparisons, either across space, or across time, also help in answering the question: how efficient are we? Benchmarking is one way of making structured comparisons with other organisations across space. Efficiency-based performance indicators allow organisations to compare their own performance across time. More broadly, productive efficiency can be further enhanced by policies that encourage investment in new equipment, better training and the diffusion of innovation.

Improving allocative efficiency requires action at a more broadly based or systemic level. According to economic theory, because competition is the great search engine of efficiency, enhancing competition in an industry (for example, by reducing regulation) increases the pressure on managers to reduce inefficiency or risk being taken over. If the return on investment does not improve sufficiently, competition will move investment into activities where a higher return can be achieved. Either way, output will be increased. In the longer run, increasing competition may change the productive parameters of firms and industries by enhancing their productive potential (for example, through innovation), although the causal links here (that is, between competition and innovation) are not as clear-cut as those between competition and efficiency-enhancement.

Beyond their structuring role, paradigms provide both commonality and power. Commonality is a factor because paradigms are the ties that bind epistemic communities – policy communities that consist of people with a common model of rationality. Power is a factor because those who do not subscribe to the paradigm can be excluded from the institutions that the paradigm serves. In policymaking contexts, economic analysis has been given the paradigmatic label of 'economic rationalism' (Pusey, 1991; Edwards, 2002). Pusey has described how, particularly in Australia and in New Zealand, in the critical period beginning in the early 1980s, the policy agenda was set by the values of economic rationalism. This was 'insider' agenda formation of a striking kind.

In every state, economic management and the direction and control of public expenditure are held tightly at the centre of power – in treasuries and departments of finance. In Westminster systems, the most powerful political office, after that of the prime minister, is that of the Chancellor of the Exchequer or Treasurer. While politics generates other priorities and values, spending agencies must always justify their bids within the framework imposed by the requirements of economic and fiscal management – a necessary discipline, of course, but one that gives great structural power to the values and world-view of treasury officials. In the 1980s and 1990s, in Australia, New Zealand and the UK, treasury and finance power rested upon, and extended, the power of economic rationalism. Thus there was a mobilisation of bias within the institutional agenda, that is, the 'do list' of government that, together with an unusually concerted political appetite for change, provided a powerful driving force for the deregulatory policies of the era.

Implementing efficiency

While agenda construction is critical, new values cannot be advanced without vectors (groups capable of transmitting the value from one sector to another), both within and outside the state. At first glance, efficiency might appear to be an unlikely candidate for dissemination because in general, efficiency is an objective more sought after for others than for oneself. Indeed the broad arguments of public choice theory, particularly its collective action variants, would have it that public policies that advance the cause of efficiency will find few allies in the polis. That this is not the case is demonstrated by the growing enthusiasm of business elites for efficiency-enhancing policies in the 20 years from 1980 to 2000. Where efficiency has suited the interests of some sections of capital, it has been enthusiastically pursued.

We can distinguish three main policy types with efficiency goals, or with major efficiency rationales:

- deregulatory policies (e.g. deregulation of labour markets, transport markets; markets for goods and services);
- policies aimed at improving public sector efficiency (such as outsourcing, or general budgetary stringency); or extracting 'efficiency dividends' from organisations; and
- 'marketising' policies, such as those that encourage (or mandate) privatisation (in the sense of selling publicly owned assets). In practice, these policy types were often combined, or overlapped, as new institutional relationships emerged.

Deregulatory policies

The economic definition of regulation is any rule that changes the behaviour of an actor. Many policies change behaviour through other means (for example through incentives). Regulation changes behaviour by changing what is permissible and can, over time, build up wide-ranging institutional patterns. By the same token, deregulation – the removal or (more usually) the changing of rules – is a powerful policy act because it often undermines long-standing assumptions and expectations. In a broader sense, we can think of these policies as redefining relationships between the institutions of government on the one hand and those of the market on the other. This choice, often constructed as purely technical, is intensely values-based in that it defines new categories of winners and losers.

Deregulation in the transport industry

Governments regulate transport in the service of a wide range of values, from safety to equity to service quality. Let us consider the example of regulation that prevents new entrants into an industry, widespread in many sectors of the transport industry for much of the twentieth century, and still a factor in some sectors (for example controls on taxi licences). This form of regulation is considered to be fundamentally efficiency-reducing, so that tracking the course of change is a good way to delineate the shift in policy values. One of the most significant sectors to be deregulated from the 1970s onwards was the airline industry. This is an industry with substantial economies of scale, so that, in small markets, maintaining adequate levels of competition can be an issue.

In the United States, airline deregulation began in 1978, during the presidency of Jimmy Carter. The regulatory apparatus headed by the Civil Aviation Board was rapidly dismantled. Competition led to significant bankruptcies in the industry and a period of prolonged conflict with unions. A review by the Government Accounting Office in 1999 found that fares had fallen overall, although more so on heavily trafficked, long-distance routes than on shorter, less well-patronised ones (GAO, 1999). As the industry continued to evolve under the impact of deregulation, firms found new ways of competing with one other, and new firms emerged, a pattern that was replicated in a number of jurisdictions. In April of 1997, full deregulation in 17 countries of the European Union led to the launch of new, cut-price airlines, and a welter of price-based competition. Ten years later, the pace of change had slowed, but not halted. While some rationalisation of the industry was expected, a number of the low-cost carriers were expected to survive (Gilroy, Lukas and Volpert, 2005).

In countries with smaller markets, however, the problems of oligopoly were more difficult to resolve. Australia's 'two-airline' policy, which ran from 1952 until 1990, is a case in point. It was designed to permit some competition, but to prevent what governments termed 'destructive' competition; that is, competition that would undermine the sustainability of the two major operators, one government-owned, the other privately owned. Why a duopoly? Policymakers believed that Australia, with its relatively small population, was naturally a two-airline country. With airline operations containing a substantial degree of fixed costs, there was insufficient demand to sustain more than two operators. At the same time, the policy prevented monopolisation. Price competition between the two airlines was also constrained. Neither was permitted to offer discount fares if to do so would lead to increases in standard ticket prices. In return, the parties to the agreement provided services to most towns and cities across the country (Dixon, 2003).

As it had done in Europe and the United States, deregulation of the domestic industry produced a high degree of instability. New entrants came and went; Ansett (one of the earlier duopolists) was acquired by Air New Zealand and collapsed in 2003, requiring extensive public intervention (in the form of a hypothecated tax on air tickets) to pay employee entitlements (Kain and Webb, 2003). From 2000, Virgin Blue Airlines moved into the market as a point-to-point operator, offering discount prices, but picking and choosing the most profitable routes over which to fly. Clearly, airline deregulation had enhanced efficiency. But other values, less easy to quantify, had suffered under deregulation. Arguably, the small size of the Australian market highlighted the difficulties involved in the transition.

Regional services had suffered to some degree, while the stability that regulation had protected, and the interests (largely those of workers and management) that had prospered in the earlier period, were now much more fragile than before. The privatisation of major airports added new layers of complexity to the mix. Interestingly passenger safety, the principal value that could not be sacrificed for efficiency, continued to be an object of both regulation and monitoring throughout this period, although it was not until 2004 that it was assigned formal priority in the work of the main regulatory authority, the Civil Aviation Safety Authority (CASA, 2004).

Privatisation and deregulation in telecommunications

The need, in an era of deregulation, for new forms of regulation was also apparent in the telecommunications industries. Privatisation of telecommunications agencies had been widely carried out since the 1970s. In Europe, beginning with British Telecom, virtually all carriers were fully or partially privatised in the years following 1990. In Asia, while Japan was the earliest to move, a range of full or partial privatisations had occurred in South Korea, Hong Kong and Singapore by 2003 (Ure, 2003).

The motivations and emphases differed from country to country. In Japan, the agenda for the privatisation of Nippon Telegraph and Telephone (NTT) in 1984 was to unleash private sector efficiencies and open the arena to value-added services, while retaining tight regulatory control by the Ministry of Posts and Telecommunications (Gottinger and Takashima, 2000). In the UK, on the other hand, the privatisation of telecommunications formed an iconic part of Mrs Thatcher's massive programme designed to change the institutional structures – essentially the power relations – of Britain.

Whatever their primary motivation, governments gradually learned that privatisation merely changed the regulatory equation, not the need for regulation itself. Technological change, in the form of the burgeoning Internet, added new levels of complexity to the regulatory task because there were now more groups to consider in devising a workable regulatory regime. Firms competing with each other to provide telecommunications services to end-users required access on reasonable terms to the cables and wires controlled by privatised telecommunications monopolies. Regulators whose overall objective was to ensure efficiency found that they had to conjure with multiple values in balancing the interests of consumers, intermediaries and the providers of infrastructure.

It is in this context that we can truly appreciate the values-balancing capacities of public ownership. When agencies operating in natural monopoly environments were publicly owned, they could pursue multiple values – for example they could cross-subsidise rural users of services in the interests of equity, and they could engage in a wide range of research, development and training activities. In a privatised environment, on the other hand, the firm's principal objective must be to maximise returns to shareholders. To this extent, the goals it must pursue are clear. But in turn this means that the public interest – a difficult concept at the best of times – must be interpreted and asserted by the regulator. The problem of values-balancing has not been removed, it has been simply displaced.

Free trade

Taxes on trade (such as tariffs) have long been used by nation-states as a means of raising revenue and to encourage investment in import-replacing industries. From an economic perspective, this form of assistance is efficiency-reducing, because (relative to the free-trade position) it moves patterns of trade away from those that reflect comparative advantage and towards those that reflect political preferences or other strategies. Gains from trade (from specialisation) are consequently reduced. Within national economies, producers in the protected industries gain at the expense of consumers. Public choice theory predicts that deregulation (in the form of tariff reductions and the removal of other restrictions on trade) should be particularly difficult to effect because of the power and relative concentration of the interests involved. Certainly, the trade restrictions that have proved most resistant to reform (those related to agriculture), have been supported by powerful coalitions of interests in the countries concerned. But there were powerful forces working for, rather than against, change. The profits to be made from globalisation and the doctrine of efficiency made powerful allies.

The liberalisation of markets for goods and (later) services dominated the international trade policy agenda in the post-war era. The General Agreement on Tariffs and Trade (the GATT), which later became the World Trade Organisation (WTO), defined arenas for the progressive reduction of tariffs and other restrictions on trade on a wide range of manufactured goods. Later trade rounds moved the spotlight to services. Multilateralism meant that agreed reductions applied *pari passu*, to all other signatories. Financial flows (both investment-oriented and speculative) also became progressively freer throughout this period. The evolving pattern of trade favoured those countries with a specialisation in manufactured goods. Those dependant on agricultural trade (many of them developing nations) fared less well. That trade policies shifted, at least in part, towards greater efficiency suggests the power of the economic paradigm, but also (within its own terms) its limitations. Many nations accepted the need for an overarching international agreement on trade, but hedged their bets when it came to specific domestic industries. Thus the WTO showed a kind of marble-cake effect, with tariff reductions proceeding rapidly in areas that were likely to survive international competition and more slowly in relation to those that would create political problems domestically.

We see this pattern particularly clearly in the case of Australia, a developed nation with an unusual pattern of exports (reflecting a reliance on relatively unprocessed agricultural and resources exports). Domestic manufacturing was largely protected from imports. However, rapid restructuring occurred as a result of progressive rounds of tariff reductions beginning in the mid-1970s. The size of the manufacturing sector reduced quickly, with the investment moving offshore or into other areas. Those areas of manufacturing with important political constituencies (such as motor vehicle manufacturing) were given assistance to restructure. But if politics guided implementation, policy formulation was as much a contest of ideas and values as it was one of interests manifested in a titanic battle over the policy agenda.

The power of the economics paradigm was instrumental in legitimating change. Assistance of any kind to industry, for whatever reason, was portrayed as 'protection', and therefore delegitimated. Just why the efficiency value proved so powerful in Australia has yet to be satisfactorily explained. But the paradigmatic power of economistic thinking certainly played a key role (Bell, 1993; Stewart, 1994). Nation-building values that had underpinned pro-manufacturing policies in the immediate post-war period were eclipsed (within the political class) by an overwhelming belief in the output-maximising properties of markets. The new Australian economy was heavily services-based and resource-based, with continuing low levels of private sector research and development and a declining national interest in science and technology. Levels of private debt rose rapidly, necessitating tight fiscal management to keep interest rates under control. Values such as balance (between sectors of the economy); decentralisation (away from major centres of population); and a degree of national self-sufficiency (particularly in strategic industries) were replaced by those of specialisation, concentration and integration with the global economy.

Outsourcing in the public sector

Outsourcing of services previously provided by public servants was a major development during the 1980s and 1990s in the UK, Australia and New Zealand. While ideology (in the form of a preference for the private over the public sector) undoubtedly played a part in legitimating change, much of the rationale for change was about efficiency and the efficiency-enhancing role of competition. The rationale was that the private sector could do it cheaper and better, but mainly, cheaper. As outsourcing was attempted in less contestable and more complex areas, however, it became apparent that the achievement of efficiency gains was a less straightforward business than many had initially assumed.

Evaluation of outsourcing produced mixed results, and the extent of cost savings was widely contested. A general study by the Australian Industry Commission in 1997 found huge variations in reported efficiencies, a finding echoed in an international study by Hodge (Hodge, 2000). In a 2007 paper, Lin, Pervan and McDermid found that in the major area of information systems and information technology outsourcing, few evaluations had been performed (Lin, Pervan and McDermid, 2007). A period of compulsory IT outsourcing in the

Australian Public Service was abandoned in 2001 because centralised contracts could not reflect the circumstances or needs of particular agencies (Humphry, 2000). Contract mismanagement and misspecification were widely blamed for outsourcing problems. But the multivalent requirements of public sector agencies must also be mentioned in this context: public organisations were not designed to be efficient but to be 'fair, open, objective, and accountable' (Lin, Pervan and McDermid 2007, p. 164). It appeared that greater efficiencies could be bought only at the expense of continuing (and high) transactions costs, as agencies struggled to maintain the control implied by their broader missions.

Quarantining efficiency in the polis

While efficiency is presented as a self-legitimating policy value, the reality is that significant areas of policy decision-making are quarantined (at least to some degree) from efficiency considerations. In certain circumstances, resources are allocated not according to cost–benefit principles, but according to principles that represent quite different values. Health and education are two sectors where we restrict the play of efficiency, often implicitly (because the importance of other values is assumed), but also explicitly, as when we restrict (or redefine) competition in order to achieve other goals (see, for example, Le Grand, 2007). It is worth identifying and discussing how and why this occurs.

Health: Budgetary rationing and the rescue principle

Economists would argue that health expenditures should be allocated where they will benefit most (for example in terms of the value of life years saved), rather than to those in greatest need. But empirical research suggests that most people subscribe to the 'rescue principle', where the most exigent conditions are treated first, regardless of cost (Nord, Richardson, Kuhse and Singer, 1995). In practice, health systems get around the problem by budgetary-rationing, a process which keeps the most pointed value judgements (about what kinds of conditions are to receive priority) off the immediate decision-making agenda. But periodically, politics intervenes, such as when the public discovers that there are not enough kidney dialysis machines to go around, and deserving cases must either wait or somehow find the resources to secure treatment outside the public health system.

Health allocation formulae desensitise as far as possible the values choices that would otherwise have to be made. Funding according to relative cost ('case-mix' funding), for example, pays hospitals according to weighted cost data, but does not question (except at the margin) the allocation of resources on the basis of historical patterns of service provision. When we consider health budget-making more generally, decisions about the resources devoted (for example) to the last few years of life, are quarantined from those relating to public health. While a dollar spent on public health may be more cost effective than one spent on intensive care for elderly patients, it would be a brave health administrator who would advocate giving more dollars to public health at the expense of health interventions for the elderly.

Education: Restricting competition

Efficiency plays relatively little role in the funding of education. Efficiency reviews may shut down schools considered to have too few students, but in general dollars go to schools on the basis of their capital expenditure needs, their maintenance requirements and the number of staff considered sufficient for the size and type of school. When public schools do their reporting, these inputs may be packaged together to constitute 'outputs'; that is, the number of children educated. But quite obviously, encouraging educational institutions to compete solely on the basis of efficiency would be to overlook the true purpose of schools – their effectiveness.

At the same time, the use of competition between schools to enhance effectiveness (for example, by publishing school performance data in so-called leagues tables) remains controversial. Competition between schools holds considerable risks for public education systems because popular schools may draw too many students away from less popular ones. In the business sector, an enterprise that is out-competed is taken over or closes down: closing down a school means unravelling many years of collective investment and community effort. The costs of travelling to a different school mitigate the risks of competition to some degree, but even so, many public systems restrict enrolment in any given school to the children of families living in the surrounding area. In some systems, great ingenuity has been shown in maintaining performance pressure while retaining services in a particular area (for example, by putting principals of 'failing' schools on notice). Use has also been made of 'charter' schools: that is, schools run by non-government entities under special accountability provisions, or 'charters'.

Services (such as health and education) may be run as businesses, but the ends that they serve are not primarily financial. Hence the environments in which they operate are deliberately maintained (largely by public policies) in a more multivalent state than would otherwise be the case. Chapter 9, which looks at universality and choice in both health and education, takes these issues further. For the moment, we should note the importance of policy institutions that do not privilege efficiency.

Trade-offs: What do we lose when we prioritise efficiency?

In the Anglo-American democracies (and in Australia and New Zealand particularly), efficiency was the great agenda-setting value of the 1980s and 1990s. It diagnosed what was wrong with economies; it established an engine for change (market competition); and it marginalised other values by circumscribing the role of government itself (Self, 1993). What were these other values, and how were they lost? What we lose, unless we specifically reregulate to retain them, are the often unspoken public values that public (and not-for-profit) organisations exist to achieve. There are many examples of the pursuit of efficiency leading to the sacrifice of other values. One of the most discussed trade-offs is that between efficiency and equity. There is certainly some evidence to suggest that deregulation (of labour markets, and for products and services) widens inequality, both within nations and also (although the evidence here is more equivocal) between them.

The mechanisms through which deregulation affects equity within countries are fairly well understood: for example, the wages of less powerful workers fall when rights to organise are curtailed or other protections are removed; economic restructuring in advanced industrial countries sends many well-paying manufacturing jobs offshore. To some degree, energetic social and labour market policies may compensate for these losses. In well-coordinated market economies, training (and re-training) programmes equip displaced or dissatisfied workers to take advantage of the new opportunities that rapidly evolving production systems provide. Such programmes, it could be argued, are synergistic with efficiency. But the reason they are there in the first place is because in some societies, equity (usually transmitted through active trade unions) is valued more highly than in others.

Apart from equity, other values may be lost when efficiency is privileged. This may not be a deliberate act: value judgements are made when policymakers overlook the consequences of their choices, as well as when they knowingly reject alternatives. If efficiency is a self-validating goal (that is, one which is considered to be relatively cost-free), this blind spot is inevitable. If we view a problem through an efficiency lens, it is not surprising that it is inefficiency that appears to be paramount. Systems for water allocation, for example, that depend upon open-access regimes defined by customary usage (as in many developing countries with monsoonal rainfall patterns such as Thailand) appear inefficient when subjected to economic analysis.

Without controlled access and pricing arrangements consumers have little incentive (so the argument runs) to save water or to invest in water-saving technologies. Without water markets based on water trading, there are no mechanisms for allocating water to its highest-valued uses. So allocative efficiency suffers. But in reality, water pricing (in Thailand as elsewhere) is just one aspect of a complex system involving historical, cultural, physical, social and political factors. Privileging the value of efficiency when the conditions for its realisation are not present risks not only other values but efficiency itself. (Molle, 2001, p. 68).

These kinds of choices are replicated within organisations. Managers with their eye on the 'bottom line' are understandably preoccupied with costs. Costs are easier to control than are revenues, which for many public organisations are set by factors beyond their control. Within the organisation, efficiency drives are usually implemented top-down (rarely bottom-up): cost-cutting is a prerogative of power. When they reduce costs, managers hope they are removing organisational fat rather than muscle and sinew. But in removing 'slack', (to change the metaphor) much that is worthwhile may also be removed. Depending on the organisation's culture, slack can be a source of flexibility, even of creativity. 'Delayering' risks loss of corporate memory and goodwill.

Relationships outside the workplace may also suffer. Efficient labour markets generate more jobs (and more growth) than inefficient ones, but highly competitive labour markets impact heavily on the number of hours worked for many employees. In Australia, very long hours of work (50 hours or more per week) became more common for full-time workers in the 20 years from 1985, particularly for men in management positions. In 2005, 30 per cent of men working full-time worked 50 hours or more per week, up from 22 per cent in 1985. Fewer women working full-time worked very long hours, but here, too the proportion increased, with 16 per cent working 50 hours or more per week in 2005, up from 9 per cent in 1985 (ABS, 2006, p. 127). Buoyant labour markets in the latter part of the period (1995–2005) meant that more people were working: part-time employment in particular grew rapidly in terms of both jobs and hours worked. Not surprisingly, problems with work–life balance, particularly for women, were widely reported (Pocock, 2006).

Organizational values, too, are affected by regulatory change. Evidence suggests that when they are forced to adopt more efficient modes of working (either directly, or as a result of competition with for-profit organisations), non-profits lose their most defining attributes – their particular ways of seeing and viewing the world. When, for example, third-sector organisations are forced to compete for resources, their external relationships and internal processes begin to change (Evans, Richmond and Shields, 2005). Organisational cultures are modified as new values (such as efficiency) are privileged over old ones (such as solidarity with clients). The process of change is both strategic (that is, based on management prescription and control) and emergent (based on negotiation, reflection and interaction).

These stresses have been reported within the Job Network, the name given by the Australian Howard government (1996–2007) to its outsourced network of for-profit and not-for-profit job placement agencies. Eardley describes how competition created serious conflicts for community-based employment agencies in relation to their use of information (Eardley, 2002). Other studies have pointed to the dangers of a simplistic rhetoric of 'partnership' between state and third-sector organisations (Kenny, 2000) and to increasing pressures on third-sector organisations to become more 'managerial' in their outlook and approach. Similarly, managerialism in higher education has proved to be a double-edged sword. Universities are undoubtedly more efficient than previously. They produce more output per academic year than in the past in the sense that student to staff ratios have risen and research quantums are up. But many of their traditional values, particularly those relating to collegial forms of governance, have been lost in the process (Marginson and Considine, 2000).

To compete successfully for students, universities have had to think more carefully about their leadership and their management – not necessarily a bad thing. But in their desire to 'run' universities, governments in the UK, Australia and New Zealand have subjected them to funding and performance management regimes that give freedom in some areas while reducing it in others. From the university perspective, the management of both freedom and control is an almost impossible undertaking. It is one of the ironies of the pursuit of efficiency (as well as of other metrics) that management power becomes more centralised, often reducing flexibility and adaptation at the teaching and research level (Duncan, 2007).

Efficiency: Flip-flops and backlashes

The operation of global markets transmits pressures for efficiency enhancement into the heart of the state. The ways in which states respond to these pressures tell us much about their institutional structures for interest mediation. It also tells us about the values they believe to be important. We have seen that, at any point in time, public policy in a given area is like a marble cake: efficiency is mixed with other values. When governments wish to change this values mix in the direction of increasing efficiency, they risk setting up strong reactions from both organised interests and voters. While it is usual to see these reactions as emanating from the loss of benefits that inefficiency entailed, there are values at work here, too.

While efficiency improvements were at the forefront of much policy-thinking in the 1990s, the extent to which they were implemented varied according to the ability of governments politically to negotiate change. The case of New Zealand is of particular interest in this respect, because from the early 1980s, the country launched a wave of efficiency-oriented reforms so wide-ranging that an experienced Organization for Economic Cooperation and Development (OECD) observer described them as constituting 'one of the most notable episodes of liberalisation that history has to offer' (Henderson quoted in Lewis, Grimes, Wilkinson and Teece, 1996, p. 1856). A Westminster-based system following majoritarian voting principles and with no upper house, the New Zealand Labour government elected in 1984 was able to push through a programme of massive change, including trade liberalisation, floating the exchange rate, labour market deregulation, and extensive public service outsourcing. While the basic contours of the social security system were kept intact (see the analysis in Chapter 3), many New Zealanders experienced a sense of outrage that a government they had assumed was of the left, would betray their trust by implementing such a degree of change without first seeking a detailed mandate (see Bale and Roberts, 2002).

The result of the economic revolution was a political one: in 1996, New Zealanders voted overwhelmingly to introduce a system of multi-member electorates, based on the German mixed member proportional (MMP) system. Under this system, each elector received two votes, one for an electorate MP and one for a party. The size of Parliament increased to 120 MPs: half would be elected in single-member constituencies (as before); the other half would be selected from party lists so that in general each party's share of all 120 seats corresponded to its share of the overall vote. The reforms were justified on the grounds of restoring trust in government. The change would refashion the relationship between voters, parties and policy outcomes, so that it would be more difficult than in the past (or so proponents claimed) for one party unilaterally to change policy (Bale and Roberts, 2002).

Interestingly, while there were retractions in some areas, the main contours of the deregulated New Zealand state were not altered. Tariffs, for example, were not reintroduced. Nor, apart from a short period immediately after the new system was introduced, were parties of what might be called the nationalist left, reinstated in power. But (perhaps ironically, given the emphasis on competition in the original reforms) a new form of political competition arguably kept governments more attuned to public sentiment on a number of questions, such as Maori rights over the seabed and over coastal fishing. More broadly, politicians and officials 'got the message' (Vowles et al., 2002). New Zealand did not flip-flop in policy terms, because it found a way of heading off public disaffection by changing its institutional structures. These changes helped to reassure voters by making the rapid, almost revolutionary reforms of the 1980s less likely in the future, unless a broad consensus existed for their adoption.

The clash of equity, fairness and efficiency are nowhere more evident than in labour–market reform. Labour market rigidities, such as those evident in many states, have often been criticised by economists. The prescription – deregulation – is often difficult to achieve. In the Australian case, an electoral backlash against the Howard government's WorkChoices programme (which would have augmented the power of employers) was a significant factor in that government's loss of power. Institutional factors both reflect, and shape, value conflicts. Some states, such as Germany from the mid-1990s, maintained competitiveness in key sectors by combining centralised bargaining with a degree of firm-level flexibility (Thelen and Kume, 2006). French attempts to 'share' work in the late 1990s represented another response, one that attempted to privilege other values (such as substituting greater leisure for monetary gain), while avoiding the greater disruption that deregulatory steps would have entailed.

The French experiment did not work as well as its proponents had hoped. Unemployment remained high – but it did show that other approaches were possible – that sharing out the benefits of regulation, rather than deregulating, was, at least an option (Hayden, 2006). In this context, the policy values pushed by Nicolas Sarkozy, elected president in 2007, were finely tuned to appeal to workers outside the state sector (where unionisation is much lower than in the government workforce). The new president was clearly a politician of the right, but not in the Gaullist mode. He created a government that according to William Pfaff included 'Socialists, centrists and an unprecedented number of women and persons of immigrant origin' (Pfaff, 2007). He negotiated skilfully with the unions, reaching a deal with striking train drivers that divided the union front opposed to his policies.

Sarkozy speedily did away with the 35-hour week, but cleverly so. Work above the 35 hours would have to be paid at overtime rates. But employers would not have to pay taxes on those additional wages (Steiner, 2007). 'I will rehabilitate the values of work, effort, merit and respect', he declared in his inaugural speech.[1] To those with memories of the Thatcher era, the values language sounded familiar, although the personal style could not have been more different. The blend of values Sarkozy represented brought together new constituents and marked a clear break with the past. But at the same time, they represented significant continuity with that same past. Like many politicians attempting to 'sell' change, he articulated a disillusion with the status quo, while trying to ensure that key constituents were not alienated by the actual policies adopted.

Economic rationalism: Means and ends

Much of the public policy debate in the latter part of the twentieth century concerned the relative roles of markets and governments as mechanisms of social choice. Both positively and normatively, forms of economic rationalism played a major role in structuring the debate and in marginalising alternatives. Public choice theory made a huge dent in the credibility and confidence of governments, particularly in the English-speaking world, by proposing that societies over time had a tendency to become sclerotic, as special interests were able to mobilise to use policy to confer benefits upon themselves, at the expense of the wider good. Normative economic analysis provided a way of framing problems and charting efficiency-enhancing solutions.

Since the mid-1980s, governments have increasingly seen their role in terms of the design of market-congruent institutions. This has not meant a decline or even a diminution of government activity, rather it has changed its form. From the point of view of the values it allocates, a state that is efficiency-enhancing is one that inscribes other realms within the economic. We see how this happens in relation to the value of equity. Economic analysis tells us that if you want to improve equity, you do not do it by trying to intervene in markets (unless significant distortions already exist). You let markets do their work, and then via various non-distorting taxes, you provide benefits to those considered to be in need.

This does not, of course, remove the values problem. It simply shifts it away from the direct trade-off area. But in doing so, it runs the risk of pushing the issue off the agenda all together. A society that deregulates its labour markets is not also one that is going to relieve tax burdens on the low-paid. Given the 'framing' role of efficiency, it is almost certainly in the interests of the poor to keep their needs 'in the face' of governments as much as possible, which means refusing to allow the value of equality to be moved away from the arena in which inequality is generated. To rely on compensatory mechanisms is to risk dilution in the values cocktail of the administrative state. Unless ways can be found to re-energize them, values may be sacrificed because societies lose the ability, collectively, to choose them.

5
Values and Policy Instruments

The key dilemma to be investigated in this chapter is the way in which public policy understands and operationalises the task of changing or controlling behaviour. Behavioural change is strongly implicated in policy implementation. This is because, when public policies are implemented, they involve relationships between agents of the state and those outside it. The ways in which these relationships are developed, maintained and constructed contain strong values-based elements. These elements reflect assumptions about the nature of human beings, both individually and in organisations.

While the range of values invoked in this way is potentially very large, I suggest that one of the most significant choices relates to the distinction between tough-mindedness and tender-mindedness. We see this distinction at the broader level of political philosophy: conservatives typically believe that people should take responsibility for themselves (the tough-minded attitude), while liberals are more inclined to see social factors as being decisive (the tender-minded attitude). I contend that toughness versus tenderness characterises both the ways the subjects of policy are constructed and the types of policy instruments that are used.

Policy design and the choice of instruments

As Peter May puts it, public policies 'typically contain a set of intentions or goals, a mix of instruments or means for accomplishing the intentions, a designation of governmental or non-governmental entities charged with carrying out the intentions and an allocation of resources for the requisite tasks' (May, 2003, p. 223). As explained in Chapter 1, policy design means matching the content of a policy to the particular context in which it is to be implemented (Linder and Peters, 1989). One of the key design choices then involves the choice of policy instruments to bring about behavioural change.

Policy design has a values-based component because the ways we attempt to change or influence behaviour depend on, in turn, beliefs (attitudes) about the reasons for that behaviour. This is obvious when we are considering policies designed to (for example) get unemployed people back into the workforce. If we believe that people are unemployed because they are lazy, we will favour policies that force them to work by penalising them if they fail to apply for jobs. If we believe they are willing to work, but lack skills, we will favour policies that build capacity through (for example) subsidised training courses. If we believe that they are willing and able to work, but lack the contacts that would help them find a job, we may favour policies to combat social exclusion.

Of course, motivation is only part of the story. Devising policies to combat unemployment may mean coming to a view about economic growth (should it be boosted to generate more jobs?), about regional disadvantage (are there barriers to investment in particular parts of the country?) or discrimination (are some groups unfairly overlooked by employers?). Or we may believe that people are out of work because the price of their labour is too high. But acting in accord with these versions of causality still involves behavioural change – in these cases, the behaviour of investors and employers.

Schneider and Ingram's classification of policy tools (instruments) is based on the behavioural assumptions that each implies (Schneider and Ingram, 1990). They see four kinds of tools, each based on differing motivational assumptions. Authority-based tools (sanctions and incentives) are required when behaviour change is likely to be resisted; capacity-based tools (such as educational programmes) are employed when the targets of policy are unable to respond to incentives; symbolic tools (such as grand announcements) give an illusion of action; and hortatory tools (such as advertising campaigns) attempt to change behaviour by changing minds.

Schneider and Ingram stress that choices between sanctions and incentives within the authority-based tools depend to some degree on the kinds of behaviours involved. Bad behaviour, for example, requires sanctions; socially acceptable behaviour attracts incentives in the form of inducements. But the two are not symmetrical. Habitual drink-driving for instance, is punished by removal of the offender's licence; we do not attempt to achieve the desired result by rewarding people for sober driving. Tax evasion is punished by penalties; we do not reward people for years of honest tax-paying. Incentives do not need to be tangible: indeed symbolic tools are frequently employed to highlight desirable behaviours. People are rewarded for undertaking activities that are considered to be socially advantageous – volunteers, for example, receive public recognition. Courageous behaviour is praised. Some kinds of activities (for example achieving success in a way that is considered socially significant) are rewarded with knighthoods and damehoods.

In later work, Schneider and Ingram stressed the connection between the types of policy tools chosen and the nature, not so much of the behaviour but of the person producing the behaviour. Thus, the poor were more likely to have their behaviour policed than the rich. Poor people might have their benefits removed if they failed to undertake certain activities (such as engaging in job training). The rich on the other hand, would rarely be required to give something up in return for tax cuts (Schneider and Ingram, 1993). Social construction provides a useful analytical tool for characterising (and comparing) quite complex policy interventions.

In choosing policy instruments, the nature of the problem, and the costs and benefits of various approaches to it are clearly important. Rational instrument choice, often based on considerations derived from welfare economics, is routinely employed when designing business incentives. But as behavioural perspectives have become more sophisticated, we often find that the same problem is tackled with more than one instrument. Think of the wide range of policy instruments that have been employed in many countries to reduce the rate of (tobacco) smoking – sanctions (for example not being allowed to smoke in public places); (dis)incentives (taxes on cigarettes); capacity enhancement (publicly subsidised stop-smoking classes); and persuasion (health warnings on cigarette packets) all figure in the mix.

Social construction of policy targets was an important factor in determining how 'tough' the mix became. The fact that cigarettes were not illegal and smoking was a widespread practice meant that instrument choice was relatively unconstrained. Addiction to other types of drugs (such as narcotics) is not viewed in the same way. These drugs were (and largely remain) illegal, with the result that very large sums of money are employed in constraining their supply and pursuing, prosecuting and incarcerating offenders. Drug takers and drug dealers are not 'us' – they are 'them'. While smokers may feel they are unfairly penalised for their habit, we do not stigmatise the users of nicotine as we stigmatise users of heroin.

Regulatory theory has advanced in tandem with the theory of policy instruments. The economic theory of regulation, as a prescriptive theory, stresses the importance of achieving (in regulatory design) an appropriate balance between risk, costs and benefits (Australian Government, 2007). Instrument choice (for example the designation of penalties) underpins the desired behaviour. But the choice of instruments does not end the story, because in implementing these choices, continuing relationships are set up between regulators and regulatees. The theory of responsive regulation recognises the importance of these relationships by advocating a move away from command and control approaches, to one based on a systemic understanding of the problem to be addressed (Ayres and Braithwaite, 1992). Thus, in implementing occupational health and safety legislation, responsive regulators will assume goodwill, before moving to 'stronger' approaches. Regulation is a constantly evolving dance between the regulator and the regulated.

Attitudes towards the targets of policy change over time – for example, in the United States and Australia, a more tough-minded approach to welfare recipients replaced an era of more tender-minded policies from the beginning in the 1980s in the United States, and about a decade later in Australia. In Aboriginal Australia, tough-minded policies were implemented in the lead-up to the 2007 federal election by the Howard government. But they drew much of their legitimation from the work and words of aboriginal leaders such as Noel Pearson who in an interview in June 2007 put the view that 'real self-determination is about indigenous people taking responsibility for the results, and I can tell you that the results that are out there at the moment are very, very miserable and shameful' (Pearson, 2007). If social policy is about who gets to construct whom, and in what ways, indigenous people were now asserting their own form of tough-mindedness.

Tough and tender

As I have defined them, tough policies employ policy instruments that are coercive and sanction-based. Tender policies are those that rely on incentives, persuasion and capacity-building. Tough policies rest on beliefs that most people are self-interested and will get away with whatever they can. Tender policies rest on beliefs that people are fundamentally well-intentioned and will do the right thing if they are shown what the right thing is. Clearly, neither view is wholly true. Some people are self-interested, others much less so. Self-interested people may behave altruistically on occasion and vice versa. Each of us represents a mix of both characteristics, and which one of them guides our behaviour depends upon a multitude of factors.

The world of public policy, however, finds it difficult to recognise these nuances. Governments tend to rely on tough policies, partly for reasons of expedience (it is easier and cheaper to crack down on bad behaviour than it is to reward good behaviour) and partly because of the strong and powerful winds of public opinion (and media interest) that that blow through any field of policy that involves making judgements about behaviour. Politicians in many jurisdictions like to show they are tough on crime and tough on drugs. But can we talk of toughness and tenderness as an important values balance crossing wide areas of public policy? How are these instrument values concretised in policy? And where should the balance lie? In this chapter, I consider five main areas of policy where this essential dilemma prevails:

- Unemployment
- Criminal justice
- Illicit drugs
- Business regulation
- Asylum seekers

Each section is a 'values vignette', bringing out notable aspects of the interactions between public policy and public opinion that tip policy balances from tough to tender and back again.

Unemployment

We saw in Chapter 3 how institutional structures affect the type and direction of value conflict in welfare, and that the value of fairness is in itself a complex relationship between policies that express obligation and those that express entitlement. These relationships spill over into policy instruments. Similarly, institutional structures shape value conflicts about how to treat the unemployed. In countries with individualised forms of social insurance, there is less scope for value conflict over policy instruments in this field than in countries where the unemployed are supported from general taxation revenue.

Within this context, the Australian story of policy towards the unemployed illustrates changing perspectives about toughness and tenderness. It is not so much that the distribution of these values in the community changes (although it is possible that it does). Rather there is a reaction against the perceived consequences of the dominant value of the previous era. In Australia, there is no unemployment insurance. The unemployed are supported out of general revenue. Until comparatively recently the 'dole', as it is still popularly called, was there for the asking. Tender-minded policies assumed that ordinary administration was sufficient to weed out the cheats and that those who were unemployed were unemployed through no fault of their own. They lacked skills or were stuck in an area where there were few jobs. When Labor was in office between 1983 and 1996, considerable effort was put into policies designed to help the most disadvantaged to find work. These labour market policies were tender-minded, in the sense that they emanated from a view of the world in which disadvantage was the compelling theme (Howe, 2007).

Through the 1990s, however, popular resentment of those who were perceived as taking advantage of the system began to grow. When unemployment was high, there might have been extenuating circumstances justifying lengthy periods on the dole. But unemployment was at historically low levels from the late 1990s and into the first decade of the twenty-first century. Apart from this, many Australians were convinced that there was a degree of wilful laziness on the part of many of those receiving benefits – the spectre of the 'dole bludger' – was frequently invoked.

By the time Howard's conservative government was elected in 1996, the mood had become entrenched. One of the first changes the new government introduced was to place much stronger activity requirements on those receiving unemployment benefits. 'Mutual obligation' summarised the tougher approach. Recipients either had to be actively seeking work, undertaking training or be engaged in community or voluntary work. Work for the Dole (WfD), a group of projects giving job experience to jobseekers, was one of the main planks of the new policy (Yeend, 2000). Mutual obligation provided an account of payees' obligations to the state, rather than the other way around and although critiqued for its philosophical one-sidedness (see Goodin, 2002), proved popular politically.

There were some immediate benefits from the new approach, as evidenced by early evaluations of WfD. Staff of Centrelink, the government's assessments and payments agency, reported that some jobseekers quickly found work when called in for a WfD referral or placement. When the programme was evaluated, it turned out that this 'incentive' effect (derived from recruitment to the programme, rather than participation in it) was one of its more immediate impacts. The longer-term objective – helping people into a job – turned out to be less easy to achieve. When matched control and experimental groups are compared, the group undertaking training had a better outcome in the short run, but over time the two converged (DEWR, 1999).

In the objective sense, mutual obligation did not have a significant impact upon the long-term unemployed. Indeed, there was some evidence that at least some of those struggling to get a job had transferred to other forms of income support. From 2003, the government embarked on a more comprehensive programme of mixed carrots and sticks called Australians Working Together. Under this programme, those receiving Parenting Payment were required to seek work once their youngest child turned 12 (Alexander, Baxter, Hughes and Renda, 2005).

The next phase of the transition – Welfare to Work – represented the tough-minded conservative in full flight. Under this programme, Parenting Payment was payable only until the recipient's youngest child turned eight, when she or he was required to transfer to Newstart Allowance (that is actively seek work). From 2006, those applying for Disability Support Pensions who were assessed as being able to work 15 hours a week or more were required to seek work (Australian Government, 2006). In moving the system towards toughness, the government had consolidated its political base and given form to its policy values. But in doing so, it had sharpened value conflict at the implementation level, both among Centrelink staff required to 'breach' (sanction) job seekers not complying with their activity requirements and also in many of the not-for-profit organisations it had contracted to provide job-placement services (Considine, 2003; Stewart, 2007). Tough and tender proved harder to separate in the ambiguous and complex world of policy implementation, than in the declaratory modes of 'political' policy.

Criminal justice

In October 2007, the French rock star Bertrand Cantat was released on parole from prison. The tribunal judge had determined that as a model prisoner, he could be released after serving four years of his eight-year sentence for murdering his girlfriend, the actress Marie Trintingant. Cantat's lawyer hoped that his client, despite the continuing burden of guilt that he would carry with him forever, would now be able to reconstruct his future (Bremner, 2007). There was intense public reaction. Trintingant's mother expressed her outrage and dismay. What kind of message did this decision send to violent men, she asked? What was a woman's life worth? asked a blogger. It was all very well for Cantat to have plans for the future; Trintingant had no future to plan for. Others pointed out that Cantat had fulfilled the conditions for early release set out in the French penal code, which stresses a balance between rehabilitation, punishment and restitution.[1]

The experiences of the famous (or infamous) draw our attention to these kinds of decisions and the difficult balancing act that underlies them. As with the case of Cantat, they also draw our attention to the extent to which popular sentiment can, or cannot, influence judicial outcomes. Much to the chagrin of criminologists and others, in no other field of public policy, with the possible exception of education, are voters so inclined to trust their own instincts as in criminal justice policy. And in a busy political market, there will always be politicians keen to feed on public fears. This is particularly so in the United States, where the principle of democratic accountability extends to popular election of many judicial office-bearers and prosecutors, and public sentiment and legislative responsiveness are deeply intertwined (Jacobs and Carmichael, 2001; Domanick, 2004).

Despite determined efforts to employ 'evidence-based' approaches to criminal justice, in making policies about crime, perceptions matter much more than realities (Roberts, 2003). But often the two coincide. In the mid-1980s, violent street crime was on the rise in many American cities, and many citizens decided that a too-lenient judicial system was at fault (see Bainbridge, 1985). The response was a widespread challenge to the rehabilitative model of correctional policy to one based on a higher degree of retribution. California's 'three strikes' legislation of 1994 was the most widely publicised example of a determination to 'get tough on crime' (Vitiello, 1997).

Conservative 'tough-mindedness' sees crime as the result of individual choice, rather than environmental factors. Offenders must pay their debt to society (the debt to be determined by the nature of the crime) rather than the history and circumstances of the criminal. Deterrence rules, rather than rehabilitation. But tough-mindedness, while politically satisfying, often defies rational considerations of cost and benefit. Incarcerating large numbers of people (disproportionately young black men from disadvantaged backgrounds) and mandating harsh minimum sentences does not make the people concerned disappear, but displaces decision-making to the 'back-end' of the system, notably to prison managers and parole officers (Wilson, 1975).

It is for this reason that calls for policymakers to consider and to discover 'what works' in criminal justice have rarely been heeded. Even if every piece of criminological research were to be meticulously inspected for its policy relevance, it is doubtful that clear lessons would emerge. By focusing on values, we come to a deeper understanding of what can be achieved. Policy flip-flops occur repeatedly in criminal justice systems, because the consequences of tough-mindedness overload the gaols, while the consequences of tender-mindedness produce conditions for a conservative backlash.

While the French system is less permeable to popular opinion than the diverse and differentiated American state-based systems, patterns of sentencing and the attention given to conditions in prisons remain strongly influenced by what Trouille calls the 'political tit for tat – repression versus liberalism' (Trouille, 2000, p. 402). It is true that the French emphasis on rehabilitation is not 'tender-minded' in the sense that it is not based on sociological models of crime. Rather, the French view is that once expiation is completed and restitution (compensation) made, the emphasis of policy should be on individual reform and rehabilitation. At this level, policy instruments do not (indeed cannot) attempt to address poverty or the underlying causes of crime. Nevertheless, in every polity, social construction, political opportunism and conflicting values provide a potent (and continuing) recipe for policy controversy.

Drugs

Sanctions are tough-minded instruments. Prohibition of illicit drug use, prosecution and imprisonment of offenders and a disinclination to distinguish between 'soft' drugs (such as cannabis) and 'hard' drugs (such as heroin and cocaine) are characteristic of tough-minded drugs policy. Education (to alert young people to the dangers of drugs), capacity-building (by addressing social deprivation and unemployment), harm minimisation (for example safe injecting rooms) and de-criminalisation are tender-minded approaches, although the motivation for their use may be as much resigned pragmatism as compassion. The drugs policy regimes of many countries show mixtures of these policies: classic values hybrids that have built up over time in response to shifting currents of public opinion, and the (often contrasting) views of criminologists, medical experts and fieldworkers. Calls for evidence-based policy are frequently made – although the evidence as to 'what works' is often equivocal or inconclusive.

It is important to recognise, however, that a 'tender-minded' set of policies is not necessarily based on a construction of the drug user as the hapless victim. Sweden and the Netherlands, for example, have drugs policies that appear initially to be complete contrasts in values terms, but on closer examination are not as different as they might at first appear. Sweden has a tough-minded, highly restrictive drugs policy based on a commitment to a drug-free society. Public opinion is reported to be solidly in favour of measures to maintain that state. Indeed there is an explicit desire that policy should reflect these values. As the Swedish Commission on Narcotic Drugs, created by the government in 1998 to evaluate policy (but within restrictive parameters) put it: preventive measures must be 'included in a system of measures restricting availability, and there must be clear rules which include society's norms and values, as well as effective care and treatment' (Lafreniere, 2002).

The Netherlands adopts quite a different stance, reflecting a different set of social attitudes. Dolin makes the point that the Dutch have a tradition of pragmatism in these matters and that the Netherlands' historical role as port and hub of a commercially minded empire ensured a long familiarity with the drugs trade. Consequently, from the 1970s, when present-day policy was first articulated, policy aimed at the 'prevention or alleviation of social and individual risks caused by drug use' (Dolin, 2001, p. 4). Policy differentiates between cannabis use (effectively decriminalised for those not trafficking in the drug) and the use of other drugs (heavy penalties exist for trafficking). Moreover, there is a strong practice of local discretion and enforcement.

The Dutch reliance on harm minimisation might appear to be a tender-minded choice, except that there is little indication in reported practice that social or economic circumstances are considered to have any relationship to drug use. The implied model is that drug use is freely chosen by individuals who are more likely to gravitate towards drugs if they are in networks that encourage this lifestyle. Thus creating separate markets for cannabis and heroin is believed to discourage users from moving from one to the other. Demand-side policy is interesting. The fact that long-term heroin users are visible on the streets is even credited with making heroin use 'uncool' among the young. But public opinion is also significant, and again there is an element of local decision-making – mayors can shut down marijuana cafes if they believe they are causing neighbourhoods to deteriorate.

There are few parallels to Dutch pragmatism in the English-speaking countries, which, in general, have more value conflict in relation to drugs policy than the countries of Western Europe. Left-liberal opinion favours harm minimisation; conservative opinion is more likely to favour action to reduce supply and to punish offenders. As a result policy presents a hybridised form, with some parts of the policy system utilising tough-minded approaches and others, tender-minded ones. But this is a somewhat unstable combination, as we shall see.

The UK provides particularly good examples of this tendency. In 1998, the Blair Labor government announced a ten-year strategy for combating drug misuse, with an emphasis (reflected in £217 million of new funding) based on prevention and treatment (Lafreniere, 2001, p. 22). The greater part of spending, however, was still going towards enforcement (police, court, probation and prisons). Ten years later, the strategy was widely considered to have failed (the incidence of drug abuse and drug-related crime continued to rise). In 2007, heroin was said to be both cheap and readily available in the streets of London. The police reported themselves unable to stem the flow of hard drugs into the country.

Viewed comparatively, we can see that the UK strategy, certainly post 1997–98, was not as tough-minded as the Swedish one, but neither did it subscribe to Dutch-style pragmatism. Cannabis use was still illegal, although police routinely issued cautions rather than proceeding further. In 2000, a Committee of Inquiry reported that more than half of arrests for cannabis possession resulted in a caution (Lafreniere, 2001, p. 9). The tender-minded elements of the strategy revolved around an implied model of misdirection or misguidedness in those using drugs and a strong belief in treatment and community-based action to correct abuse.

As James Q. Wilson observed as long ago as the mid-1970s, even if it could be conclusively demonstrated that social conditions, or for that matter, psychological predispositions caused drug abuse, such findings contained little of relevance to public policy, whose available instruments were unable to change such things. Wilson's view – the classic 'pragmatic' tough-minded approach – was that drug users (he focused on heroin users) were, for the purposes of public policy, best regarded as rational beings who responded to cost–benefit comparisons. If the costs of drug use rose, they would be less inclined to pursue it. Treatment programmes were unlikely to appear (to an addict) as increasing the costs of drug use, and should, in consequence, be viewed with some scepticism (Wilson, 1975).

The Australian experience presents another variation on this theme. When Howard came to office in 1996, he announced that his government would be 'tough on drugs'. This meant, in practice, giving more money to the Australian Customs Service and to the Australian Federal Police to prevent importation of heroin and, on the domestic front, empowering new voices in policy communities close to the prime minister (such as Christian organisations with long experience in dealing with drug abuse). As Australia is a federation, the prime minister could not stop the States from using harm minimisation policies. But where he had the power to stop such initiatives (as he did in relation to the Australian Territories which do not have the sovereign powers of States), heroin trials and injecting rooms were forbidden (Stewart and Maley, 2007).

The Australian public favours tough policies towards illicit drugs – any politician who could be portrayed as being 'soft on drugs' would be electorally at risk. Knowing this, no politician would publicly support policies that featured harm minimisation at the expense of prohibition. At the same time, no government can afford to consign the problem of drug use to the criminal justice system. In practice, policy must tread a fine line between punishment and control on the one hand and harm minimisation on the other. Consequently, so-called national strategies on drugs are a mishmash of many different kinds of activities, each with its professional and bureaucratic proponents. Nevertheless, the perceived stance of governments, and in particular, whom they admit to the key circles of policymaking is important in signalling where, and whether, the values balance has shifted. For example when, in 1998, the prime minister established a new federal advisory body, the Australian National Council on Drugs, it was under the chairmanship not of a member of the medical profession, but of a serving Salvation Army officer with wide experience in practical drug rehabilitation programmes.

Regulating business

While business people are generally positively constructed in Western societies, business itself is heavily regulated in the public interest, the result of more than a century of continuing political struggle. From the character of the regulation applied to them, we must infer that business managers are trusted neither by their workers nor by their shareholders. They are required by law to ensure a safe workplace for their workers, and they must put shareholders' interests before their own. Their products must be safe to use, and they must refrain from attempting to fix prices or to rig markets. Much of the regulation affecting business concerns permits and permissions, the bureaucratic apparatus of accreditation. But some have a more obvious value content. At times the values stance can seem somewhat schizophrenic. Governments encourage business to be aggressive and competitive, but then wring their hands when businesses overstep the mark. The result is an uneasy equilibrium between toughness and tenderness, as the example of the United States most readily demonstrates.

In 2001, the US energy company Enron filed for bankruptcy, owing some $90 billion. The company's books were in such disarray that they could never be properly deciphered. The following year, WorldCom imploded, having overstated its financial results by $3.8 billion. These companies were simply two of the most notorious examples of corporate malfeasance that, by the middle of 2002, had resulted in some $900 billion of worth of corporate losses (Turner, 2006). The public outcry was so great that a previously reluctant Congress was forced to act. The Sarbanes–Oxley Act toughened corporate governance by creating an independent regulator to oversee the accounting profession, ensure the independence of auditors and set auditing standards. No longer would the supposed disciplines of the marketplace, and the professional standards of the accounting profession, be considered sufficient. Public policy was getting tough with business. But for how long and to what effect? The credit crunch of 2008 suggested that many deficiencies remained.

At the same time, many policies towards business are tender-minded and some types of business are constructed in much more socially favourable ways. Small business, for example, is often viewed as particularly deserving of assistance. Nevertheless, the public continues to demand regulation that will reduce risk (to itself). The result of this continuing action and reaction is that, over time, the build-up in the regulatory load is appreciable. In 2006, an Australian taskforce found a welter of rules that were imposing costs on business: in many cases, they were rules that business had been complaining about for years, with no action being taken (Australian Government, 2006a). But costs and benefits (the preferred calculus of the analyst) tell only part of the story. What weight must be given to the need for public protection from risk, as against the need to foster (or at least, not to impede) business efficiency?

A growing body of academic (and practical) thinking seeks to discover how best to proceed in these circumstances. From a broad perspective, regulatory theory discerns how state, law and society intersect and interact to produce complex implementing systems. But research rarely produces definitive answers as to how these priorities should be set. At the practical level, leaders and managers must make informed guesses about what will work. Failure to comply with the rules usually means a sanction of some kind may be imposed. This kind of tough-mindedness however, creates a framework that must itself be turned into a workable system by those responsible for putting it into practice.

Detecting and prosecuting even a fraction of the cases of infringement is beyond even the most vigilant and well-resourced regulators. In practice, agencies set priorities as a way of achieving outcomes through the resources entrusted to them. They will concentrate on some types of cases rather than others; they will launch high-profile prosecutions to act as a deterrent to others. They must also choose how to balance their deployment of policy instruments. They are equipped to implement sanctions but they will also, if they are wise, devote some of their budget towards the education of those they are supposed to be regulating. Following from this, there will be choices to be made in relation to the types of people the agency will employ. Will they be enforcement-minded people, or will they be communicators, able to build relationships with clients and with the associations representing clients' interests? Some, the authoritarians, will opt for tough action on the basis of the assumption that those who are subject to the law will want to evade its provisions. Others, I will call them the liberals, will take the view that most people in business want to do the right thing, and if the law is administered fairly, they will cooperate of their own free will.

As there is no clear way of striking this balance, organisations tend to either segment themselves into different values or oscillate from one to the other, often reflecting prevailing political currents. These political currents in turn reflect unresolved problems from earlier regimes. As the UK's principal revenue-collecting agency put it, apart from those who comply because it is the right thing to do and those who habitually do not conform, 'there are people who will weigh up the benefit of non-payment against the likelihood of getting caught' (HMRC, 2007, p. 8). Consequently, 'get tough' periods (often involving increases in penalties) succeed periods where the regulated have been getting away with it. But toughness must itself be qualified in the light of evidence that increasing penalties does not, of itself, lead to increased compliance (Devos, 2004). The perception of rigorous and effective enforcement is often linked with voluntary compliance, not because regulatees believe they are more likely to be caught, but because they perceive that others are paying their fair share.

The values choices that are available do, however, depend fundamentally on the nature of the regulatory problem – itself an interpretation of the desired and desirable relationship between the public interest and the interests of business. Regulators must be able to penalise behaviour that is proscribed, but the nature of the relationships underlying the behaviour will itself determine prospects and modes of detection. Consequently, the regulatory choices of competition watchdogs (agencies that police anti-competitive behaviour) differ in important respects from those of revenue-collecting agencies (such as tax offices).

Competition watchdogs face a difficult equation. They are trying to prevent firms from engaging in behaviour (anti-competitive conduct) that will advantage themselves, but also disadvantage other firms and consumers. Regulators must detect proscribed behaviour and punish those engaging in it. At the same time, there will be many thousands of infringements of the law, as strictly interpreted, which will go undetected or if detected, will not be prosecuted because the issues involved are judged to be too difficult or too complex to yield a finding favourable to the agency.

Watchdogs choose to prosecute those cases where public benefits (including deterrent value), will be greatest. But the tough–tender balance applies here, too. What proportion of their resources should they devote to educating businesses about the law? Within the parameters of the legislation they implement, how should they interpret cases where anti-competitive conduct is moderated by mitigating circumstances (as for example might occur when a group of small firms selling to a powerful purchaser band together to share the work among themselves)? Where is the dividing line between competition and legitimate cooperation?

Values about the role of business in society critically determine these balances, both across countries and over time within the one country. Comparative work has shown that in Japan, where traditionally cooperation was valued more highly than competition, a softly-softly educative approach has been taken to competition regulation. In other jurisdictions, offering immunity from prosecution in return for giving regulators information about collusive practices has proved fruitful (see ACCC, 2005).

While competition watchdogs are attempting to prevent firms from colluding, tax offices are trying to ensure that companies and people do not evade paying tax. If wage-earning individuals are left with little room to manoeuvre, business entities and the wealthy self-employed are engaged in often-protracted 'games' with tax authorities regarding their tax liabilities. Entrepreneurs selling avoidance schemes flourish in the loopholes of tax laws that grow, almost daily, in complexity. Typically, periods of lax enforcement of taxation law alternate with others in which the rhetoric of enforcement has been to the fore. Political will to 'get tough' is important in underpinning confidence that others are not flouting the law, but at the same time, perceived heavy-handedness, particularly if subsequent court action goes against the tax collectors, undermines their own credibility.

Unlike competition watchdogs, who never know how much collusion they may be missing, tax agencies have ways of estimating the amount of money they should be receiving, and comparing it with actual assessments. They therefore have some sense, through their risk assessment practices, as to where their most cost-effective efforts will lie. Pursuit of the 'big fish' is both cost-effective and politically popular. At the same time, the activities of the 'little fish' cannot be neglected if the system is to retain its credibility, even if the amount of tax evaded is relatively small. When the tax office bases its compliance policies on heavy fines and a high risk of detection, implemented by auditing businesses under suspicion, it is being tough-minded about tax evasion. When it opts for a softly-softly approach, creating relationships with taxpayers that encourage compliance, it is being tender-minded.

In practice, the Australian Tax Office (ATO) features a regime based on encouraging voluntary compliance with the law – a version of President Truman's dictum 'tread softly but carry a big stick'. Survey and other work suggested that modelling taxpayers solely as rational utility maximisers overlooked the fact that 'they also behave in ways that are consistent with different attitudes, beliefs, norms and rules' (James, Murphy and Reinhart, 2005, p. 187). Responsive regulation proposed a sequential values balance that acknowledged the importance of nurturing the capacity to comply before proceeding to more punitive options (Braithwaite, Healy and Dwan, 2005).

Voluntary compliance meant blending tough- and tender-mindedness: establishing relationships that were based on goodwill, but with the backup of hard-headed risk management. As the ATO's compliance programme put it 'the art of good tax administration is to create an environment which supports high levels of voluntary compliance. This is achieved by managing the inherent risks in the system by focusing on those areas that pose the highest risks in terms of non-compliance with the tax law' (ATO, 2006). Implementing the compliance model does, however, create problems for officers who, after developing a relationship with (for example) a large taxpayer, must be able to be tough when the occasion demands. As Job and Honaker put it, '[f]or some, to be both "soft" and "tough" was to exhibit "questionable behaviour"' (Job and Honaker, 2003). As with many street-level bureaucrats, there was perceived security in compliance-oriented behaviour based on command and control values. More nuanced decision-making created values dissonance.

Asylum seekers

Nowhere does the tough and tender balance manifest itself more clearly than in immigration policies generally and policies towards asylum seekers in particular.

According to the 1951 Geneva Convention, a refugee is a person who has a claim on the goodwill of others because of a well-founded fear of being persecuted (in his or her own country) for reasons of race, religion, nationality, membership of a particular social group or political opinion. Illegal immigrants are those (other than refugees) who enter a country without appropriate approval: a simple distinction conceptually. But of course, the problem for public policy and for those who must administer public policy, is determining who a 'genuine' refugee is.

A troubled and politically volatile world generates large numbers of people who are desperate to leave countries that have been torn apart by war, have governments that do not respect the rights of minorities, or which are simply impoverished. As Greta Uehling argued in a sensitive and extensive paper published in 2004, assumptions that those moving from one country to another, irregularly or even illegally, were motivated solely by the attractiveness of their destination were often misplaced. On the basis of the testimonies of migrants moving through Ukraine, she formed the view that it was the horrors of their own country that were the principal motivating force. In the case of asylum seekers (that is, those seeking acceptance on the basis of persecution in their home country) this motivation was particularly pronounced (Uehling, 2004).

In the absence of international migration regimes that allow some sort of overall order to be imposed on increasingly chaotic situations, nation-states that are the preferred destinations of asylum seekers must develop and enforce policies that balance the human rights of asylum seekers to be treated fairly and humanely, against the need to manage entry according to national priorities and to deter illegal entry. While there is a large body of writing giving the human rights viewpoint (see Weber, 2002), and considerable discussion of social construction issues, the relationship between public opinion in the host countries and the development of policy remains a difficult area for researchers. Polls in the UK suggested that public opinion towards asylum seekers hardened in the 2000s (Carvel, 2004). In Australia during the same period, many people came to see asylum seekers as either impostors (that is economic migrants rather than genuine refugees), or as queue-jumpers using people-smuggling operations to reach their preferred country of asylum.

From the point of view of policymakers, there were the very real difficulties of producing a decision-making regime that would deal effectively, but also humanely, with illegal arrivals. Two case studies will give some sense of the values-balancing involved and the importance of administrative history and context in shaping responses. Australia, traditionally a country of immigration, is generally considered to have the most tough-minded approach to asylum seekers of any Western nation (Phillips and Millbank, 2005). By way of contrast, the UK, not traditionally a country of immigration, when faced with increasing numbers of asylum seekers, found it difficult to deal decisively with an increasingly difficult political and humanitarian situation.

United Kingdom

Politics, shaped by events, determines who is considered desirable and who is not. The Immigration Act of 1971 effectively ended immigration from the countries of Britain's former empire, except where patrial status (that is, having a parent or grandparent born in the UK) could be demonstrated. On the other hand, during the period of the Cold War, defectors from the Eastern bloc were viewed as prizes, rather than burdens. The far more fluid circumstances of the period after the collapse of the Soviet Union, and the challenges (both internal and external) posed by militant Islam changed both attitudes and practice. Britain, along with most other host nations of the European Union, became much more restrictive in its security-related immigration practices, both during the 1990s (Bank, 2000) and even more so after the attack on the United States in September 2001. Policy was tightened progressively through the 1990s, by giving immigration officers more discretionary and police-like powers.

In the UK in the period up to 2000, as reported by Bank, asylum seekers could be detained if immigration officials considered that they were at high risk of absconding if granted temporary admission (Bank, 2000, p. 263). While the percentage of applicants placed in this category was relatively low, for some nationalities it represented a high proportion of claimants. Whether detained or not, most applicants were refused refugee status. But the rate at which failed applicants were deported consistently fell behind the number of failed applications being produced. This caused the Home Secretary to announce, in 2005, a 'tipping point' performance target: by the end of the year, the number of asylum seekers being removed would exceed the number of failed applications being made (Clarke, 2005). (In other words, the build-up of failed claimants would be progressively reduced).

The role of public opinion in precipitating or at least, encouraging these changes was substantial. Asylum and immigration were campaign issues in 1997, 2001 and 2005 (ICAR, 2005). The media overwhelmingly presented asylum seekers in a negative light. Many failed asylum seekers were housed in properties near Council housing estates, fuelling resentment. In 2002, Home Secretary David Blunkett agreed that Britain was being 'swamped'. The problem was not only the numbers arriving (over 100,000 in 2002), but the fact that many failed applicants evaded deportation by disappearing into the system, often for years on end (Casciani, 2003). We do not know if public attitudes towards those seeking asylum changed (in the sense that people changed their minds), or whether those whose values had not been reflected in policy began to exert more influence: probably something of both. It is undeniable, though, that in the period after 2001, the values balance in the instruments of policy towards asylum seekers in the UK moved towards a much more tough-minded regime. Despite this change, however, the stance of policy remained far less tough-minded than in Australia.

Australia

During the Howard era, policy towards asylum seekers became a battleground between two opposing camps. On the one hand (at least as the government saw it) were the policy elites, who supported multiculturalism and championed a 'tender' or compassionate approach to arrivals, on the other were the great majority of people, who wanted the strongest measures of deterrence applied to those arriving without permission. While the first view was widely and passionately expressed, the second was the one that held sway in policy terms (Lewis, 2007). The tough-minded policies went very far indeed, ultimately to the point of excluding from the migration zone a number of islands to the north of the Australian mainland. This meant that even if asylum seekers reached the jurisdictional shores of Australia, for the purposes of the immigration act, they had not done so. They could then be processed offshore from where (if they were found not to be refugees) they could conveniently be returned home or resettled elsewhere.

There were two key events in the evolution of these policies. The first was the turning-back of the *Tampa* in August 2001. The *Tampa*, a Norwegian cargo vessel, had picked up 400 people, mostly Afghanis, from a sinking vessel in the seas north-west of Western Australia. The captain, under some pressure from those he had picked up, requested permission to dock on Christmas Island, but was refused. The resulting stand-off highlighted for many Australians the potential extent of the asylum seeker problem. The second incident, the so-called children overboard affair, occurred in the lead-up to the November 2001 election, when public opinion was inflamed by reports (uncorrected by the government) that, in their desperation to be picked up by Australian naval vessels, asylum seekers had thrown their children into the sea (Weller, 2002).

These events had the effect of focusing public attention on the problem of unauthorised immigrants arriving by sea from the north and their subsequent treatment at the hands of Australian authorities. In fact, mandatory detention (for unauthorised arrivals) had been inaugurated (in 1992) by the Labor government that held office federally from 1983 until 1996. It became contentious in the period from 2000, when asylum seekers (many of them from Afghanistan and Iraq) began appearing on the northern Australian coastline. Most had flown to countries such as Malaysia, from where they made their way to Indonesia, within striking distance of northern Australia. In Indonesia, people smugglers procured places for them, often on dangerously unseaworthy boats, for the short but perilous journey to Australia (Phillips and Millbank, 2005).

Why, with relatively few asylum seekers, did Australia have such very tough policies towards them? Public opinion clearly played a crucial role, as it did elsewhere. Moreover, there was a clear conduit for its transmission to politics and strong incentives for politicians from both major parties to respond to it. In Australia, with its system of compulsory voting and relatively frequent federal elections (every three years), public opinion translates in a very direct way into votes. Public policy therefore reflects, not just the values of policy elites (who tend to favour more liberal treatment of asylum seekers) but also those of the larger mass of working people, who as a rule are in favour of tougher approaches. Political parties cannot afford to ignore these waves of public sentiment.

Conclusion

We have seen that toughness and tenderness are useful ways for understanding policy stances and policy changes in the field of regulation. Governments do not have many options in relation to their choice of policy instruments, which is why the balance between those that are based on tough-minded approaches and those that are more tender-minded in character is so important in shaping outcomes. While public opinion in these matters is easily excited, the origins of the attitudes that are reflected in the policy values are complex and operate at a number of levels.

To some degree, toughness and tenderness may reflect individual personality characteristics – 'tough' people being characterised by aggression and dominance, tender-minded people by less hard-edged attitudes and greater levels of empathy. At the extreme edge of the spectrum, Adorno's theory of the authoritarian personality depicts a kind of aggression based on fear and hatred of 'the other'. At the group level, a wealth of psychological research suggests that individual attitudes are mediated through collective processes of public opinion formation in ways that are subject to many cross-cutting factors (Taber, 2003, pp. 449–50).

As analytical devices, toughness and tenderness encompass ideas about the relationship between human responsibility and social and political conditions in the context of the causal reasoning that underpins policy. On the one hand, there is the view that behaviour stems from individual calculation and preference, independent of the environment in which the person was brought up. On the other, there is the view that human behaviour is a product largely of these circumstances. The first view produces policy based on incentives (or disincentives). The second produces policy based on adaptation, learning and harm minimisation.

What causes these balances to change? The way we attempt to control each other in society, through collective means, reflects a melange of factors. Among the most significant are the prevailing values of the time, and the extent to which popularly held values are transmitted into decision-making. Public policy with regard to (for example) the sentencing of criminals reflects popular attitudes towards crime in the United States to a far greater extent than in many other countries, because of the fact that those exercising the prosecuting powers of the state are elected, rather than appointed officials. This propinquity is in contrast to those countries where the criminal justice system is largely in the hands of trained elites. The values analysis also reminds us of the prime importance of social construction in shaping instrument choice. Enlightened forms of business regulation stress the importance of mutual trust and an approach that stresses outcomes rather than processes. Those with less power and fewer resources find this kind of flexibility much harder to come by.

6
Where Policy Meets the Personal

We have seen how, through paradigms (such as that of efficiency) and the administrative routines of implementing organizations, public policies allocate values even when these same values are often not clearly or explicitly expressed. But what of that policy terrain where values are omnipresent, religious groups are both watchful and active, and states must find a pathway through what is often an ethical minefield? The issues involved are complex and tenacious.

Some actions (such as abortion) have long been the subject of state regulation and, until relatively recently, prohibition. Others, such as voluntary euthanasia, have emerged as areas of controversy, as advances in medical technologies make it increasingly likely that citizens will live beyond the point where they are able to enjoy any quality of life. While not itself a matter of life and death, more freely available divorce requires ever-closer engagement between the state and families as policies must be developed for the support of children. Gay marriage (the legal recognition of same-sex unions on the same basis as heterosexual ones) challenges the traditional state-sanctioned understanding of marriage. In addition, medical science and its associated technologies have raised ethical dilemmas for which no precedent exists, such as the regulation of assisted reproduction and of stem cell research. Further scientific advances will create ever more difficult regulatory issues to resolve.

These are examples of a class of policy problems in which we search for what Mark Sagoff has called 'principled decisions' – in other words, ethical or moral concerns are obvious and important enough, to become the context within which reasoning about action occurs. Sagoff points to many policies where these considerations have applied, such as racial segregation, the war in Vietnam and capital punishment. Costs and benefits may be calculated, but they are rarely decisive (Sagoff, 1991).

Governments struggle with these issues even when deliberative forums are available for considering them. Where the regulation of science is involved, for example, governments may attempt to find principles that will guide or rationalise decision-making. Bioethicists and philosophers contribute their perspectives. Committees deliberate and inquiries report.

But focusing on this type of discussion may be misleading, as it concerns the 'input' side of decision-making. How are the values realised after the public policy choices are made as implementation takes place? Do we find the same patterns in these value-laden areas as in others? To answer this question, I consider four areas – all of them controversial – in which deeply held beliefs, interests and values permeate policy-making: abortion, euthanasia, reproductive technologies and marriage and child support.

In general, because of the personal nature of the decisions involved, these are worlds in which 'policy' emerges in the interstices of the law, and public administrative agencies are not directly involved. (An exception is post-separation child support, in which, increasingly, securing the interests of children involves administrative rather than court-based decision-making). Where the context is purely scientific or medical, law and public policy construct a variety of interactions between the state, professionals (such as doctors and scientists) and citizens. The values governing these interactions are legally prescribed, and vary from state to state. At the same time, value conflict is mediated by a variety of strategies that allow practical decision-making to occur, while not directly confronting religious values.

Abortion

Abortion law and policy provides a good example of states (through public policy) finding ways of balancing religious and secular values. In terms of policy values, states must balance the right to life of the embryo against a woman's right to choose. They must also consider the stark reality that many women will risk injury and possible death procuring an illegal abortion, rather than proceeding with an unwanted pregnancy. Typically, public policy avoids explicit value conflict through a variety of mechanisms, while still (in almost all states) liberalising access to abortion. For example, (as in most Australian jurisdictions) access to abortion may be safeguarded by liberal judicial interpretation of existing statutes, and the privacy of the doctor–patient relationship, while remaining a criminal offence in the formal sense (Drabsch, 2005).

In permitting abortion, however, states must choose when to allow it to occur. In devising a practical regulatory regime, they must come up with a number of gestational months beyond which prohibitions (or tighter criteria) apply; they must decide who will decide, and on what grounds. In effect, in states with liberal abortion laws, regulation makes the values choice by authorising the rights of individuals to make the choice themselves. But in states where religious traditions remain powerful, the value conflict itself is never finally resolved. In general, abortion law has become more liberal in most countries since World War II (Cook, Dickens and Bliss, 1999), so the balance has shifted in favour of choice. Of course, considerable differences remain between countries, the result as Michael L Gross puts it in a summary of the comparative literature, of 'underlying religious, historical and cultural factors' (Gross, 2002, p. 203).

While public attitudes have generally been more liberal than those of religious groups, it has taken principled action, sometimes by individual doctors, sometimes by proponents of social change, to bring about new possibilities, especially for the less well-off. This is one area of public policy where the women's movement has made a decisive and enduring difference (Stetson, 2001). But values supporting gender equality did not come solely from the women's movement. In Catholic Italy, abortion in the first trimester has been legal since 1978, largely the result of the influence on public policy of secular, left-wing parties (Calloni, 2001). In a country noted, up until that time, for the power of the Church in politics, the very strength of the papacy created the conditions for a strong reaction against Church influence.

But law itself, while obviously of critical importance, was a poor guide to the ways in which practical choice-making was managed. In federal states, the pattern of decision-making often reflected the practical schizophrenia of federalism. As Howard Palley points out, Canada has a clear policy at the federal level to permit abortion as a 'medically necessary service'. But provinces routinely limit access to abortion, both directly through public policy and indirectly by allowing local health authorities to impose restrictions. Policy conflict comes into play as 'provinces and local health officials contend with local political forces that oppose federal policy' (Palley, 2006, p. 568)

In the United States, while some States have relatively liberal laws, others do not. Moreover, in 2001 federal funding for abortions was prohibited by the Bush administration. Nevertheless, the general framework permitting abortion continued to be guaranteed, on the grounds of the privacy of the doctor–patient relationship, by the

Supreme Court's interpretation of the Constitutional position in Roe v Wade. In Australia, which does not have a constitutional Bill of Rights, access to abortion remained wholly within the regulatory jurisdiction of the States and Territories, allowing for some variation in the law. In the Australian Capital Territory, early-term abortion was explicitly decriminalised. In other states, it remained on the criminal code (Drabsch, 2005). Nevertheless, in a more pragmatic polity than the United States, abortion continued to be (relatively) freely available. Private clinics were able to operate, because the law allowed abortion where the mother's mental and/or physical health was at stake, and no one could prove that this was not the case, without violating the confidentiality of the doctor–patient relationship.

During the period of the Howard government (1996–2007), there was some disturbance to the status quo. Federal funding for abortion continued to be available through Medicare (the compulsory financing scheme for primary health care), but key members of the government (including frontbencher and former seminarian Tony Abbott) wanted to reduce the number of abortions. Religious values and political interests coincided. From 1996 until 2006, in order to shore up its position in the Senate, the government restricted the availability of the abortifacient drug RU 486. Later, when Abbott became health minister, the government used its control over the funding of abortion counselling services to include the welfare arm of the Roman Catholic Church in the management of the contract (ABC, 2007). But Prime Minister Howard was careful not to allow the debate to run too far, a trait shared by his State government counterparts. Opportunities to discuss the policy issues that would be involved in changing the law (that is the competing values questions that would then have to be discussed) are not generally welcomed by politicians – certainly not in the run-up to an election. Politicians understand very well that public opinion generally favours abortion, certainly in the first three months of pregnancy.

For political managers, though, public opinion is only part of the story. While right-to-life and family-values parties command only a tiny number of seats, politics attracts many with strongly held views on these questions. The saving grace is that pro- and anti-abortion views are represented on both sides of politics, giving both a reason and an excuse to relax party discipline. Indeed in 2006 when a private members' Bill to hand ministerial power over all drugs approvals to the Therapeutic Goods Administration (thereby effectively ending the ban on RU 486) was brought before the Parliament, the prime minister allowed a conscience vote on the issue. The Bill was passed with clear majorities in both Houses, with women senators and members voting overwhelmingly in favour.

The debate about RU 486, as its proponents emphasised, was not a debate about abortion but who should determine the safety of the drug (Khadem, 2006). By not constructing the issue in terms of abortion, while permitting a conscience vote, political managers avoided overt value conflict. Religious values, or to be more accurate, values emanating from religion, continued to be expressed by anti-abortionists, without forcing a return to the pre-1970s situation. While some parts of the law remained unchanged, public policies worked because they were able to combine values ambiguity with a clear, liberalising regulatory regime.

Voluntary euthanasia

If choices in relation to abortion were (in most instances) confirmed, those in relation to euthanasia continued to be heavily constrained in most jurisdictions. In 2005, voluntary euthanasia (meaning doctors may intervene to bring about death at the request of a patient) remained illegal in all countries except the Netherlands. Physician-assisted suicide (in which doctors provide the means of death to patients requesting it) was legal (in the sense of being the subject of explicit legislation) only in Oregon (United States) and in Belgium (Pakes, 2005). In contrast to the situation where abortion remained nominally illegal, but where the law was rarely, if ever invoked, governments continued to be willing to prosecute doctors who openly provided their patients with the means of death.

The pressure of what would otherwise be an intolerable situation was mediated by casuistic practices – the case-by-case decision-making of doctors, sometimes acting on the instruction of patients, sometimes in consultation with the families of the terminally ill. There are many instances of terminal sedation, where the patient is in so much pain, that the line becomes blurred between the alleviation of suffering and the deliberate ending of life. Passive euthanasia (where treatment is withdrawn from a terminally ill patient) is also widespread. However, casuistry cannot encompass voluntary euthanasia, which describes the situation where a doctor actively ends the life of a patient who wants to die.

In these circumstances, explicit change in the law is required to protect the doctor from being charged with murder, and few politicians have been prepared to weather the controversy associated with reform. Even where reform has been achieved, it has proved vulnerable. In Australia's

Northern Territory, where in 1996 a committed politician successfully brought in the so-called right-to-die legislation, the legislation was subsequently overturned by the federal government. As Francis Pakes notes, the fact that voluntary euthanasia and physician-assisted suicide are legal in so few countries, is at odds with what is known of public opinion on the subject. But public opinion in itself is insufficient to bring about change in institutions and practices that in most jurisdictions, substitute case-by-case or casuistic decision-making for explicit policy.

As in the case of abortion, those with religious objections to euthanasia are unlikely ever to be reconciled to liberalisation. Moreover, in contrast to the case of abortion, public policy has fewer resources to draw upon in bypassing and defusing value conflict. Because active euthanasia involves the taking of extant life, regulatory liberalisation within the context of the doctor–patient relationship is not possible. Legalised euthanasia invariably requires authorisation by more than one doctor and hence a much more 'public' authorising regime – a values minefield into which few politicians are prepared to venture. Until the elderly themselves, aided by sympathetic doctors, are able to bring about change, this situation seems likely to continue.

Reproductive technologies and stem cell research

Changes in social values are not the only stimulus for policy change. Increasingly, science itself provides the need for regulation. As there is no regulation to begin with, a genuine *tabula rasa* confronts policymakers. In the recommendations they make, and the responses adopted by governments, how will values be articulated and implemented? Two key medical technologies dominated regulatory agendas in the period from the early 1980s onwards: *in vitro* fertilisation (IVF) and, later, therapeutic cloning using embryonic stem cells (that is, the production of therapeutic stem cell lines based on the patient's genetic make-up). The UK's Human Fertilisation and Embryology (HFE) Act (1990) represented one of the first regulatory regimes for IVF. How were value-based questions handled in this legislation?

First, a quick review of the technology is necessary. Technologies to assist reproduction, such as IVF, involve the production of 'excess' embryos that are not needed for implantation in a given cycle of treatment. Two regulatory questions arise: first, until what point should the embryos be allowed to develop before they are frozen and stored; and second, how long should embryos that are not required for treatment purposes be permitted to be stored, before they are destroyed? From the religious viewpoint, life (in the sense of personhood) begins at the moment of conception. Indeed in Catholic theology, gametes (sex cells) are to be considered in the same way as embryos. In permitting *in vitro* at all, therefore, the law (from a religious perspective) entails some destruction of human life. From a pragmatic, secular point of view, there is no compulsion to believe that life begins at conception, but at the same time, a reasonable person would not countenance 'growing' embryos beyond a certain point.

The founding principles for the UK Act were enunciated in the Warnock Report (Warnock, 1984). The inquiry that produced the report, chaired by Dame Mary Warnock, took submissions from hundreds of interested individuals and organizations, highlighting, as the British Official Publications summary puts it 'the wide range of often conflicting moral, ethical and religious views prevailing in society on this sensitive and controversial issue' (BOPCRIS, 2007). The UK Act defined a specific point beyond which embryos might not be kept or used: this is the appearance of the 'primitive streak', defined as 'the end of the period of 14 days beginning with the day when the gametes are mixed' (§3a). Neither gametes nor embryos are allowed to be stored beyond a statutory maximum period: 10 years in the case of gametes and 5 years in the case of embryos (§14).

Crucially, the Act controlled the application of *in vitro* technology (and responsibility for the implementation of its restrictions and requirements) by establishing a licensing regime, to be administered by a statutory authority. The statutory authority has a long history in public administration as a vehicle for removing from direct ministerial purview the activities that it undertakes. It is intended to depoliticise decision-making, and to remove the minister from the pressures that would otherwise be applied were the activity to remain within a Department of State. In the case of the HFE Authority, however, the motivation was a form of administrative values-balancing that, compared with regimes based on legal regulation alone, enabled new questions to be addressed within a deliberative forum that commanded considerable legitimacy. At the time (the early 1990s), the prevailing ethos of public management was that public business should be carried out according to businesslike management principles. The regulation of the *in vitro* regime was clearly not to be likened to a business.

But what should be its governing ethos? This was a matter that could not be defined by the Authority alone, but evolved in response to the changing scientific and human agenda. The UK Act provided for the members of the Authority to be appointed by the Secretary of State.

Its operations were governed by the prescriptions contained in the Act regarding medical and therapeutic activities, as well as the conventional accoutrements of public sector accountability (that is, the production of accounts, and of an annual report). The utility of the Authority soon became apparent when, in 2001, the original legislation was extended by the introduction of the HFE (Research Purposes) regulations to enable embryonic stem cell research and its regulation by the Authority (Stewart et al., 2007). The House of Lords passed the regulations, but also initiated its own inquiry into stem cell research.

The Report of this inquiry supported the regulations, noting in its discussion that '[c]laims that the embryo is a person from the moment of fertilisation are hard to reconcile with standard views of human and personal identity' (House of Lords, 2002, §4.11). The House of Lords report also recommended the setting up of a national stem cell bank to manage stem cell resources: an independent steering committee was to evaluate all applications to deposit and access stem cell lines. A code of practice outlined the criteria that should be used when deriving and using human stem cell lines (Stewart et al., 2007, p. 261).

In making policy for the regulation of IVF and, later, stem cell research, British policymakers established a governance regime offering new opportunities for scientific research. In allowing therapeutic cloning (in which an embryo is created that is matched to the tissue of a specific person) this regime was among the most progressive in the world. In values terms, by constructing the issue in what might be called morally informed utilitarian terms, 'public policy', in this case at least, bypassed what would otherwise have been the constraining influence of religious values.

At the same time, the HFE Authority's status as a non-departmental public body, together with the requirement of its Act that the Chair, Deputy Chair and at least half of the Authority's members should be neither doctors nor scientists involved in embryo research or infertility treatment, signalled that the interests and motivations of the regulated should not dominate the Authority's work. The prevailing ethos might be described as enlightened common sense. The Authority's Annual Report referred to the importance of generating and maintaining a consensus by working closely, in policy work, with stakeholders and with members of the public. A strong emphasis on the needs and interests of patients was also apparent (HFEA, 2007). These values – fairness, consensus, and a concern for patients – show the importance of process and orientation in the administration of difficult, complex and contested fields that are also changing rapidly as new discoveries and techniques proliferate.

In its approach to stem cell research, the United States showed a rather different pattern predicated on its federal structure and more volatile politics. Rather than seeking to establish a federal institutional framework, in 2001 the Bush regime effectively prohibited the use of federal funds to create new stem cell lines. This would ensure, according to the administration, that federal funds would not be used to create stem cell lines derived from newly destroyed embryos, nor would they support the creation of embryos for research purposes (Johnson and Williams, 2004). At the same time, the private sector was able to continue to fund stem cell research, subject to widely varying State government regulatory regimes (Johnson and Williams, 2004). The State of California's law, enacted in 2002, expressly permitted and encouraged research involving the derivation of human embryonic stem cells and cloned embryos. Other states, such as Nebraska, legislated to forbid the use of state funds for stem cell research.

In the United States a multivalent federalism allowed for many kinds of answers to the problems posed by the need to regulate stem cell research. The structural form of deliberative politics in the United States produced an outcome which in itself, mirrored the dimensions of the values conflicts involved. This type of values pluralism is characteristic of federal systems and, as a normative principle, constitutes one of the key dimensions of federal theory. As a non-federal state, the United Kingdom demonstrated a quite different pattern. A more centralised, prototypically Westminster-based government both required and enabled a more exclusionary politics. This form of politics facilitated a deliberative construction of the issue based on a framework of secularism.

The interpolation of professional public servants (articulating and servicing the work of the Authority) was of key importance here, particularly in balancing the interests of scientists (and of scientific research), with the needs and wishes of infertile couples and those of the broader community. Of course, this did not mean that values questions were defused. The Authority's working environment continued to be a challenging one, involving not only research questions, but the rights of those born as a result of reproductive technologies. As time went on, the needs of children conceived as a result of donated sperm, eggs or embryos, began to feature more strongly on the policy agenda and in 2005, the law was changed so that donor anonymity was no longer protected. There are, however, limits to the extent to which an unelected body can carry the weight of regulation in these contested and constantly changing areas, without fresh mandates from the legislature. Pre-implantation genetic diagnosis (PGD) is a case in point.

PGD is a procedure that, through the use of IVF technology, allows couples at risk of having a child affected by a genetic disease, to choose an embryo that will be unaffected by that disease. Because PGD became available after the HFE Act, the Authority had to make policy on the issue. It chose to allow PGD in cases of serious disease (but an exact definition of 'serious' remained elusive). It also licensed 'saviour siblings': the selection of an embryo that is a tissue match to an existing sibling affected by a life-threatening disease. However, because these decisions involved selecting some embryos and rejecting others, they remained intensely controversial from the perspective of religious groups. A Bill for an amended and updated HFE Act was introduced into the House of Lords in late 2007, in large part to define more precisely the basis for screening and selecting embryos for both treatment and research (Shepherd, 2007).

The Australian situation, in which during the 1980s and 1990s regulation of research was largely carried out by the industry itself (supervised by a special committee of the National Health and Medical Research Council), shows the close connection between the 'who' of values administration, and the values themselves. This relatively free regime permitted the rapid development of the industry, but gave little scope for the incorporation of other interests and values. An early pioneer in the development and application of assisted reproduction technologies, the State of Victoria relied initially on the industry-based regime, but in 1995 created an Infertility Treatment Authority to administer both research licensing and record-keeping, including the maintenance of a donor register. The guiding principles of the Infertility Treatment Act 1995, stressed the importance of the rights of children created as a result of the procedures, as distinct from those of infertile couples.

Meanwhile, at the federal level, the Council of Australian Governments (COAG), a body comprising the leaders of the State, Territory and Commonwealth governments, began to address what had become a bewilderingly inconsistent patchwork of regulation in relation to stem cell research. This resulted, in 2002, in legislation that allowed some stem cell research under a strict regulatory regime, but banned therapeutic cloning using stem cells. In 2006, after an extensive inquiry, the Australian Federal Parliament passed amended legislation that permitted therapeutic cloning, a result applauded by the then Victorian Treasurer as giving much-needed support to his State's 'knowledge-driven high skilled' sectors of biomedical research (Brumby, 2007). In this case, the extended arena of the federal system had permitted the values balance, from the perspective of the State of Victoria, to swing in favour of scientific research.

Marriage and child support

As divorce has become more freely available, the relationship between the state and the family has become more multi-stranded and complex, forcing public policy and law into ever-more difficult and contested areas. New values have been enacted and interactions with others have multiplied, creating a need for new policies. In particular, the needs of children in post-divorce situations have resulted in the creation of new kinds of bureaucracy, designed to implement administered forms of child support. As a result, the values-balancing previously undertaken by courts becomes the domain of professional public servants – in turn constructing more detailed relationships between the state, the family and individuals.

The way in which this change occurred is a useful example of one of the paradoxes of modernity. As 'black and white' law based on traditional religious values is superseded by legislative individualism, so the need for additional regulatory activity by the state increases. As this regulatory activity grows in extent, so does its values complexity. In every western democracy, in the years since World War II, marriage laws have become more liberal (while almost always stopping short of permitting gay marriage). At the beginning of the twenty-first century, no fault divorce was available in most of the countries of Western Europe, as well as all the States of the United States, the UK, Canada and Australia (Simon and Altstein, 2003). This shift in policy and law marked a profound shift in social attitudes. Marriage as an institution reflected more individualistic values, and for women, an end to the traditional bargain in which equality was sacrificed for economic protection.

The introduction of no-fault divorce and its intersection with existing social security systems, however, created a situation in which the support of children post divorce was falling increasingly to the state and to custodial parents (usually mothers), rather than to non-custodial parents (usually fathers). Children, it became clear, were among the casualties of this environment. Post-divorce, their living standards often declined dramatically. By the end of the twentieth century, after several decades of relatively freely available divorce and with marriage no longer being seen as necessary to 'legitimise' children, there was a growing recognition that improved mechanisms for child support were required. For those not wanting to turn back the clock, it had become apparent that the state would have to become more, rather than less, involved in what had traditionally been considered the private domain of the family. Child support agencies reflected the response of a number of governments to these developments. The movement (in the UK and in Australia) from court-reliant maintenance action, to the setting-up of administrative agencies to undertake (or at least to oversee) much of the work, was justified on the basis of values (non-custodial parents had an ongoing enforceable obligation to their children); and resources (the payment of social security to custodial parents would be reduced). The values-based case for intervention, however, then had to be translated into an effective set of administrative policies, a task of considerable difficulty. Indeed, these agencies had one of the most difficult jobs in public administration. On the one hand, they were in effect debt collectors. On the other, if they were not to be overwhelmed by complaints, they were required to be attentive and responsive to clients or 'customers'. It is worth contrasting the implementation histories of the British and Australian agencies, as they show the importance of policy design principles, both in supporting compliance and in establishing successful relationships with stakeholders.

The UK agency ran into considerable problems at least in part because of a disconnect between the obligation (to pay) and the receipt of money. Whereas in Australia, payments from fathers were collected by the agency and passed on to the custodial parent, in the UK, the money was collected by the Treasury, and social security payments adjusted to reflect the additional resources. The Australian system not only put the Child Support Agency (CSA) in the middle of the custodial relationship, it also enabled the Agency to know, and to show, exactly what was happening to payments. Relative to its UK counterpart, the Australian agency showed a clearer alignment of administrative practice with the perceptions of clients (while retaining strong powers of enforcement where these are needed).

Within the Australian agency, values conflict was handled in a number of ways. First, there were sequential changes of emphasis. Later, as the agency grew larger, the division of labour made it possible for different parts of the organization to pursue conflicting goals. In its earliest years (from its foundation in 1988 until the mid-1990s), the Australian CSA was located in the Australian Tax Office (ATO), underlining the importance of its enforcement role. 'The Agency's mandate was to assess, collect and transfer child support payments as efficiently as possible' (CSA, 2006). Subsequently, the emphasis shifted to encouraging voluntary compliance, as both a cheaper option, but also one that engaged (and constructed) clients as 'customers'. Even when it was located within the ATO, the complexity of the issues that had to be determined meant that there was extensive phone-based contact between clients and public servants. As the Agency developed further, it worked out ways of segmenting its client base, so that different parts of the organization specialised in different aspects of the assessment and payment management process.

But trouble was brewing. At least some non-custodial parents (mostly fathers) were embittered by what they saw as a bias within the system towards the interests of their ex-partner, largely because the legislation stipulated a flat percentage of the non-resident parent's adjusted income as a child support liability. This inflexible approach, they argued, caused multiple problems. For example, non-custodial parents were required to make payments, but had little say in how they were allocated. Moreover, although they might wish to spend more time caring for their children, if they did so, their payments were not adjusted to reflect this fact (Ministerial Task Force, 2005). The solution that was adopted, which was to vary the formula based on the respective parents' 'income shares', added more layers of complexity to the assessment task. But it is a good example, not only of the practical ramifications of perceptions of 'fairness', but also of the administrative consequences of public engagement with highly personal and emotive issues. As a ministerial taskforce report of 2005 put it:

> [I]t [the Child Support Scheme] seems to act as a lens for intensifying personal resentment on the part of those who feel aggrieved by court decisions on children's living arrangements and the division of property, or by the circumstances that resulted in separation, or the unplanned birth of a child. Even in the absence of conflict between the parents, it may prove difficult to develop a mechanism that both parents will consider fair'.
>
> (Ministerial Task Force, 2005, p. 79).

The CSA's history shows that, as Cyert and March observed in relation to business firms, organizations have a capacity to deal with multiple goals by pursuing them sequentially (Cyert and March, 1963). But this example also demonstrates the additional stresses placed on public agencies when they must deal administratively with interests and values that are as inextricably mixed together as they are intensely felt.

The values-balancing routines and techniques observable in most other policy fields are even more important in these contexts.

Science, social change, religion and the state

In the areas of principled decision-making reviewed in this chapter, we can see that public policy has a complex relationship with changing social attitudes and values. Where old practices change, we have evidence of a new value, or values shift becoming manifest. The removal of legal prohibitions on abortion, and the availability, in most advanced countries, of forms of no-fault divorce, suggest the weakening hold of religious values on the apparatus of the state, particularly in the period from the end of World War II until the 1980s. States are complex engines of collective will, and many mechanisms are available for registering, constraining or facilitating change. Even where decisions are made that impact upon the most intimate aspects of people's lives, mechanisms must be found to convert choices into administration.

The fact that voluntary euthanasia continues to be illegal in almost all jurisdictions despite evidence of considerable public support for right-to-die legislation, suggests not that the principle is unacceptable, but that practical mechanisms for making it available do not accord with prevailing professional norms and interests. Right to die forces doctors to acknowledge that life is not the only value relevant to their practice – a confronting proposition. When it is invoked, political will can release or absolve professionals from the pressure of conscience, as occurred when the Belgian government obliged church-owned hospitals to implement its euthanasia laws, on pain of losing their licences (Delkeskamp-Hayes, 2006). The French government put some steel into the pharmaceutical industry when in 1989 it forced Roussel Uclaf, the pharmaceutical company it part-owned, to proceed with the distribution of the abortion pill RU 486 in the face of concerted opposition from pro-life groups (Smolowe, 1993).

The state, in upholding the value of choice, distances itself from religious values that would preclude choice. But the values dilemma never ceases, because of multiple interaction effects. Where divorce becomes more frequent, the state finds that it needs to go further than court-ordered maintenance in order to improve support for first families of separated parents. As experience in Australia shows, in the administration of child support, governments find themselves sucked further and further into the bitterness and emotion of family breakdown, as the need for vindication raises the question of fault in another guise.

The range of choices confronting governments has undoubtedly been expanded by the march of science. But science itself, for example in relation to stem cell research, juxtaposes its needs with pre-existing regulations governing assisted reproduction and even abortion. States do not need to be consistent and few are. Even technologies as novel as gene technologies can be absorbed into a pre-existing regulatory framework, if that is what prevailing interests want.

Given the overall argument of this book, it is not, perhaps surprising that changes in the involvement of governments in issues of the deepest personal moment and complexity, should be so contingent upon circumstance, political opportunity and pre-existing institutional structures. The more difficult the issue (as with euthanasia), the more sedulously is it avoided. In some cases, administrative structures reflect and assist this kind of strategy. In others, (for example in the administration of child support) very difficult questions are pushed into the administrative realm.

A resurgence of religious values?

For much of the twentieth century, commentators assumed that the modern state had effectively removed itself from the reach of religious values. The analysis in this chapter has suggested that, while there has been a growing 'secularity' in public sentiment in most, although certainly not all, western nations, religious values continue to be present in the layers of public policy, and religious groups continue to assert both their influence and their right to exercise it. The resurgence of the Christian Right in the United States and to some extent in Australia showed that religious values were by no means extinguished as a policy force. Moreover, as Islamic populations increased in the states of Western Europe, cultural and political factors introduced new complexities into the relationship between the state and religion.

Could the values balances that have been achieved through broadly utilitarian ways of thinking themselves be vulnerable? If we imagine a theocratic state at one end of an imaginary spectrum, and a communist state at the other, the liberal democratic state occupies the most difficult position, as it must make public choices about many issues that go to the hear of personal belief, without a guiding ideology other than liberalism itself. But liberalism, as it evolved in response to the identity politics of the latter part of the twentieth century, had an increasingly ambiguous relationship to secularness. Secular principles began increasingly to be overlaid by intellectual trends towards relativising values, often manifested in the form of multicultural policies.

The controversy about religious dress illustrates the point. Many Moslems, while not supporting radical forms of Islam, became more insistent upon female veiling as the political confrontation between Islam and the West became more strongly marked in the first decade of the twenty-first century. In France, the wearing of the hijab created enormous controversy. In 2004, after a decade of conflict over the issue, legislation was passed banning the wearing of all religious symbols in state institutions (Robinson, 2004). In supporting the law, President Jaques Chirac referred specifically to the secular traditions of the French state (Aljazeera, 2003).

Interpretations differ as to what liberalism might mean in this context. Authorities such as Warnock have argued that public policy in the liberal state allows no room for religion. In a paper published in 2005, Warnock, the chair of the UK's initial inquiry into IVF, put forward her view that religious belief had nothing to contribute to the formation of public policy, even where the policy was concerned with matters agreed to be matters of morality (Warnock, 2005, p. 33). Public and private morality could not be divorced from each other, she argued, but at the same time, the main principles of policy-making had to rest on the weighing-up of harms and benefits, the formulation of the 'least unjust' course of action, with a clear eye to the enforceability of the regulations that were put forward.

On the other hand, Julian Baggini points out that when (for example) we decide under what circumstances abortion should be allowed, religious and secular values are in constant contention and the role of the state is to maintain a neutral public space in which, as far as possible, differing views can be discussed (Baggini, 2006). While supporting this kind of discussion in principle, though, few liberals would want the question of abortion policy reopened. Fortunately, public policy, as a practical phenomenon, cannot afford too much theorising. It must respond to needs, interests and enunciated values, by producing a workable regulatory response – a values balance. Of course, this values balance is never conclusive, but is itself part of what Sagoff calls 'a complex and deliberative cultural, legal and political process' (Sagoff, 1991). The capacity of public policy to absorb, deflect and even to blur value conflict is an important resource in keeping these processes within incremental bounds.

7
Values and Public Management

Public organisations enact values when they implement public policies. They do this in ways that are both intended and unintended, conscious and unconscious. Enactment occurs in a number of modes, as the values that policies aim to achieve are translated into organisational forms, practices and interpretations. 'Policy', therefore, from the perspective of the public agency, is a multi-layered phenomenon with many decision-making sites. These sites are, most obviously, associated with the programmes the organisation is paid to administer. But programme administration is, in turn, conditioned by organisational policies, both overt and covert, long and intricate histories involving key stakeholders and arching above all of them, the policies of public administration itself. In assessing the role of values in public management, it is important to consider how the 'policy' of public administration relates to all these activities.

A public policy that makes grants to businesses for research and development (for example) directs resources towards the value of 'innovation'. In making the payments the public organisation makes many choices about how it interacts with the businesses it assists – how they are informed of the existence of the programme, the kinds of information made available, whether applicants deal with a shopfront or a website (or both), whether there is someone trained to help with more complex queries, what kinds of information are kept as the program is implemented and so on. But there is also a subconscious administrative realm. The culture, resources and accountabilities of the organisation shape the way these decisions are turned into practice: whether 'street-level bureaucrats' go out of their way to be helpful, or whether they are instructed simply to impart particular kinds of information and no more.

Given the many different tasks public agencies perform, there is scope for countless variations on these themes. Over time, agencies build up a history or tradition, a memory of dealing with the kinds of programmes with which they are entrusted. They deploy what March and Olsen call a 'logic of appropriateness' (March and Olsen, 2006) as they tussle within themselves and with other agencies (particularly budget agencies) to deliver what is required. Regulatory agencies, in particular, develop orientations towards those they regulate that is often values based: some favour a strict 'by the book' approach, others are more focused on outcomes.

Surrounding these decisions, though, is a far more political world. Depending upon the structural, contractual and conventional relationships between the political and the bureaucratic executives, the influence of elected politicians on administrators may be extremely powerful and direct, or much more diffuse. There may be rules or traditions about public service neutrality that protect public servants from politicisation. Or (as in American-style presidential systems) the upper layers of the public service may change as the party-political regime changes. The way these settings are organised and managed by political executives and the most powerful agencies of the bureaucracy – the 'policy' dimensions of public management (Christensen, Laegreid and Wise, 2002) – places another framework around public organisations that determines a good deal about what they can do and the way they behave.

It is the values inherent (or explicit) in these frameworks and the impact of administrative reforms upon them that I explore in this chapter. Inevitably, because of their salience in English-speaking countries, I focus on the changes that go under the general heading of 'new public management'. Although there is a vast literature on this subject, few studies have focused on the ways in which public organisations have dealt with key areas of value conflict in the transition from traditional forms of public administration to public management.

Taking up the schema put forward in Chapter 2, I discuss how four Westminster-based countries – New Zealand, Canada, the UK and Australia – have experienced, responded to and managed this type of change. Two major axes of value conflict are considered: responsiveness versus neutrality, and flexibility versus control. Coping strategies, both emergent and planned, to deal with these conflicts are then examined: I focus particularly on managerial responses such as attempts to manage values directly, and the pervasive emphasis on leadership. Before embarking on this analysis, however, it is important to locate the experience of the four Westminster countries within the broader context of public administration.

From public administration to public management

Writing about public management in the Anglo-American world sees (very broadly) two major phases in the policy of public management: the era of traditional public administration (which lasted, broadly speaking, from the mid-to-late nineteenth century and through the 1980s) and the era of public management (from the 1980s to the present). In the late nineteenth and early twentieth centuries, the era of public administration, the emphasis was on merit and professionalism, as an antidote to the 'spoils' or patronage era that preceded it (Henderson, 2004). This, traditional, period was (in its own time) characteristically normatively based (in the sense that norms were seen as central to the identity of the civil servant), although the character and emphasis of these norms differed from one national tradition to another. The later period, while not abandoning these earlier norms, emphasised performance as the basis for evaluation.

The Northcote–Trevelyan report, which formed the basis for the reform of the British civil service in the mid-nineteenth century, described a public administrator (invariably male) who was appointed on the basis of merit and carried out his duties in an apolitical way. In the United States, the Pendleton Act of 1883 provided for merit-based employment but without the British emphasis on the generalist, well-rounded official. Similarly, in Australia and New Zealand, where public agencies carried out a good deal of developmental work, there was a greater emphasis on technical expertise compared with the British model (Henderson, 2004; Caiden, 1965). The changes that began in the 1980s (referred to, for convenience as 'new public management') reflected a shift away from these values in two major ways. Firstly, there was a reaction against the perceived degree of public service autonomy that they entailed – the public choice critique. Secondly, there was a critique of the capacity of traditional public bureaucracies to do their work efficiently and effectively. This was the managerial critique of public administration.

The two critiques diverged in their understanding of the problem of organisational design. Public choice theory emphasised the need for increased control of bureaucrats by politicians, in order to prevent self-serving behaviour by administrators. Managerial theory stressed the need for greater flexibility, in order to 'let the managers manage', which implied increased devolution and decentralisation (Aucoin, 1990). When it came to practice, the two streams converged to form a kind of hybridised paradigm generally known as 'new public management'. Public servants (it was argued) should be both more responsive to political direction from above, and more receptive to consumers and clients from below. Achieving these objectives entailed structural changes (such as in the UK the separation of agencies into policy and administrative components) and process-based changes, such as the outsourcing of service delivery, the implementation of performance measurement and the use of contracts for specification and control.

During the 1980s and into the 1990s, the Westminster-based English-speaking countries were in the vanguard of these kinds of changes. But practice varied even within this group, largely because of the intimate relationship between the ideology of the party in power and the pace of administrative reform. In the United States, with a differently constructed relationship between the political and the administrative, the emphasis was on more creative ways of working, particularly the use of co-production with the private sector. Moreover, if we look beyond the circle of the English-speaking countries, we see how closely the expression of reform was dependent upon the point from which it started. While many European countries embraced the values of NPM, their actual expression varied considerably from country to country. And there was a further, deeper division – that between the European *Rechsstaat* traditions and those of the Anglo-Saxon countries.

In the *Rechsstaat*, to use Pollitt and Bouckaert's words, 'the state is a central integrating force within society, and its focal concerns are with the preparation, promulgation and enforcement of laws' (Pollitt and Bouckaert, 2000, p. 53). Civil services are the vehicle of law, and their administrative cultures reflect this priority. Indeed, in the sense that it both carries out and embodies the law, the civil service *is* the state. In the Anglo-American tradition, the public service is not identified with 'the state'. Indeed, the use of the term 'the state' is rare within originally Anglo-Saxon countries. The term 'government' is preferred, to denote the more dependent nature of power. In turn, the civil service is seen as an arm of government, with complex relationships between the political and the administrative within that concept.

Legal traditions notwithstanding, both custom and culture determine a great deal about the way civil services operate, and also about the way change is conceptualised. Where (as in France for example), it is not unusual for politicians to have been members of the grand corps of the civil service, the relationship between elected politicians and unelected officials is less likely to be a motor for change. Indeed the managerialist reforms of the Anglo-American democracies had no clear analogue in France. Other European countries followed change agendas that reflected their party political and institutional histories. The Netherlands, for example, with its traditions of consensual democracy, developed loosely articulated modes of engagement between elected politicians, civil servants and academics (Pollitt and Bouckaert, 2000: 54)

If we consider Asian countries, the relationship between civil services and the objectives of the state (particularly in relation to economic development) is clearly marked. Japan in the 1960s and 1970s and the Asian economies (Taiwan, Singapore, South Korea and Hong Kong) that industrialised successfully in the 1970s and 1980s, showed how familiar institutional forms could take on new and more extensive roles (Stewart, 1994). The example of Singapore, a Westminster-derived presidential system, is interesting in this context. The structure of the Singapore Public Service reflects the powerful role of the state in managing and developing the economy. Singapore's Economic Development Board has a formidable reputation as a practically oriented and strategically sophisticated agency. At the same time, the public service is firmly meritocratic and successive governments have been at pains to ensure that it remains corruption free. Services are delivered efficiently because that is the best way to keep the wheels of production turning.

The context of reform, and the values that are expressed through it, express the character of the state, its history and traditions and the nature of power within it. The comparative context helps us to see how significant the Anglo-American approach to government is for public service reform, and in particular, its perspective on desired and desirable relationships between the public and the private sectors. But if the Anglo-American countries form a group, it is important also to acknowledge their differences. Canada, Australia, New Zealand and the UK are characterised by the close parliamentary–executive nexus of the Westminster tradition. The United States has a presidential system. Canada, Australia and the United States are federal systems, while New Zealand and the UK are not. Within the Westminster group, there are differences in the style, pace and thoroughness of reform (Halligan, 2001).

New public management and the process of change

Pollitt and Bouckaert make the strong point that 'the administration of public programmes commonly exhibits deep-seated and recurring types of dilemma and contradiction' (Pollitt and Bouckaert, 2000, p. 151).

They identify ten 'candidate contradictions' within the field of new public management: aspects of reform that cannot simultaneously be achieved (that is must be traded off against each other), or which represent decision-making dilemmas for managers. As the authors note, these structural contradictions are conceptually distinct from (although related to) problems experienced in the implementation of change (Pollitt and Bouckaert, 2000, p. 154). The values-based analysis applied here, in focusing on implementation, brings out significant relationships between initiative, structure and response in the new public management story.

It is important to note that 'new public management' is an academic construct: practitioners of change did not usually talk about change in these specific terms. Rather, they identified particular practices that impeded efficiency, or which prevented managers from taking the kinds of decisions that were needed to bring about change. In some instances, the activities of particular groups (such as public sector unions) were seen as inimical to change. Thus, the agenda for reform varied, even within the group of English-speaking countries that spearheaded change.

In the struggle for power in the practical world, it was necessary to delegitimate the old order. Thus (to varying degrees), winning the debate about change in the public sector depended upon portraying the negative face of the traditional values. This contrast is easiest to demonstrate in the case of the United States, where writers such as Hummel saw traditional American public administration as displaying, ineluctably, a narrow, rigid and self-serving bureaucratic mindset (Hummel, 2000). Other proponents of change questioned the notion that public servants might serve the public interest, arguing that the public interest could never be objectively identified, and only politicians had the mandate of election justifying their actions (Keating, 1990; Shergold, 2007).

There were many sites and contexts for action. Practical work (by managers) as well as much academic fieldwork and commentary focused on organisational culture (and associated values), because there was a perception that the organisation's culture was 'wrong' or needed changing. The desiderata of new public management supplied a kind of checklist against which practices could be compared, but inevitably there was a degree of selectivity involved. Typically, 'old' cultures based on established practices and prescribed ways of thinking were contrasted with the possibilities of a 'new' culture that identified new kinds of roles and accountabilities. Many organisations prioritised a culture of customer service as a way of improving performance by overcoming bureaucratic mindsets (see, for example, Claver et al.).

The value conflicts that accompanied implementation were sometimes clear to those 'on the ground', but more often there was a sense of trying to find one's way through a plethora of issues. Civil servant and academic David Good identified a state of organisational flux – expectations were changing faster than managers could find robust organisational forms for them. As Good put it, 'Throughout this period [the 1990s] the old values of traditional public administration – accountability, neutrality, anonymity, and consistency – were rubbing up against the new values of the new public management – client (for some, customer) service, responsiveness, innovation, performance and results' (Good, 2003, p. 49).

The fact that the 'old' values were becoming clearer, even as they were being superseded, was not coincidental. One key effect of the NPM movement was, perhaps ironically, to bring the question of the old values to the fore. The traditional values had been implicit within the practices of traditional public administration, but with those practices now being changed, other mechanisms had to be found to retain them. Thus, for Westminster-based systems, new public management presented a Janus face: on the one hand, it looked towards augmenting the power of elected politicians vis-à-vis non-elected officials, as a means of enhancing political responsiveness. On the other, it sought to enhance the power of managers to run their agencies in accordance with agreed objectives. The two pressures collided at the imagined intersection of politics and administration.

Politico–bureaucratic relationships: Responsiveness versus neutrality

Administrative systems rarely express their values directly. Rather, they are contained in conventions, structures and rules that set expectations and govern behaviour. Westminster systems are constructed on a supposed separation of politics and administration reflected, in turn, in a doctrine of public service neutrality, meaning that professional public servants were expected to serve governments of different political persuasions equally effectively. Traditional public administration then, proposed a structural separation between the two value domains of politics and public administration. Ultimately, policy decisions rested with the minister. But public servants were expected to be 'frank and fearless' in the advice they gave. To ensure this independence of mind, senior public servants enjoyed various forms of tenure: the bottom line was they could not be dismissed by the minister. Thus there was a kind of balance of power, between minister and civil servant, implicit in this paradigm.

Reforms intended to improve the effectiveness and efficiency of public organisations did not necessarily interfere with this balance. 'Managerialism' stressed the importance of clarity and transparency in relations between the political and bureaucratic executives (see, for example, Scott, 2001). But the extent to which the creation of this kind of space was accompanied by a dismantling of the traditional protections for public service neutrality varied considerably from country to country. The cases of Australia, New Zealand and the UK are instructive here.

Australia went furthest towards redefining the minister–public servant relationship in favour of augmenting ministerial power. The incoming Labor government of 1983 took the first steps by winding back the tenure of secretaries, most of whom were henceforward employed on a quasi-contractual basis. In 1994, formal contractually based employment was introduced: by now, all tenure at the seniormost level had ended. Appointments were made by the Prime Minister, acting on the advice of the Secretary of the Department of Prime Minister and Cabinet (PM&C). There was no formal role in the process for the Public Service Commissioner, although in practice the PM&C Secretary usually consulted with the Commissioner before making a recommendation (Shergold, 2007). There was no obligation to consult anyone before removing a departmental secretary.

In New Zealand, despite what was, in many ways, a more stringent form of managerialism, the appointment process for chief executives was a much more formal affair. The process for drawing up a list of candidates and managing the appointments process was the responsibility, under the State Services Act, of the State Services Commissioner. The role of ministers was certainly more prominent than in the past (the decision as to whether to accept the recommendation was made by the Cabinet and approved by the Governor-General in Council), but also more transparent in the sense that if the Commission's recommendation was not accepted, the government was obliged to notify the fact publicly through the government gazette (Boston et al., 1996). Despite some difficulties, this system remained intact over the ensuing decade.

In the UK, departmental secretaries retained their tenure and were still known as 'permanent secretaries'. While Mrs Thatcher's government, in Dowding's words (Dowding, 1995), made the mandarins more manageable by managerialising them, the role and powers of the top echelons of the civil service remained intact throughout the Thatcher era. Consequently, the all-important strategic space between ministers and departments remained jointly controlled by both politician and civil servant. While political advisers came to play a much more prominent role, particularly in the Blair era, their numbers remained relatively small. In 2005, ministers in the UK appointed about 70 specialist advisers, who might not supervise 'permanent' civil servants (Talbot, 2005).

By contrast in Australia, in 1999 there were 152 specialist ministerial advisers, whose influence reached well into the body of the public service (Maley, 2000, p.51). The greater prominence of ministerial advisers in Australia brought political values deeper into the public service, increasing value conflict in many ways. In interviews I conducted for the Australian Public Service Commission (APSC) in 2006, addressing the issue of the future of public service as a profession, many participants mentioned this tension between political and other imperatives. As one middle-ranking public servant put it, it was difficult at times to know when she was expected to be a government servant and when she was expected to be a public servant.

The values analysis perspective described in Chapter 2 further illuminates the situation. Traditional public administration made a clear distinction between 'politics' and 'administration', a distinction not really tenable in practice but one that nevertheless served to mark out a kind of structural separation between the political and bureaucratic executives. Politicians were political; public servants were apolitical or neutral. It is important to recognise that the value of neutrality was not abandoned in the move to new public management. Indeed, the new Public Service Act of 1999 stated that 'the APS is apolitical, performing its functions in an impartial and professional manner'. The Act also enunciated the value of responsiveness to government in providing 'frank, honest, comprehensive, accurate and timely advice'.

In fact, the Act effortlessly hybridised a wide range of possibly conflicting values. The problem was that the world of practice was not so straightforward. With the breakdown of the traditional way of handling the politics–administration problem, the resulting value conflict required casuistic responses – that is, advice for public servants on what to do in particular circumstances. In a 2006 publication, the APSC addressed a number of problem areas that had arisen in practice. The expanding role of ministerial advisers caused many difficulties because advisers regularly communicated directly with public servants.

In these circumstances, the APSC advised employees always to check that an instruction comes with proper authority:

> It is Ministers, of course, who have final authority and accountability to parliament, and APS employees, through their Agency Head, are responsible to them. The relationship between the APS and Ministerial employees needs to always recognise this final authority. APS employees must, if in doubt, check that directions conveyed by advisers have ministerial authority and that professional APS advice has been conveyed to the Minister.
>
> (APSC, 2006)

If public servants were constantly reminded of the importance of values, no such guidance had been issued to politicians. What if a politician asked for a briefing to be changed in order to give the impression that a particular political course of action came from the 'independent' public service? The APSC advised that in these cases, briefings should not be altered. What if a minister ordered a public servant to do something illegal? 'When making decisions, APS employees must act in accordance with the law, including the APS Values and Code, and with any government policy and decisions. If a conflict arises between government policy, agency guidelines and the law, the law prevails' (APSC, 2006, p. 52). Of course, implementing these prescriptions in an environment in which ministerial control was absolute, might be another matter entirely.

The emphasis on 'values' in discourse about public administration did not necessarily mean that the values were being upheld: it could mean that they were under threat. Conversely, a more muted approach to values did not mean that there was necessarily a cause for concern. In New Zealand and the UK, where traditional public administration was hybridised with more obviously contractual forms of NPM, there was much less talk of values than in Australia. But as we have seen, the structural underpinning of the values was arguably more intact in New Zealand and the UK than in Australia. The Canadian case furnishes more evidence on this point.

The extensive discussion of public service values in the Canadian literature (both academic and practitioner-based) represented a sense of disquiet, rather than one of satisfaction (see Kernaghan, 2003; Langford, 2004). The shifting sands of politico–bureaucratic relations at the federal level had created many accountability problems that were interpreted as being threatening for traditional values. The Canadian Task Force on Public Service Values and Ethics observed that the purpose of its 1997 report was 'to help the public service think about and, in some cases, rediscover and understand its basic values and recommit to and act on those values in all its work' (Task Force, 1997, p. 1). The report identified a number of clusters of core values – relating to responsible government and the rule of law, professional impartiality and efficiency, ethical conduct, and 'people values' focusing on respect and caring. In similar vein, the report of the Gomery Royal Commission (2005) into various irregularities in the administration of the so-called Sponsorship Program underlined the importance of clear roles and responsibilities as an underpinning of ethical governance.

Codes of conduct and statements of values, particularly when they are intended as guides to action (that is, they are used casuistically) may result in more confusion than illumination. The important point to note is the extent to which 'values' (in this case the values of political neutrality on the one hand and responsiveness on the other) are themselves bound up in structures. While public organisations must always be the servants of multiple values, those that apply to public servants themselves are particularly dependant on supportive frameworks for their development and exercise. I will return to this point in a later discussion of public service professionalism.

Dilemmas of flexibility and control

Reform affected (and was intended to affect) the relationship between patterns of change, management decision-making and the broader apparatus of accountability and control. How were the traditional administrative values affected as reformers sought to bring in new techniques that would enhance flexibility? The key dilemma of public bureaucracy is how to make public organisations strong enough to do the work that is required of them, without, as Kettl puts it, making them so strong that they 'threaten the very system they are supposed to support'? (Kettl, 2006, p. 367). The general answer to this conundrum of competing needs lies in the mechanisms of accountability, both political and bureaucratic. Traditional Westminster theory aligns the accountability of public servants with that of ministers, who are accountable to Parliament and (ultimately) via elections to citizens.

But this model is clearly insufficient for the complexity of modern public administration and the very real decision-making power that lies in the hands of bureaucrats. Even within traditional public administration, institutions and agents of accountability, such as administrative law, public accounts committees and external auditors, had been added to the basic model. All these methods, however, in emphasising compliance, tended to sacrifice performance to control. The strong argument for managerial methods was that they allowed for a more productive relationship between the three dimensions of accountability – control, assurance and improvement (Aucoin and Heintzman, 2000). By measuring and reporting performance, clarifying expectations and offering incentives for improvement, managers would be empowered to achieve results. This was the rationale behind performance management at both the individual and the departmental level.

In moving towards greater flexibility, however, NPM produced a values hybrid. We can see this most clearly in relation to financial management. Some aspects of departmental financial systems (such as accruals and outputs-based budgeting and reporting) were intended to give effect to the new order. But other aspects (to do with the appropriations framework, the cornerstone of parliamentary accountability) continued to be hard-wired into the system. On top of this, government requirements for overall expenditure control and for translating policy priorities into spending outcomes, meant that central budgetary and finance agencies continued to exercise quite detailed controls over spending agencies, particularly in Australia and the UK. In the UK, Treasury engaged in 'cycling' – sometimes increasing control, sometimes decreasing it, but always retaining its pre-eminent position (see Parry and Deakin, 2003).

In New Zealand, the devolved system of agreed outputs created difficulties for the Treasury in negotiating and imposing overall limits. The largely bottom-up nature of the process meant that there were gaps in strategic elements of the picture (Scott, 2001). In Australia, the federal structure of the polity (although with a highly centralised financial structure) created further difficulties, because of the high proportion of departmental appropriations at the federal level that were 'passed through' to other levels of government, or to implementing agencies outside the purchasing agency. These 'administered' appropriations continued to be annually based, and were related to particular programs, rather than to designated outputs. (New Zealand by contrast, was able to make full outputs-based appropriations).

Consequently, the output prices presented in Portfolio Budget Statements were essentially artificial constructs, representing amalgamations of estimates of program costs, staff costs 'mapped' to the output, plus a (usually proportionate) allocation of fixed costs. It is a curious effect of the rationalising pressure imposed by outputs/outcomes budgeting and reporting, that rather than encouraging agencies to think of program costs as being a part of an output which they themselves produced, if anything the distinction between funding that goes beyond the agency, and funding that stays within it, was more sharply emphasised.

This meant that there was a continuing, short-term cash substructure to the outputs-based system. Further, this system substantially affected the behaviour of public managers, who had to (at estimates committee hearings, for example) account for 'what they had done with cash' in the previous year, rather than for the overall progress of a multi-year project. The politics of parliamentary accountability continued to trump good management practice. Opposition senators on estimates committees were more interested in finding information that would embarrass the government, than in reviewing achievements and problems. At the same time, critics of the system argued there was sufficient 'give' in the departmental appropriations for expenditures that could be represented as 'non-program' to escape parliamentary scrutiny all together (Harris, 2006).

Apart from these factors, the new techniques, by attempting to construct analogues to the financial aspects of management in the business sector, overlooked a number of very real differences between public and private organisations. Public organisations that deliver unpriced services (such as paying pensions or benefits) do not seek to make profits from doing so. Where surpluses are accrued as a result of improved efficiency, they are considered to belong to the central budgetary agency, or are extracted mechanically through 'efficiency dividends'. Where they represent an implementation failure (funds were not expensed in the time anticipated) they indicate a design or management problem (or both).

Moreover, at the purely technical level, outputs of public sector organisations are notoriously difficult to cost accurately (Robinson, 2001). Outputs are heterogeneous, and necessarily input driven – that is they consist of many different kinds of activities, which can be costed only according to what was spent on them. There are continuing difficulties in establishing convincing output prices (Scott, 2001). In any case, for budget-funded agencies, the objective is to translate desired projects into winning bids for revenue. Costings must be defended, but they are shaped by the programme, project or entitlement, rather than the other way around.

Establishing analogues to competitive markets through forms of internal contracting does not greatly help in the quest to find 'prices' to charge customers. Brookfield observes that 'quasi-markets' (such as the purchaser–provider relationships in the health sector) cannot generate 'quasi-costs', even with the assistance of activity-based costing methods, because the costs of a particular activity (and its associated overheads) reflect institutional structures, which in turn reflect evolutionary factors (Brookfield, 2001). From this perspective, the rules and habits of organisations represent the implied savings from repeated internal contracting, so that trying to construct (or elicit) transfer prices from 'within' as a way of comparing in-house with outsourced provision becomes an exercise in futility.

The measurement of costs and its use in management decision-making in the public sector takes place in (and can only be understood through) a perspective on the agency concerned that gives due weight to the environment in which it operates. As we have seen, the environments of public organisations are characterised by high levels of ambiguity and complexity. Managing for results attempts to simplify this complexity through a form of technicisation, that is, a way of overcoming value conflict by emphasising instrumental rationality. But technicisation, as a means for handling differing values, marginalises those that do not fit into the particular frame being applied. In the most 'managerial' polity, New Zealand, managers expressed a sense of frustration with performance indicators and outputs specifications that did not sufficiently allow for, or reflect the 'complexity, ambiguity and intellectual challenge that are key features of public sector roles' (Norman and Gregory, 2003, p. 46).

Dealing with value conflicts

By using values analysis, we begin to see differing patterns of tension within the new public management hybrid. It is noticeable that some of the strongest forms of value conflict occurred where rules and conventions had been abolished or made redundant by change. These rule changes, as we saw in the Australian case, left public servants exposed to heightened forms of the dilemmas that are intrinsic to public administration, with few counteracting or compensating mechanisms available to them.

Can values themselves help people to deal with this kind of ambiguity? Dewar describes values as 'standards to help us measure progress, decide perplexing questions and choose between alternative courses of action'. But as Langford points out, almost anything desirable can be described as a 'value'. He estimates that over 50 'core' values were identified in the Centre for Management Development task force report referred to earlier in this chapter (Langford, 2004). Nevertheless, if the core values are stripped down to the essential institutional values of public service they would, according to Aucoin, be primacy of the rule of law; impartiality in administering public services; and public service as a public trust (Aucoin, 1997, p. 37). Henderson discusses the following core values: neutrality and objectivity; professionalism and expertise; transparency and accountability.

But managing through values is difficult. Most public sector organisations have mission statements that emphasise organisational values. But these values are espoused, rather than those that are necessarily embraced by employees of the organisation. Codes of conduct are intended to be more specific, but are still aspirational, rather than means for practical guidance. If they are to be made useful, values need to be related to the organisation's systems and processes – and there should be credible sanctions for violating them. Reviewing values statements across the English-speaking democracies Kernaghan found that the APS had the most explicit presentation of values, with the Public Service Commissioner being given a role in upholding their implementation. In an annual state of the service report, the Commissioner reports on the values through staff surveys, including the investigation (by agencies) of suspected breaches of the code of conduct.

One of the difficulties of values management is that the values are piled on top of each other. The Australian Public Service Act (1999) contains the following values basket: the APS is apolitical; bases its employment decisions on merit; has the highest ethical standards; is openly accountable for its actions; is responsive to the government; delivers leadership of the highest quality; provides a fair, flexible, safe and rewarding workplace; and is a career-based service. But the basket contains values of different types. Some relate to individual qualities and decisions (such as the obligation to demonstrate 'high ethical standards') while others must be developed organisationally. For example, a key value such as merit-based employment is collective in character and can only be implemented in a systemic way; that is, by HR departments and senior managers working together to ensure that decisions are made in accordance with the value.

The implications for implementation are considerable. Organisational values cannot realistically be covered by induction programs, because they need specific attention and reinforcement at regular intervals and at a variety of points in the organisation. Moreover, the degree to which one rather than another organisational value might be emphasised will vary according to the role and function of particular parts of the organisation. Importantly, responsibility for the transmission and observance of the value becomes part of a manager's role rather than that of a values trainer or educator. While section 35 of the Public Service Act enjoins members of the Senior Executive Service (SES) to promote the values 'by personal example and other appropriate means', a wider ambit of engagement would help to identify practical opportunities for doing so.

Some aspects of APS professionalism relate to forms of knowledge and practice that are difficult to specify in general terms. For example, the importance of legislation in decision-making is part of the legal aspect of public service professionalism that cannot readily be incorporated in a list of values. It may be necessary to reinforce familiarity with key pieces of legislation and the decision-making that goes with them at regular intervals in specified parts of particular agencies. Again, responsibility for this activity becomes part of a manager's duties, as a key aspect of the expression of his or her professionalism.

The role of leadership

A number of academic commentators, as well as practitioners, have stressed the importance of leaders modelling and promoting ethical behaviours where rules are not clear-cut (Kernaghan, 2003). It is notable that of all the Westminster-based civil services, the APS puts the most emphasis on leadership, both in the interpersonal and the strategic senses. We can see this emphasis as both a requirement of the new public management, but also a reaction to it.

One of the key problems is that as the upper echelons identify more and more with ministerial agendas, a gap arises between the leadership and the rank and file. But what seems to be praiseworthy responsiveness at the Senior Executive Level, looks like a betrayal of public interest values to those further down. As the Canadian Tait report put it, there was a 'fault line' in the public service, a perception that senior managers did not, in their own behaviour, model the values that were said to be essential to public service (Tait, 1997). Yet it was through their actions that the core values had to be transmitted.

Public service as a profession

One way in which values are related to action is through professional identity. The values attached to a professional way of life carry an emotional resonance with those who identify with it. The realities of change are always political in this sense – they signal a reassignment of the right to define what is valuable. In times of rapid change, we would expect that the capacity of public servants to define themselves professionally would be an important resource both in setting boundaries and in mediating change.

Romzek stresses the institutional relationships involved in the exercising of control and the giving or rendering of one's account. These relationships have two dimensions: firstly, the extent to which public officials are autonomous in their activities and secondly, the extent to which they are held accountable by actors outside their own organisations. Four types of accountability system emerge: hierarchical and professional, and legal and political (Romzek, 2000). As we move away from traditional, hierarchical civil services (that is, as power is devolved to managers), the locus of accountability rests on professionalism, rather than on hierarchy. As sources of control become external, rather than internal, they may be prescriptive (such as entailed by legal requirements, and/or by audit), or they may reflect chosen modes of responsiveness to political and other stakeholders. Romzek stresses that these modes of accountability may conflict (for example, when political responsiveness conflicts with legal obligation).

Writing on professionalism is much stronger in the North American, than in other public service traditions. It is also interesting that the cast of this literature is much loftier than its counterparts elsewhere. This seems curious, when there is more overt politicisation in the American system of government than in any Westminster system. Yet it is an overt, rather than a creeping politicisation. And it exposes officials both to more temptation and to more opportunity. In these, more fluid systems, civil servants are expected to take more upon themselves. If we consider the writings by Pugh, van Wart, and by the Canadian Task Force chaired by John Tait, we see a list of values that stress the civil servant's role in democratic governance, his commitment to ethical conduct and so on (Pugh, 1991; van Wart, 1998; Tait, 1997). In Australian publications of the Howard era, on the other hand, the public servant is not represented as the upholder of a particular tradition but as a manager serving the wishes of government (see APSC, 2004).

We see further differences in the content and style of professionalism between the civil services in the Westminster-based democracies. While recruitment and staff development powers are devolved to departments in the UK civil service, there remains, nevertheless, a strong sense of the civil service as a collectivity expressing particular values. This sense of an administrative class based on the ideal of the educated generalist is both culturally ingrained and is also institutionally supported by the close working relationships (so ably parodied in Yes Minister) between ministers and departmental secretaries. The concept of an administrative class flows into training arrangements. The UK's National School of Government (the former Civil Service College) stresses courses in leadership and professional skills in government. The professional skills for government framework 'sets out the expectations the Civil Service has of its leaders, both individually and collectively'.[1]

In New Zealand, individual departments are responsible for their own recruitment, but there is a strong role for the State Services Commission in the sense that it is the employer of the SES and has an important part to play as adviser to the government on general management and personnel issues. Since 2005, the State Services Commission has overseen the implementation of state services development goals, covering not only excellence in the performance of public servants, but a range of organisational objectives relating to trust, networking, coordination and employer of choice. Significantly, the word professional comes into the overall goal of '[a] system of world class professional State Services serving the government of the day and meeting the needs of New Zealanders' (SSC, 2005).

Unlike the UK, Australia does not possess a professional administrative class, defined as possessing generalised management skills, loyalties to the system greater than those to the organisation they currently manage, a sense of career as an administrator; extensive authority; and a strong sense of professional community developed during long years of education and training with other careerists. Despite the formation of the SES as a cross-service body, the trend since the 1970s has been to entrench a departmentally focused managerial competence. Public service leaders have responded to these challenges by emphasising the importance of departments working together (through whole of government initiatives). A recent emphasis has been there on skills that are dispersed across agencies, such as project management and expertise in implementation (Shergold, 2003). The Public Service Commissioner, Lynelle Briggs, has spoken eloquently of a 'passion for policy' – being prepared to take a risk to put forward new ideas and to see them through (Briggs, 2005).

Nevertheless, participants in focus groups I conducted for the APSC in 2006 felt that there was an insufficiently clear conceptual connection between these expectations, the APS values, and the skills and qualities that individual public servants are called upon to demonstrate in practice.

In an organisational profession it is the rewarded behaviours that are replicated, and there are ever-present dangers that agencies (or parts of them) will become 'stuck' in practices that are counterproductive, as occurred in the Department of Immigration, Multicultural and Indigenous Affairs (DIMIA).

An official inquiry into the detention by the department of an Australian citizen in 2004 found that the pressures being applied to the department and the framework within which it was required to operate had given rise to a serious cultural problem within DIMIA's immigration compliance and detention areas, a culture that was described as both overly self-protective and defensive (Palmer, 2005, p. ix). More broadly, the report described a department with many managerial and leadership deficiencies, required to operate within a highly charged environment and as a result unable to cope with the complexity or systemic demands of its workload. The impression one gains from this report is of a Department that was neither a competent, compliance-oriented organisation of the old school nor a managerialised, results-oriented business of the new.

Public management and the public interest

How should public services be evaluated? The view from the academic world is that accountability is one of the key measures. But accountability has many dimensions. And as Simon noted, the balance between them changes over time. Writing in 1950, he described accountability as 'those methods, procedures and forces that determine what values will be reflected in administrative decisions' (Simon in Lynn, 2003, p. 20). We have seen that new public management, in giving greater power to elected members of the executive, placed a stronger emphasis on political values than was the case in more traditional forms of public administration. Public service values were modified to take account of this emphasis by the addition of 'responsiveness' to the list.

But what happens, in these circumstances, to the role of public servants in relation to the public interest? In the Australian model, the public interest was defined as being co-extensive with the wishes of politicians. Public servants could advise and warn – but they must have no expectation that their views carried any particular weight. When it came to implementing policy, however, as we saw with DIMIA, these formulations proved somewhat thin. The New Zealand model also tipped the balance in favour of politicians, but not to the same extent. It emphasised much more strongly the 'craft' of public service – the development and deployment of particular skills in the service of the public (see SSC, 2005). The craft model stresses the creation of public value within existing constraints (see Lynn, 2003). But presidential systems allow far more scope to bureaucrats to strategise their own political space than the Westminster world affords.

We know that public organisations are capable of containing huge amounts of value conflict, and that senior public servants have always had to be proficient at handling ambiguity (Halligan, 2003, p. 106). But some conflicts are more easily dealt with than others. Those that have to do with the ideals of public service itself may be particularly difficult because they relate to concepts of self-identity and self-worth. When a value (such as responsiveness) tips over into politicisation (preferment rests on conformity with ministerial wishes) some of the most valuable motivations may be lost. This is not a value conflict, so much as an important value losing its institutional underpinning. My own work with public servants suggests that many are attracted to public service by a desire to serve the public and, with that service, to play a role in defining and developing a view of the public interest. It is these public servants who feel most acutely the value conflict entailed by politicisation.

Politicisation would not matter so much if the political executive were made more accountable and/or if the new management approach itself engaged directly with the political dimensions of public service. It is difficult to find much evidence of greater political accountability flowing from new public management. The main way in which this might have occurred was through performance information supporting a more informed Parliament. But what evidence we have, suggests that the performance reporting of public management proved impenetrable or useless when it came to parliamentary scrutiny of administration. In shifting the axis of accountability for public servants, new public management seemed to depend upon a politics–administration dichotomy that could not be sustained either in terms of theory or in practice. Crucially, new public management lacked a theory of the political.

Politicisation cuts two ways. It means that public servants have less autonomy than would be implied by a managerial system. A managerial system requires (as far as possible) a separation from the political. At the same time, it makes efficacy inseparable from the political. Thus in the Australian case in the 1990s, we find a situation of some ambiguity between the political and bureaucratic executives, where favoured public servants worked closely with ministerial employees and with insider groups to craft policy. It is almost inconceivable that an apolitical ethos would be sufficient to guide this kind of activity. Moreover, where politicisation comes in, it is virtually irreversible. A drift towards an American-style situation might be one resolution. Or it is possible that a new 'hyper-political' administrative group, a little like the French *grands corps*, could conceivably emerge.

The future of public administration

There is no 'right answer' in the policy of public administration. But in identifying the key value conflicts, we can better see where the points of tension are. How durable, then, is new public management likely to be? We have seen that the history of public management is in many ways a history of changing values concepts. Public management carries with it the hopes of the societies that it serves and (whatever its actual achievements) must necessarily reflect those ideals in the rhetoric it uses about itself and in the way it is set up and operates. At the same time, new public management is an exemplification of a paradigm shift, a movement in thinking and ideas as much as a change in practice (Gow and Dufour, 2000). The idea of new public management enabled people to see more clearly what it had replaced. But the new paradigm did not stray far from its roots in public administration (that is the study of the practical business of government). It did not interrogate the possibilities of new relationships between public bureaucracies and the societies they were intended to serve.

In this sense, NPM was an agenda of power of the state engaging in internally generated reform, rather than a transformation of the state by newer forces. Certainly, NPM was reformist in character: the old bureaucratic public services were widely seen (both by politicians and practitioners) as no longer meeting the needs of modern governance. But the values-in-use were those of rationalism rather than those of participation. NPM came from above, rather than from below, an attribute that coloured much of its subsequent history.

We can say that the new techniques offer part of an answer to Peter Wilenski's question, 'how should administrators behave if their decisions are to be consistent with generally accepted views on democracy, efficiency and social justice' (Wilenski, 1986, p. 51). They have shown administrators how to be efficient, and they have given them new tools for thinking about the purposes of their organisation. Public administration is a less arcane and more logical activity as a result.

In some important ways (notably a consciousness of customers) it has become more accountable than in the past.

But the value questions persist. Indeed, the advent of governance, particularly in its more diffuse forms, restates the problem of administrative values in an even more trenchant form. The issue of defining a public interest becomes ever-more pressing when power shifts downwards and outwards, and public officials must learn to manage across boundaries as never before. A public service that is capable of different modalities of power is clearly one that needs to be self-confident and self-critical. It is doubtful whether polities that allow little or no room for public service self-definition, that is where public servants must be 'thought for' by politicians in relation to their role and responsibilities, can manage this kind of transition. If governments are to become part of the solution, rather than part of the problem, newer and more nuanced types of accountability will need to be devised. Leaving it all to 'leadership' is a poor substitute for a collective discussion of the issues.

8
Greenness and Growth

Environmental issues in general, and climate change in particular, present unprecedented threats to the very future of humanity. While science-based technologies are looked to for solutions, improvements in administrative and decision-making technologies will be needed just as much, if not more, if real progress towards environmental stabilisation is to be made. Can values analysis shed some light on the kinds of changes that might be needed?

This chapter assesses past decision-making technologies using and developing the techniques discussed in Chapters 1 and 2. Specifically, it addresses the ways in which policy systems have responded to the challenge of reconciling 'greenness' and economic growth. The main thesis of the chapter is that, at least up until the end of the twentieth century, environmental concern was typically dealt with by adding to, or modifying, existing bureaucratic structures and processes in order to create versions of environmental governance. While these forms showed increasing sophistication in terms of addressing values conflict, the characteristic modes of response suggested that true transformation (that is, a new synthesis) remained a long way off.

Before proceeding, it is important to define what is meant by 'greenness'. Environmental philosophies contain and expound many types and shades of green consciousness, from the radical to the managerial (Dobson, 1995). In this context, however, 'greenness' simply means environmental concern. Thus, anti-pollution policies give effect to green values because they are intended to lead to cleaner air, water or soils. Policies for protecting species habitat (for example by preventing deforestation or land-clearing) also give effect to green values by preventing actions that would harm the environment. 'Greenness' in this sense (that is as a range of valued objectives realised through policy) differs from environmental values embodied in discourses about the environment, or as contrasted with material values. Environmental values, expressed through movements and pressure groups, provided the pressure for new approaches. But it is what happens once pressure is turned into policy (that is the formal or institutional agenda of government is invoked) that concerns us here.

'The environment' as a source of value conflict

Chapter 2 discussed, broadly, the ways in which value conflict drives policy change. So it is important to establish its dimensions in relation to the development of environmental policy. That unregulated economic growth impinges adversely upon environmental values is clearly true – pollution, congestion, loss of amenity, species loss, over-exploitation of resources are all clearly observable by-products of growth. Value conflict is also evident when choices must be made between valued aspects of the environment (wilderness, biodiversity, iconic landscapes) and the needs of housing, traffic and industry. Given the fundamental nature of the environment as a 'commons', such conflict is to be expected. Rivers, air and soils transmit the consequences of individual and corporate decisions far and wide.

Land-developers in favour of increased housing densities point to the advantages of growth for first home buyers and young families and for the construction industry. Existing householders worry about loss of views, landscapes and amenity. In these situations, where costs and benefits have zero-sum characteristics, the clash of values is particularly intense. But the conflicting values run deeper than this, because the costs of mitigating growth are unevenly spread. Indeed, analysts such as Paehlke have pointed to the existence of an environment–equity–economy value conflict (Paehlke, 2003). Growth is the driving force of this conflict.

In developing countries, the preservation of important species and habitats runs directly counter to the interests of those who believe that they can improve their living standards by establishing cattle ranches and logging enterprises. In doing so, of course, their desires mimic those of their counterparts in the developed world, whose need for growth destroyed or at least severely modified large tracts of natural environments in Europe and North America. Ultimately, growth in the developed world created the conditions for improved equity but at huge environmental cost. The conflict continues in developed, as well as in developing countries. Attempts to mitigate environmental damage through (for example) taxes on carbon emissions are a case in point. In car-dependant societies, such as Australia and the United States, increases in fuel costs impact most severely on the poor, who are just as car dependant as the rich but have less capacity to absorb the increases.

Similarly, deliberate rationing through prices (you pay more for what you use) is often urged upon governments in order to reduce water consumption. Yet once again, those least able to pay are impacted the most – unless 'command and control' mechanisms are used (such as restricting garden-watering to certain times of the day). But these methods, in turn, raise efficiency concerns because those who are prepared to pay more to keep their gardens alive are prevented from doing so. To complicate matters further, environment–equity problems must be resolved, as Paehlke points out, 'in the context of a globalized economy and political reality' (Paehlke, 2003). The resolution of these issues must necessarily be political, in the sense that they will require choices to be made at the individual, local, regional, national and international levels. But the trajectory of these choices is strongly determined by the values they contain. As we saw in Chapter 1, values and interests are intricately linked through politics.

Environmental values and the policy agenda

While environmental values have, to varying degrees, become institutionalised within the structures of the state, the prominence of environmental issues on national (and international) policy agendas fluctuates over time. All public policies are, to some degree, subject to this phenomenon. But the particular character of green values, and their complex relationship with economic growth, makes these dynamic changes of particular significance, particularly when the future direction of values pressure is being considered.

Anthony Downs first pointed out the contingent nature of agenda prominence in his 1972 paper 'Up and down with ecology' (Downs, 1972). When the adverse consequences of economic growth impinge strongly on the public's consciousness, environmental concern rises, and dissipates when action (whether symbolic or real) is taken. There is also a relationship with the business cycle. Environmental concern tends to be relatively stronger when economies are functioning well and to dissipate when concerns about unemployment become more intense (Durr, 1993). At the same time, conservative political sentiment, even in good times, can override environmental concerns. In the United States, the Reagan era (1980–8), was notable for a distinct lack of enthusiasm, verging on antipathy, for environmental projects.

Calculations of electoral advantage clearly played a key part in these attitudes. The identification of green values with the left (or liberal) end of the political spectrum does not encourage parties of the right to develop green policies. But in Australia at least, both major parties, at both federal and state levels, tended to de-emphasise green policies in the 1990s (Economou, 1993). After the high point of the campaign to save Tasmania's Franklin river from being dammed in the early 1980s, there was a suggestion among voters of fatigue with 'greenies' as a political species, a sense that environmentalists, certainly the more extreme wings of the movement, were pursuing personal agendas that had little resonance with the needs of ordinary people.

While the environmental movement was far more complex than this reaction suggested, to a significant degree, environmentalists were included in the backlash that propelled politics towards the cultural, as well as the economic, right in Australia in the 1990s (and in the United States in the same period). Until the advent of water shortages in the drought years from 2000 onwards once again reinstated it on the agenda, environmental concern showed some evidence of values 'flip-flop' – that is of alternating prominence with growth-oriented values. The pressure on governments to acknowledge new values is, therefore, far from constant, but tends to ebb and flow. As a result, there is a disjunction between the public agenda (matters debated and discussed publicly) and the formal (institutional) agenda, which tends to follow the trajectories of bureaucratic politics.

Paradigms as governance mechanisms

While there is considerable scholarly and political debate about the extent to which growth and environmental values must (inherently) be traded-off against each other, in the world of institutionalised policymaking we are discussing here, the contrast is marked. Not only are the policy systems and state apparatus of advanced industrial societies built around the importance and the requirements of economic growth: growth is also the dominant paradigm. Growth produces jobs, and jobs keep governments in power. Attempts to introduce environmental values into public policies must therefore confront (or at least come to terms with) an overwhelming bias in favour of growth. This is not to enter the argument about the extent to which belief in environmental improvement is 'post-materialist' in origin. Rather, it is to make the point that policy regimes institutionalise patterns of values, and that the introduction of new, or different values, challenges these patterns.

As we saw in Chapter 4 (economic rationalism) and in Chapter 7 (new public management), paradigms (or ways of thinking about problems) play important roles in managing values. In the broad sense, paradigms provide a framework of meaning (Cotgrove, 1982, p. 26; Howlett, 1994). But, particularly when harnessed with the power of professional expertise, they act as ways of framing reality so that alternative approaches are excluded. One of the ways in which paradigms do this is by imposing a technical or instrumental rationality on issues that are much more complex.

This simplifying stance has significant practical advantages when professionals are confronted by value-based problems, as they often are. Professional paradigms play a role in technicising decision-making about these problems – that is they enable professionals, using the frame provided by their professional training, to measure and compare valued attributes in ways that aid decision-making. To see how this works, four key paradigms are explored in relation to decision-making about the environment – economic rationalism, planning, science and law. The basis for the exploration is the way these paradigms underpin professional involvement in policy and the values attributes that they bring to bear on policymaking.

Economic rationalism

As I argued in Chapter 3, the paradigm of economic rationalism, with its prevailing value of efficiency, tends to sideline other values. Economic rationalists (such as Bjorn Lomborg) may favour a 'business as usual' approach to the environment, arguing that continued growth is the best (most efficient) way of tackling environmental problems (Lomborg, 2001). But economic rationalism, through the theory of externalities, also gives an important normative handle on the environment, as the Stern report on climate change notably demonstrated (Stern, 2007). If the environment is a factor that normal prices overlook (a market failure), it is possible, through price-based instruments to address this omission through an evening up of the balance of incentives confronting decision-makers.

From a technical viewpoint, price-based instruments have the major advantage that they allow environmental remediation to be prioritised according to relative cost. In the case of water management, for example, price signals to consumers help to encourage economy of use and where entitlements to water can be traded, the resulting markets re-allocate uses away from activities that generate few benefits relative to their costs and towards those that are more cost-efficient. Other types of price-based instrument (such as rebates) have been used to encourage the use of green energy, through the adoption of solar hot water and solar power generation. As a disincentive, price instruments have been used in pollution abatement, in water management and have been widely advocated as a means for reducing greenhouse gas emissions.

From a values perspective, price-based instruments have the advantage that they enable 'the environment' to be written within the professional paradigm of economic analysis – that is, they do not involve major paradigmatic change. In turn, because of the policy dominance of this approach, 'the environment' can be mainstreamed without changing familiar forms of calculation. But at some point, externality-based arguments run up against the prevailing winds of economic growth, fanned by the interests of industry and (ultimately) of consumers. To some degree, the conflict can be hidden, but ultimately, has to be confronted.

For polluting industries, cap and trade schemes are less disruptive than so-called green taxes, which (even when they are passed onto consumers) impact more heavily on profits. From an industry point of view, therefore, new taxes have been vigorously resisted. Janicke describes this as 'structural' resistance to change – a point at which major industries, occupying key positions in the economy, are able to use political power and lobbying experience to delay or to water down new initiatives (Janicke, 2004). The acceptability of cap and trade schemes may rest more on their intricacy (and hence potential negotiability) than upon their effectiveness.

Of course, problems arising from the power of industrial interests should not be laid at the door of economic analysis. But at the same time, to the extent that economics permeates the policy thinking of a global world, effective responses to environmental problems may be hindered rather than helped. Economic analysis prides itself on the utility of its prescriptions for growth, while ecological economics lies uncertainly on the frontier between science and the economy. As a means to an end, economic rationalism provides many useful policy tools. As a guide to values, as many have observed, it is circumscribed by a certain narrowness of vision.

Science

The paradigm of science – the search for verifiable knowledge – plays an ambiguous role in public policy. On the one hand, scientists have been crucial in raising the alarm about climate change. Scientific knowledge and the data underpinning it are indispensable for the management of ecosystems. On the other hand, science does not produce certain knowledge. Scientific conclusions will always be hedged about by acknowledgment of the limitations of data or of methodology. For managers needing to know 'what will happen if I do x rather than y' this equivocation can be maddening. At the same time, different fields of science, by framing problems in particular ways, lead to differing conclusions about the value of particular resources. Consider the very different orientations (and often, judgments) of forestry scientists and ecologists when each considers the value of a particular type or area of forest.

As policy professionals, scientists are often at a disadvantage in the cut and thrust of decision-making at the heart of government. Scientific data supports decision-making in the field, but is less helpful when it comes to structuring problems in ways that are relevant for policy analysis. The length of time required for orderly research frustrates policymakers, who want immediate answers, rather than the raising of more questions. Where finance, cost and efficiency dominate the policy calculations of governments, science speaks of interconnection, probability, and complex modelling.

Ironically, while this marginalisation of science makes scientists outsiders in the policy game, it is this very position that enables them to voice their views with wholehearted conviction, whether through the media, or through international scientific bodies and congresses. The voice of science has become the voice of the planet, but it is a voice that, when pressed into the service of policymaking, is necessarily qualified by the uncertainties of its conclusions. Even when the evidence seems overwhelming (as with the connection between increased concentrations of greenhouse gases and climate change), it is difficult for scientists to give precise advice on mitigating strategies, an issue often seized upon by those advocating cautious, steady-as-you-go responses to environmental crises.

Planning

Planning is a particularly important example of the technicising role of paradigms. While urban planning is not usually considered under the rubric of environmental decision-making, the principles of planning and associated law continue to underpin the ways in which conflicts between interests – as they manifest themselves spatially – are settled. Planning rules, in the form of conditions governing development approvals, express values in a way that can be operationalised by builders and architects. These professions, in turn, favour clear and unambiguous statements about what can be done, with (at the same time) sufficient flexibility to enable unforeseen problems to be addressed or opportunities to be exploited.

Those affected by development want clarity, because it means they know what to expect. The language of values becomes a double-edged sword in these circumstances. When values related to outcomes are suggested as a guiding principle for granting development permissions, they create difficulties for those administering planning rules, because of the relationship between values and interests. For example, a developer might see a particular building as 'fitting in' with its environment. Those required to live next door to it, might think otherwise.

Those aspects of values that can be quantified win over those that cannot. It is possible to legislate for the amenity of a room by requiring that it should include a window of a minimum size. Aesthetics, unless they can be observed under the banner of 'heritage', are a different matter. Specifications of heights, widths and depths, as the instantiations of particular values, are under constant pressure from change-minded interests. As a result, planning law, like tax law, is an incrementalised palimpsest of values: which value will be observed in practice is often difficult to predict.

Law

Law, as a paradigm for arbitrating between interests, enshrines and defines rights, remedies and due process. In fact legal thinking gives values a voice by shaping the apparatus of process, through the determination of sequence, standing and protocol. Very often, it is only through the law – for example, by identifying a slip-up in failing to follow some aspect of due process – that environmentalists are able to exercise any kind of countervailing power to the bias inherent in growth-oriented systems. But law (as economists are wont to observe) works slowly and often ineffectively. In policy terms, its identification with command and control, with sanctions and limits, transmits information much less smoothly than relative prices do.

Law recognises only with difficulty the need for jurisdictional integration. Where law and science meet (for example in environmental impact assessment (EIA)) the scientific paradigm is pressed into a quasi-adversarial framework to which it (in turn) is ill-suited. Law represents the state in its most adamant frame of mind, but also its most compromised. Where (for example) environmental values are recognised through the imposition of conditions on development, the result (particularly in controversial situations) may satisfy no one. For those outside the circle of power, the result often resembles absolution, rather than resolution, as both monitoring (for compliance) and ongoing management (for sustainable outcomes) are often neglected.

Governance, sustainability and value conflict

Academic opinion is divided on the implications of what has been termed the 'repertoire of administrative rationalism' (Dryzek, 2000). Bartlett has described EIA as a 'worm in the brain' of the administrative state, pointing it in the direction of greater responsiveness (Bartlett, 1986). Dryzek, on the other hand, remains sceptical of the capacity of conventional administrative systems to deal with the complexity, uncertainty and risk inherent in environmental problems.

'Sustainable development' represents the most concerted attempt to overcome these limitations. From the values perspective, sustainable development represents a hybrid paradigm – a way of encompassing the values of both greenness and growth. The paradigm is an attempt to 'inscribe' one value in terms of the other. When we look at the way this paradigm is actually deployed, however, we find that, while it has allowed some rebalancing of decision-making to occur, it has not proved truly transformative.

This is not to suggest a cynical stance. Many in government want to promote sustainability. The problem is that government itself, in its multivalent interactions with the economy and with society is itself part of the problem. Sustainable development offered a new way of configuring and projecting existing activities, without the need to alter established values-handling practices. To see how this occurred, it is necessary to explore the architecture of sustainability and specifically to review how policymakers tried to give it an organisational dimension. In the next three sections, I describe three general modalities, or tropes, through which the administrative state attempted to generate new institutions for this purpose: firstly, through structural separation; secondly, through integration; and thirdly, by giving the environment a 'voice'.

If we see these institutions as mechanisms for avoiding or rationalising conflicting values, rather than as activities or functions, we gain an additional perspective on their likely longer-term evolution. Initially, environmental values were 'add-ons' to agencies with growth-oriented functions. In the next phase, separate agencies emerged to regulate problems such as pollution: the era of structural separation. Later, the need to find ways of bringing environmental criteria to bear on a wider range of decision-making, led to forms of integration. In policy instrument terms, there were parallel developments. Following Tews, Busch and Jorgens (2003), I distinguish between an initial phase, in which regulatory approaches were adopted across the Organization for Economic Cooperation and Development (OECD) to control water and air protection and waste management, and a later phase, in which market-based instruments began to be used increasingly.

Structural separation

As we have seen in other contexts, one way of managing value conflict in governance is to establish a separate agency to 'carry' the new value. In environmental matters, we see this pattern in relation to two areas of policy: the creation of national parks and the regulation of pollution. It is worth, briefly, reviewing the history of representative examples of the bureaucratic entities that were created to carry these ideas forward and to place them in the perspective of other administrative developments of the time.

In all nations, we find an enormous variety of land uses with different designations, different legislative protections and different values evident in their management. All major cities, for example, have recreational spaces where building is not allowed, even if the natural environment within these parks is virtually non-existent or has been heavily modified. But recreational parks are defined by the needs of urbanised families with little space for gardens. National parks represented one of the first attempts by governments (pressured of course by their citizens) to create, or at least to preserve, greenness. The beginnings were modest and tangential to the vast bureaucracies devoted to allocation and to growth.

Preserving parts of the natural world because they are beautiful or distinctive represented a new and different direction in human thinking and initially at least, concentrated on areas where the opportunity cost of preservation was low. Even in countries where 'greenness' had a relatively long history, the setting-aside of areas from economic purposes focused on those parts of the environment not already taken up by production. Thus the first national parks were created, not where farming could have taken place but in rugged areas of obvious natural beauty where the claims of crops and animals were minimal.

The tasks of managing these small enclaves could easily be absorbed by existing organisations. As specifically 'green' values have developed, however, their administrative expression tended to require separate organisations, with their own ethos and training. In the history of environmentalism, the formation of agencies that could 'carry' a value into the apparatus of the state was a development of major importance. In the United States, the National Park Service was created as early as 1916 (Klyza, 2002). In the UK, the National Parks Commission, established in 1949, had charge of all areas designated as national parks (preservation of particular habitats came under the Nature Conservancy). In Australia, where (somewhat confusingly) national parks come under the jurisdiction of state governments, separate National Parks Services were established in each of the Australian states in the post-war period.

Bureaucracies for pollution control

The creation of separate, regulatory agencies for pollution control had a number of advantages in preventing value conflict: within a traditional, functionally organised governing bureaucracy, it represented the new value in a way that could be accommodated within the general parameters of bureaucratic politics. We see this mechanism employed in many contexts in the 1970s and 1980s, as regulatory solutions to specific problems (for example, pollution caused by motor vehicle exhausts) were devised and implemented. At this time, the facts of environmental air pollution (smog) were becoming apparent in many cities, not only those of Europe and North America, but also in Japan and the newly industrialising countries of East and South East Asia. In every case, the mode of attacking this problem was to create an environmental protection agency to administer anti-pollution legislation. I take as the locus classicus of this approach, the US federal Environmental Protection Agency (EPA).

Founded in 1970, the EPA was itself a mechanism for bringing together numerous existing federal initiatives for protecting the environment. The EPA's battle to implement its legislative mandates in relation to water and air pollution, pesticide use and other environmental problems saw it initiate prosecutions of polluters (including many US cities) in its first few years of operation. Point-source water pollution proved easier to counter than air pollution problems occasioned by automobile use. When it came to supporting action that called into question unrestricted automobile use, public opinion was more equivocal than opinion polling had suggested (EPA, 2007). As the EPA itself came to realise, whatever its legislative arsenal, its ultimate power to act depended upon gaining (and retaining) public support.

Nevertheless progress was made through the development and promulgation of ambient clean air standards, and the approval of state and regional plans to meet the prescribed standard. By 1973, the EPA and auto manufacturers had agreed to adopt the catalytic converter as a means to reduce automobile emissions by 85 per cent in 1975-model cars. Having established a broad framework of operation that was scientifically validated, the EPA was able to move ahead strongly where major targets could be identified, and incrementally where action started to sharpen value conflict among the citizenry.

Mechanisms for integration

Structural separation could only go so far. As the complexity and importance of environmental problems began increasingly to be understood, it became necessary to find ways of modifying mainstream forms of decision-making so as to make room for the needs of the environment. I trace these developments by exploring the principal forms of integration developed to implement the new ways of thinking: firstly, structural coordination and secondly, strategic planning. Structural forms of coordination seek to bring diverse organisational practices together, whereas inter-organisational forms of strategic planning (such as those evidenced in the Dutch National Environmental Policy Plans (NEPP)) are more process-based (Carter, 2001, p. 274).

The coordinating capacity required to create an overarching commitment to sustainability, by working within and between the myriad agencies whose activities affect it, is formidable. Each agency does its best, but cannot go beyond its immediate mandate. We see this in the Australian case, where concerted efforts were made in the 1980s to establish a policy agenda for ecologically sustainable development (ESD), defined as 'using, conserving and enhancing the community's resources so that ecological processes, on which life depends, are maintained, and the total quality of life, now and in the future, can be increased' (ESDSC, 1992).

Several volumes of reports were produced in the 1980s, one for each of nine major industry sectors, and two for cross-cutting issues. The language of the reports was moderate, their aims modest. The more radical wings of the Australian environmental movement found these limitations difficult to accept, particularly where they affected forestry and both the Wilderness Society and Greenpeace withdrew from the process. Ultimately, the reports morphed into a National Strategy for Sustainable Development, which in turn underpinned an Intergovernmental Agreement on the Environment.[1] Under this agreement, governments at all levels undertook to ensure 'that environmental issues associated with a proposed project, program or policy will be taken into consideration in the decision making process'. However, at the same time, the same governments would ensure 'that measures adopted should be cost-effective and not be disproportionate to the significance of the environmental problems being addressed'.

When the implementation of ESD principles by the Commonwealth agencies was assessed by the Australian Productivity Commission in 1999, the agencies were able to report many initiatives they could relate to the sustainability objective. In one case, the management of the Commonwealth-controlled fisheries, sustainability objectives and principles had been incorporated in the governing act (Productivity Commission, 1999, p. 45). However, the Commission was disappointed to find that overall, implementation of ESD principles had been patchy and was often missing from key stages of the decision making process (Productivity Commission, 1999, p. 63).

As an integrative paradigm, ESD had proved to be more rhetoric than reality, a way for agencies to reframe and to some degree reorient what they were doing, but providing an insufficient remit for effective interagency negotiation. Put through the administrative values filter, ESD was not so much transforming, as reassuring. Comparisons with other policies more in keeping with the ruling economic paradigm of the early 1990s, such as the National Competition Policy (NCP), suggested further reasons for this. Curran and Hollander propose a number of reasons for the relative lack of penetration of ESD, including its lack of definitional clarity, and the absence of strong prime ministerial support (Curran and Hollander, 2002). From a values perspective, we can see another reason for the stronger currency of NCP – its firm emphasis on a single value (efficiency). While the NCP helped to resolve value conflict by marginalising alternative views, ESD was worryingly heterodox.

A similar phenomenon has been observed in European states, where, despite the existence of national strategies for sustainable development (for example in Sweden, Norway and Germany), constant political pressure and involvement at the highest levels is required to prevent reversion to the dominant values set (Niestroy, 2007). In the right conditions, however, the resilience and adaptability of this values set is formidable, as the Dutch example demonstrates. The importance of clear goals and strong political support in giving a practical edge to sustainability is evidenced by the Dutch NEPP, the first version of which was promulgated in 1989. The NEPP aimed to 'make environmental problems manageable within 20 to 25 years' by launching a concerted attack on the sources of environmental degradation (Bennett, 1991). It set targets for reductions in emissions and goals for waste management that reflected the requirements of sustainable development. These plans were carried out by identifying key systemic points of intervention and bringing together government, business and community in networks that embraced shared understandings or covenants as to what was to be achieved.

The imperatives of the Dutch environmental situation, and the strong traditions of consensus-based planning in Dutch governance, undoubtedly provided necessary preconditions for these developments. Whether they represented a decoupling of environmental improvement from economic growth, however, remained uncertain. The most cost-effective reductions in pollutants had already been made. Future improvement would require more thoroughgoing transformation, including radically changed behaviours from consumers and householders (Connelly and Smith, 2003, p. 324). The pathway to this stage – that of transition management – remained shadowy, if tantalising.

Environmental impact assessment

As practised in most jurisdictions, EIA offers a way around contentious decisions by technicising them; that is by placing values problems within a framework of scientific appraisal and measurement. The idea is that by quantifying the impacts on the environment of proposed developments, a clearer and more objective assessment of the costs of proceeding can be obtained, and where necessary, actions can be modified or even prohibited in order to protect the environment. In practice, the benefits of EIA have fallen well short of the promise. Bartlett, reviewing the US National Environmental Policy Act two decades after its initiation, reported that too many EIAs were used to justify decisions already made, and that the process, by virtue of its 'one-off' iterative nature, did not allow for the cumulative effects on the environment of many projects (Bartlett, 1986). Goldberg, reviewing Australian experience from the perspective of the mid-1990s, came to similar conclusions (Goldberg, 1996).

The deficiencies of the process as a way of mediating conflict reflect both the biases that are built into it (much of the investigatory process is carried out by the development proponents), and the fact that the collection of scientific information and its use in decision-making is itself a politically charged process.

Integrated resource management

Integrated environmental management means combining the various elements of resource management into a coherent whole. Initially, experiments were made with hybrid organisations, that is, bringing together agencies with separate, although related functions. For example, in three Australian states during the 1990s, agencies for managing natural resources were assembled in order to bring together activities such as catchment management, aspects of land administration, water infrastructure, and national parks (Stewart, 1997). Significantly, policy responsibility for production agriculture continued to be located in a separate department, reflecting a continuing separation between farming considered as an industry and farming considered as an ecologically significant activity.

Where one agency was created to arbitrate between production-based and ecological values, the pressures upon it could prove overwhelming. The Australian case of the Resource Assessment Commission (RAC), created as a political expedient at a time when mining development was prominent in Australia, is a case in point. The RAC made a number of recommendations on contentious issues, but its lifespan was limited, precisely because it tended to highlight, rather than to defuse, value conflict (Economou, 1993). More robust efforts focused on process, rather than structure. New Zealand's Resource Management Act (RMA) 1991 offers an excellent example of a form of governance designed to incorporate environmental requirements into an overall decision-making system.

The Act was unusually wide-ranging, so it is worth considering the ways in which it moved beyond the technicising aspects of planning, towards a more holistic framework. The Act covers land, air, water, coastal, geothermal and pollution management. The framework of the Act is based on a single purpose, which is to promote sustainable development of natural and physical resources. Part II of the Act contains a comprehensive statement of values, listed under the heading 'Matters of National Importance'. This statement requires 'the preservation of the natural character of the coastal environment[. . .] The protection of outstanding natural features and landscapes from inappropriate subdivision, use and development; the protection of areas of significant indigenous vegetation and significant habitats of indigenous fauna'. Under the headings 'other matters', the Act requires decision-makers to have 'particular regard to [. . .] the efficient use and development of natural and physical resources'.

Section 5 of the Act also states that consideration must be made of the maintenance and enhancement of amenity values, defined to mean 'those natural or physical qualities and characteristics of an area that contribute to people's appreciation of its pleasantness, aesthetic coherence and cultural and recreational attributes'. This pattern of values is to be turned into choices through the operation of statutory plans, with rules governing consent requirements. Regional authorities produce plans for natural resource management. Regional and territory planning systems have to conform with superior regional policy statements (Smith, 1996).

Evaluations of the operations of the Act suggest that it has had a limited, although still worthwhile effect, on decision-making. In particular, the section relating to 'amenity values' has proved important in urban contexts, where there is often not a clear biophysical bottom line to protect, and the quality of life of residents depends on tree preservation and the designed 'feel' of particular streetscapes. However, the New Zealand Parliamentary Commissioner for the Environment reported in 1998 that the adversarial nature of the permitting processes was discouraging public participation. Moreover, a lack of performance targets meant that the concept of sustainability could not reliably be observed in decision-making (Smith, 1996, p. 9).

Writing in 2002, while observing the pressure placed on the RMA by neo-liberal political ideologies, Memon observed the fundamental problem was 'the challenge of crafting a definition of sustainable management that can enable decision makers (elected councils, the Environment Court, the Minister for the Environment) to reconcile the spectrum of values different groups accord to the environment in a plural social setting' (Memon, 2002, p. 303). Experience showed that in practice, decisions were being pushed down to officials and politicians in regional and local settings. We would expect that these officials would use the strategies outlined in Chapter 1 to make decision-making doable within the resources available to them. The kind of values-balancing that occurs in these circumstances tends to be ad hoc and inconsistent. Nevertheless, despite its shortcomings, the New Zealand Act, with its emphasis on the local level, does at least suggest the shape more balanced decision-making might assume.

Giving the environment a 'voice'

We have seen that environmental values are represented only with the greatest difficulty in conventional decision-making systems. One technique that overcomes this problem, at least partially, is to give environmental values a 'voice' in decision-making. This can be done in a number of ways. One model is for the state itself, so often ranged against the interests of concerned citizens, to take their part in legal proceedings. In Sweden, the state may play this role in environment courts used to determine permits for large installations. Legislation such as the US Endangered Species Act of 1973, promotes the voice of endangered animals into the actions of federal agencies.

Other kinds of measures allow (or even encourage) citizens to articulate their own concerns as part of a pluralistic strategy to even out the balance between growth and green values. In many cases, this means finding ways to oppose government agencies, or decisions made by them. In New South Wales, Australia, the citizens of the small village of Bungendore were able to use the Environmental Defender's Office (a network of not-for-profit community-based legal centres) successfully to represent their interests in an action in the Land and Environment Court against a local government body that had permitted a land development in the village that contravened its own requirements for water availability and sewage disposal.

Another mechanism is to use public power or public funds to give resources 'back' to the environment. A number of attempts have been made in regulated water systems where water has been over-allocated to give (or return) water to the environment by means of designated environmental flows. In Australia, as a result of a fortuitous combination of political events, an agreement was reached in 2002 to return to the Snowy River a small fraction of the water diverted from it for irrigation purposes. Until drought put an end to the practice, regular discharges were made from dams in the Australian Capital Territory to maintain a level of flow in the Murrumbidgee River.

On occasion (non-human) environmental users of water have been given rights within conventional allocation systems. In the management of the Macquarie Marshes, a wetland in northwest New South Wales, water allocation was nominally made to the marshes for the purpose of sustaining a breeding ground for waterbirds. The waterbirds had become part of the human decision-making matrix for the marshes (Stewart and Jones, 2003, p. 24). Similarly, Wiering and Arts' account of Dutch integrated water management – using the discourse of 'giving the river room' – suggests the incorporation of new policy actors into a previously closed, technocratic system (Wiering and Arts, 2006).

But the limitations of governments are everywhere apparent. Public servants follow dominant paradigms and, despite the values melange within which many operate, prefer risk aversion to the hazards of insider activism. Moves to initiate change come from concerned conservationists – while they may lack the luxury of public regulation and resources, they have the advantage of values coherence, at least when they are campaigning on a particular issue.

Resolving value conflicts

As we have seen, governments have many ways of accommodating new values without altering the basic power structures too much. The story of the accommodation of the state to 'the environment' shows all these resources in action. But it is also true that environmental issues place these power structures and entrenched ways of making decisions under enormous pressure, precisely because it is these structures that are themselves part of the problem. Those seeking change or even redress often find that existing mechanisms for resolving conflict do not meet their needs. Governments must come up with forms of governance that mediate, settle or contain these clashing values if policymaking is to proceed.

Action through the courts can be effective where rights to a particular resource are contested by other interested parties. In the United States, much of the framework of water governance has been established through a combination of interstate litigation and negotiated compacts (Lord and Kenney, 1995). As a conflict resolution method, though, the law does not recognise the rights of 'the environment', or those concerned about the environment. It recognises only the rights of those who have been injured by the uses made by others of the environment. Thus it is possible to launch a legal action against a neighbour who is spoiling your view, but not against the developer of a giant tower that is despoiling an entire neighbourhood. When these kinds of events occur, the resulting conflicts act out the fundamental value conflict of greenness and growth.

Regional Forest Agreements

Australia's Regional Forest Agreements (RFAs) show both the potential and the limitations of state capacities in these contexts. Put simply, RFAs are formal agreements between the Commonwealth and state governments whose aim is to balance the conflicting claims of conservation and development in Australia's native forests. The agreements describe and give effect to, a number of balances, or compromises: between the Commonwealth and the states on the one hand and between conservationists and economic interests (miners, loggers and processors) on the other. As such, they demonstrate key steps in the creation of environmental governance.

In specific terms, the Agreements provided for the setting up of a 'Comprehensive, Adequate and Representative' reserve system whose aim was to preserve from logging representative examples of every forest ecosystem type, together with management plans for the conservation of rare and endangered species. They also set out, for a period of 20 years, the basis on which forest industries, on both public and private land, are to be managed and developed.

There were separate RFAs for each state with substantial native forests and in some cases, for areas within states. While each agreement reflected the particular situation of the area to which it applied, the underlying structure of all RFAs was similar. They relied essentially on a form of land use planning in which certain areas of forest were allocated to wood production, while others were placed in conservation reserves. The criteria governing these allocations, the so-called JANIS criteria, covered the conservation of forest biodiversity, old-growth forests and wilderness, using a formula derived from the Montreal process (JANIS, 1997). This formula provided that a minimum of 15 per cent of the pre-settlement extent of each forest type should be preserved, together with a minimum of 60 per cent of extant old growth forest. Once each RFA was signed, the Commonwealth exercised no further direct influence on the timber industry in that area – an important development in an area where the Commonwealth–State relations had been extremely bitter.

Conservationists wanted as much forest as possible to be protected from logging. The timber industry wanted guaranteed amounts of wood, so that firms could make investment decisions with some degree of certainty. Unions and employee groups wanted jobs to be protected and employment prospects enhanced. Where neither of these things was possible, they wanted compensation. Governments wanted forests off the political agenda and, depending upon their political interests, continued support from key constituencies.

Immediate conflict was cooled by setting aside areas (called deferred forest areas) about which participants could 'agree to disagree'. The formal process also involved a major investment in gathering and collating data, which would form the basis for later agreements. While these agreements varied from state to state and from area to area, each specified 'who gets what' in land-use terms and required the state government in each case to legislate to give effect to the resulting reserve system. The proportions of each identified forest type contained in reserves were also specified. There was provision for annual monitoring of implementation, and for a five-yearly review of outcomes.

The Commonwealth played a major role in steering the process in each case, seeking to ensure that the resulting agreement met its own criteria, while confronting a different political scenario in each state. But the Commonwealth's concerns and those of the state could not always be resolved. After initial agreement, political change led to a stand-off in relation to Western Australia's RFA. In Queensland, the process stalled because the Commonwealth and the state government could not agree on the desirability of a deal struck between conservationists, the timber industry and the state government, which involved phasing-out public native forest logging in favour of plantation resources (Brown, 2001).

The experience of the RFAs shows the importance (but also the limitations) of value conflict in driving change. Where a more or less sustainable solution occurred, the resolution of the conflict involved reducing areas of multiple-use forests (managed by one agency) and replacing them with separately managed conserved and intensely harvested areas. This deal had the effect of meeting green values, but at the expense of forest-based logging communities. From a values perspective, the balance had been altered from the multiple-value forestry pursued by the Forestry Agencies, to a new form of structural separation, in which some areas were clearly managed for conservation values (in National Parks), while others were given over to intensive forestry. Outright conflict had moved the values balance, with larger physical areas of forest being preserved as part of the deal. While sustainability (in the sense of generating areas of sustainably managed forest) remained doubtful, as a political mechanism, the RFAs had undoubtedly proved their worth.

International environmental governance

International organisations have produced many values-based statements about the importance of harmonising the environment with development. The problems of value conflict are, however, if anything even harder to resolve at the international level than they are within nations. This is because there are fewer mechanisms for constructing the kinds of environmental governance observable at the national level. Moreover, nation states on the international stage cast themselves in particular roles (although the same nation may play a different role in different circumstances). Norway, for example, exemplary environmental citizen in many ways (and whose Prime Minister Gro Harlem Brundtland gave her name to the first major international report on sustainability) offends the sensibilities of many, in other ways much less green states, when it comes to whaling.

As with forms of governance emerging within nation states, international treaties operate most unambiguously where there is an identified problem (such as acid rain), with a solution that fits within the prevailing growth paradigm. Even here, persuasion may be more important than regulation. The 1979 Geneva Convention on Long-Range Trans-boundary Air Pollution (the LRTAP) represents forms of governance based on what Levy has called 'tote-board' diplomacy, rather than the exercise of collective regulatory power (Levy, 1993). The LRTAP refers to the desire of contracting parties to limit pollution, and establishes procedures for consultation between states affected by air pollution, and those producing the pollution. Within the LRTAP progress has been made because leading states have been able to shame laggards into action (UNECE, 2007).

Problems such as climate change create far more controversy because they pose obvious difficulties for the paradigm of persuasion. A much wider-ranging convention than the LRTAP, the UN Framework Convention on Climate Change provided, similarly, for good intentions rather than mandated actions. The Kyoto Protocol, however, offered a mechanism for a number of states to move beyond good intentions to targets for reductions in emissions of greenhouse gases, as we see in the following extract from the Protocol.

> The Parties included in Annex I shall, individually or jointly, ensure that their aggregate anthropogenic carbon dioxide equivalent emissions of the greenhouse gases listed in Annex A do not exceed their assigned amounts, calculated pursuant to their quantified emission limitation and reduction commitments inscribed in Annex B and in accordance with the provisions of this Article, with a view to reducing their overall emissions of such gases by at least 5 per cent below 1990 levels in the commitment period 2008 to 2012.
> (UNECE, 2007)

The bald language masks the fact that international agreements of this kind displace value conflicts onto their signatories. Those seeking to meet their targets must find ways of doing so without sacrificing the economic growth that no government, politically, can afford to do without.

At the same time, the global version of this fundamental conflict, the one described by Paehlke as environment–economy–equity, is left to one side (Paehlke, 2003). While ever-developing countries are allowed to find their own path towards sustainability, value conflict (about the relationship between equity and effectiveness) can be deflected. In the world of realpolitik, this may be the price for not alienating these countries. Nevertheless, in the longer run, avoiding value conflict in this way may be counterproductive.

The way forward: Ecological modernisation?

Humanity is obviously at a crucial juncture, not only in relation to our impact on the biophysical world, but also our understanding of that relationship. Policy practitioners (and academics) are searching constantly for frames within which to understand what is (or may be, or could be, or should be) happening. Ecological modernisation, a particularly powerful set of compounded concepts, represents one such general-purpose frame. In its strong form, it presages a transformative path, in which (despite continued subservience to growth) adjustment creates its own alternatives (Dryzek, Downes and Hunold, 2003, p. 169). In its weak form, ecological modernisation suggests the pragmatic incrementalism of 'business as usual', with new technology 'squaring the circle' between economy and environment (Connolly and Smith, 2003, p. 68). Some commentators have pointed to a state in which it is possible to maximise both values, and growth and the environment are 'de-coupled' (Christoff, 1996, p. 479).

Whether 'de-coupling' of the two values is technically possible has been vigorously debated. However, when we look at the values perspective, the prospects for a transformative path for ecological modernisation appear limited. I make this point on two grounds: firstly, the monumental nature of the challenge of climate change creates new sources of values conflict for the environmental movement. Secondly, the huge values ambiguity that can be contained within administrative states, will mean that pressures for change can be contained and/or sidelined for some time to come.

Much of the momentum for policy changes comes from those outside government. The pressure on governments of public opinion, energised by those arguing from an environmental consciousness more fully developed than the norm, has been crucial (Blowers, 1997). Yet paradoxically, as energy policy becomes more pre-eminent in the battle to contain global warming, the environmental movement has to face a curious difficulty: its warnings about the unsustainability of current productive systems have been richly vindicated; on the other hand, the fact that energy policy is now so central, means that 'the environment' as a set of values becomes sidelined in the drive to contain greenhouse gas emissions.

In turn, these developments mean the environmental movement will have to confront its traditional aversion to nuclear power, or risk losing its way politically. In the 1990s, the German Greens succeeded in turning the entire policy system away from nuclear energy. Yet despite its obvious problems, nuclear power represents one of the few possibilities for effective carbon-free energy generation. Renewables are widely acknowledged to be only part of the answer. Wind farms in particular, scar the wild beauty of coastal landscapes, and hinder the free passage of birds. Sometimes favoured solutions merely displace problems. Plantation forestry, widely promoted as the best alternative to the continued logging of Australian native forests, created its own problems as rural farmscapes that had previously been pleasingly open, were now occluded by softwood and hardwood forests of monotonous uniformity and mind-boggling extent.

In facing these dilemmas, environmentalists themselves are forced into values trade-offs that may undermine their political 'edge'. Thinking globally and acting locally has never been so difficult. Growth, on the other hand, retains all its advantages. It is relatively monovalent, and highly compatible with the market mechanisms of capitalism. Whether growth is capital intensive, or labour intensive is immaterial. Measures to reduce carbon emissions (such as those proposed in the Stern Report of 2007) use mechanisms developed for other forms of air pollution. These mechanisms, by technicising environmental problems, enable their connection with economic and population growth to be set aside.

The ultimate value of growth, however, may be that it obscures the sharpest edges of Paehkle's environment–economy–equity trade-off (Paehlke, 2003). While growth is steady, we do not have to think too deeply about how it is shared. If environmental problems are, deep down, problems about equity (both within nations and between them), we can continue to believe that we can solve them within the dominant paradigm by pretending that economic growth and environmental protection are not only compatible, but even complementary. By continuing to believe that we can harmonise 'greenness' and growth, we can fudge the implications for equity of the green taxes and charges increasingly being promoted (by mainstream as well as green groups) as a way forward in relation to problems such as climate change.

Conclusion

We have seen that environmental values, construed in the broad sense of concern for the integrity of the natural world and the sustainability of ecological systems, have been translated into the language and organisation of public policy in ways that have brought about adaptation to ecological risk, but have avoided more fundamental change. When it comes to governance, therefore, 'the environment' is processed in much the same ways as other values. It is absorbed into the giant morass of competing values that constitutes the state. But if the environment really is a different kind of issue from others that we have discussed, this kind of response will not only continue to disappoint environmentalists: it will simply not be good enough in the sense of maintaining other values (such as amenity and quality of life) for most people.

We have seen that environmental issues *are* different, in that they do confront the growth-based state. Proposals for integrated management have generally foundered on the rocks of bureaucracies still operating in traditional ways. Price mechanisms have proved more useful, largely because they are a way of distributing ecologically relevant information that bypasses bureaucratic confines. Nevertheless, whether price-based mechanisms can 'do it' seems doubtful. It is true that strong theories of ecological modernisation stress the need for devolved and decentralised systems, the deliberative democracy that lies beyond bureaucracy. At the same time, to implement reductions in carbon emissions requires the single-minded, top-down attention of governments overcoming fundamental problems of collective action and trust.

Without a dramatic shift in consciousness, it is difficult to see governments combining these desiderata of bottom-up and top-down, while remaining democratic. When they have done so in the past, as dictatorships, the results have been catastrophic. Modern states, like punching bags, can absorb huge amounts of values conflict. In one sense, that is encouraging. We can go far in the direction of modernisation while still stoking the fires of growth. But if a true resolution means that the environment must trump growth, it cannot do so within the system that gave rise to it.

9
Universality and Choice in Health and Education

As the discussion in Chapter 3 highlighted, in developing policies for looking after the aged and the unemployed, welfare states display a balance between obligation and entitlement. In this chapter, I show how the values pair of universality and choice structures decision-making in health and education. Hospitals and health care centres provide services that safeguard life and promote well-being, while schools prepare the next generation for work and citizenship. In meeting these goals, similar policy problems emerge: the nature of the relationship between the public and private sectors; the extent to which citizens may choose between providers; and the degree to which equality of access and equality of opportunity are underwritten by the state. 'Universality' (equal provision and open access for all) and 'choice' (provision based on personal preference) describe the two key values shaping the relationship between the citizen and the state in both these sectors.

The concept of policy design – the selection of 'elements of a policy intended to achieve certain goals', to use the phrase of Linder and Peters – suggests how these values play out in the construction of policy (Linder and Peters, 1984). All countries find difficulties in managing and regulating the relationship between public and private, and many design-related questions are involved. Should the public system provide for those who cannot afford to purchase services, while the rest pay? Or should the public system offer good basic services to all, with 'top-ups' for those who can afford them? To what extent should public systems include for-profit and not-for-profit providers operating as agents of the state? To what extent should private systems receive public subsidies? Do the same accountability criteria apply?

The values of universality and choice describe the main options involved. On the one hand, policy-makers might design a fairly cheap and efficient system that delivers basic health services and a basic education to everyone, regardless of their income, status or wealth. Such a system represents the value of universality. On the other, they could design a system that allocates these services in much the same way as private markets do – through competition and choice. They might have to even out the ability to choose, because clearly some citizens will be better placed to exercise choice than others. But essentially, providers would compete with each other for the customer's dollar. Broadly speaking, these are the positions of the left (favouring universality) and the right (favouring choice). But in a democracy, no one system totally dominates the other. Over time, public policies and forms of governance acquire elements of both values, depending on the way interests are organised, how powerful they are and the ability of political parties to organise and capture votes.

As ever, the interesting part comes when we consider how change occurs. In Chapter 2, which discussed value conflict and policy change, we saw how opposing value pairs tend to play off each other. Achieving one tends to create a demand for the other, particularly where there is a trade-off between the two. In the case of universality and choice, the trade-off is particularly demanding because the disadvantages of universality (for example, lack of responsiveness and flexibility) are the advantages of choice (and vice versa). No matter how the balance is struck, stability rarely ensues. Introducing choice into a universal system (or vice versa) tends to create friction at the values interface – usually (although not always) where public and private sectors meet.

Powerful interests line up along these divides. Because health and education have a large public presence (in the sense of large public sector workforces in most countries), they generate powerful unions. They also generate powerful private interests with a stake in public policy decisions. In explaining why some features are present and others absent in particular countries, many accounts stress the activities of organised interests. See, for example, James Gillespie and Nicholas Laham's accounts of the role of the medical profession in Australia and the United States, respectively (Gillespie, 1991; Laham, 1993). Moreover, the conflicts generated in each field carry a moral force that is powerful. It was partly for this reason that the Australian physician Sydney Sax memorably called health a 'strife of interests'. People die if health care goes wrong. Education, too, arouses passionate engagement, because it impacts so heavily on our children's futures. And everyone has an opinion about education, because everyone has been to school.

There is huge self-awareness in these industries, reflected in the variety and plenitude of writing that they generate. The political importance (of health in particular) draws forth a plethora of government-generated and think tank–generated reports and studies. Communities of practice in both health and education are substantial, well-organised and professionalised. While professionals are clearly often self-interested, they also see themselves as having a wider duty to the people they serve and to the public. Schoolteachers are not only 'in it for the money'; otherwise, many of them would be doing something else. Doctors are usually well-remunerated, but all but the most venal are, surely, motivated by a desire to help others.

There is a further similarity between health and education that becomes apparent when we consider the ramifications of opting for universality. Universality may preclude the activity of choice by consumers, but not the need for choices to be made. In a universal system, the problem of choice (in the sense of which kinds of treatments or what kinds of education to offer) becomes one of allocation within a public budget, rather than of private preference expressed through a market. In theory, equity objectives should be easier to achieve within a budgetary system. In reality, budgets impose an inexorable logic of their own. To what extent should resources follow need (that is, seek to redress disadvantage) and to what extent should they be assigned according to cost-effectiveness? In the case of health, problems of allocation become particularly acute, because of the need to assign priorities to different kinds of conditions, each with its own framework of costs and resource demands. And politics, in the form of public opinion, is never far away.

Public policy determines, not only the relative dimensions of public and private choices but also, within public choice, it must rationalise values-based decisions of the utmost complexity and delicacy. Governments attempt to control costs through various forms of rationing (for example, by providing only a limited number of expensive pieces of medical technology). Governments may also attempt to use price-related rationing (for example, by not subsidising the cost of some medications or treatments). But political pressure – the expectation that a person with a disabling condition should have access to the best treatment available, regardless of their means – places considerable pressure on governments to approve subsidies. I use the recent experience of four countries – three English-speaking democracies (the UK, Australia and the United States) and one European democracy (the Netherlands) – to illuminate the tensions involved. While the range of countries is obviously not comprehensive, each shows a different combination of universality and choice, and each shows different mechanisms through which the value conflict between the two is handled. Obviously, health is a huge and multifaceted field of activity. I focus on two key aspects of the health system in the four countries chosen for comparison: the way in which hospital services are provided and the nature, values and assumptions underpinning the financing of health.

Health systems compared

How are universality and choice related in terms of policy design? If we imagine a continuum from a universal system on the one hand to a choice-based system on the other, the British National Health Service (NHS) would personify universalism. The NHS subordinates private interests in health to the public good. Despite its difficulties and failings, it is deeply popular with the British public. Even Mrs Thatcher's governments did not interfere with its basic values, although its detailed architecture changed considerably in order to introduce a degree of quasi-market discipline.

The NHS is taxpayer-funded, and its health professionals are either public employees or are contracted to the public sector. The NHS projects a high level of universality, for both medical and dental care, although the extent to which dental care meets the level of need has been deteriorating (Laurance, 2008). All residents of the UK are eligible to access the NHS after a six-month qualifying period. Although its governance is both complex and contested (Morrell, 2006), this is in many ways an indicator of the publicness of the system; that is, the degree to which health is considered to be the public's business. A public matter involves self-reflexive regulation, that is, institution-building; a private one concerns itself alone (Borghi and van Berkel, 2007, p. 358).

Publicness generates open puzzling. The NHS has been subject to numerous reviews and evaluations, and White Papers (announcing new policy directions and changes) have been regularly produced. In contrast to the ferocious political battles that have characterised health policy in the United States, the NHS has evolved forms of governance that allow for considerable structural change without violating the fundamental architecture. At the same time, these structural changes have had a powerful values dimension, partly as a result of political entrepreneurship, partly because of tensions created by previous changes. The NHS is 'visible' in ways that a less public system would not be. Its problems are public property.

Successive governments have attempted to attenuate universalism by offering greater degrees of choice, if not in the form of direct consumer choice, then by freeing up the options of those choosing on behalf of consumers. Under Conservative governments, the NHS was disaggregated along 'purchaser–provider' lines, with an emphasis on the creation of 'internal markets'. These internal markets were characterised by multiple providers; for example, directly managed hospitals were replaced by hospital-based 'provider' units designated as NHS trusts. Larger-scale units, the health authorities, purchased health services from the provider trusts.

Over time (and particularly when New Labour came to power) the number of provider trusts diminished as mergers between them took place. On the purchasing side, New Labour replaced both the health authorities and the general practitioner (GP) fundholders of the Conservative era, with more numerous Primary Care Trusts (PCTs), each serving a population of about 100,000. The PCTs were supposed to underpin choice at the local level, but (as most health professionals had predicted) they proved too small for the allocative job they were required to do. Local choice created a patchwork of services and a huge monitoring problem for central government. Over time, the PCTs, in turn, underwent numerous mergers with each other (Talbot and Johnson, 2007). In the NHS, efforts to harness the power of choice were undertaken within an overall framework of universalism, which in turn limited the degree of choice that could be efficiently retained.

When we turn to the United States, we see the reverse occurring – a choice-based system struggling to come to terms with its lack of universalism. Health care policy in the United States is both far more devolved than in the UK (in keeping with its federal structure) and more varied in its governance and organisation. Public expenditure accounts for only 45 per cent of total spending on health. Public hospitals constitute less than 20 per cent of the total (OECD, 2006; US Census Bureau, 2006). There is no universal health insurance. The elderly and the poor have publicly provided insurance; for those in employment, health insurance premiums are paid by their employers although, increasingly, co-payments are required from employees.

With its commitment to private enterprise, it is not surprising that choice should be the design value of emphasis in the United States. There is choice in the sense of variety of service and freedom to choose from within that variety. But choice itself is not evenly distributed. In practice, the United States system offers choice only to those with health insurance. And health insurance, increasingly, cannot be afforded by the working poor. As many commentators have pointed out, cost control is almost impossible to maintain in these circumstances. Competing providers of for-profit medicine and health insurance do well out of the insured section of the population (generally those with jobs that include employer-financed health insurance), but as health costs continue to rise, the only way the basis for choice can be maintained is by continually increasing premiums.

Unfortunately, as premiums increase, the privately insured percentage of the population falls – from 75 per cent in 1987 to 68 per cent in 2004, according to US Census Bureau figures. Those with special needs and the means-tested elderly receive government-provided health insurance (Medicare and Medicaid) but a rising proportion (15.7 per cent in 2004) has no alternative but to be at the mercy of any hospital willing to treat them (US Census Bureau, 2007). While repeated efforts to reform the system have been made, all have foundered on the rock of organised interests in Washington. The points of conflict show not only in the fate of the non-insured, many of them in direst poverty, but also in the difficulties faced by hospitals giving treatment to uninsured patients. In these circumstances, they cannot receive payment (from governments) for doing so. Ironically, where choice and markets are conflated in this way, the cause of choice itself is not well-served. A system based on choice ends up by removing choice.

The Dutch healthcare system has been put forward as a role model for the United States, because it allows a degree of choice that is not possible in more universal systems such as the NHS. But in contrast to the UK, in the Netherlands the public sector is not the main engine of provision, or even of service delivery. Private provision is strong on the financial side, too. The Dutch system is publicly regulated, but overwhelmingly private-financed. It reached this point as a result of successive evolutions and compromises. Three distinct phases have been identified: firstly, a corporatist system characterised by a strong commitment to solidarity; secondly a state-dominated period, in which cost-containment dominated; and thirdly, a more market-oriented system, characterised by regulated competition (Helderman, Schut, van der Grinten and van de Ven, 2005).

How, then, is the value of choice operationalised in this environment of regulated competition? Citizens can choose their doctor and choose their hospital (not a logistically difficult problem in a densely populated country of 16 million people). General practitioners work for themselves, not the state, and there is a diverse range of hospitals and clinics. But there are significant areas of non-choice. You cannot choose not to insure against sickness. And the extent to which insurance companies can risk-rate their clients is also restricted: premiums are regulated for those who are elderly or are chronically ill. There is a strong element of managed care: the insured receive benefit-in-kind entitlements provided by contracted health providers (den Exter, 2005).

The Dutch health care system retains a high degree of both universality and choice, by using regulation to maintain the publicness of the system, independent of ownership. This construction of publicness contrasts with the Australian case in health, in which publicness rests upon an uneasy balance between publicly owned and privately owned parts of the system. Consequently, the overall balance between universality and choice lies somewhere between the examplars of the UK and the United States. Moreover the balance between the two has been subject to constant political change, most recently during the prime ministership of John Howard (1996–2007), when concerted efforts were made to re-engineer the public–private balance, largely in the name of choice.

In comparison with the UK, Australia has a health system that is characterised by extensive private involvement. It is a hybridised system in which 40 per cent of hospitals are privately owned (ABS, 2007). These hospitals are linked with the public system in many instances (for example in my city of Canberra, a private hospital delivers emergency services in the northern part of the city, under contract to the territory government). But although deeply enmeshed with government (in terms of regulation, for example), private hospitals are significantly more autonomous than are public ones in the types of treatments they offer and the market segments they target. Private providers tend to concentrate on the most profitable procedures (such as elective day surgery), leaving public hospitals with the more difficult and expensive cases (Pratt, 2005).

Apart from decrying the dysfunctional nature of Commonwealth/ State relations in health, debates about health in Australia (at the national level) tend to revolve around health financing. Australia has a universal system of insurance for public hospital care and medical services (general practitioners and specialists) known as Medicare. First introduced by the Whitlam Labor government in 1974, it remains highly popular. Citizens prefer it to the previous system, which relied on private insurance funds.

But Medicare is expensive, because of the constantly rising costs of health care. Costs are controlled in two ways: firstly, by rebating a fixed amount for each visit to the doctor. Doctors may charge more, but it is not possible to insure to cover the gap. Secondly, public hospitals (which are usually free at the point of service) are funded through special legislation (Medicare agreements) that provide the state governments (that operate the hospitals) with a budget for doing so. State governments decide how the public hospitals money is to be allocated – most use variations on so-called case-mix models, in which hospitals are funded according to the benchmarked cost of particular procedures (varied to take into account different levels of fixed costs). Budgets therefore reflect the mix of procedures that the hospitals deliver in a particular period of time. With a relatively fixed funding model, but variable patterns of demand, hospitals respond by rationing services. This means that for non-urgent procedures, waiting lists can be very lengthy.

As health insurance premiums are community-rated (high-risk groups such as the elderly are not charged more than low-risk groups), there is an obvious problem for the private insurance industry. The young and healthy, who are much less likely to need services than the elderly, are not inclined to join up. Government has intervened by weighting the scales in favour of private health insurance, through a mixture of carrots and sticks. Private health insurance premiums are reduced by means of a taxpayer-funded subsidy to those paying them. Those with incomes above a specified threshold, who choose not to take out private insurance, are required to pay a surcharge on their Medicare levy. In addition, funds are required to charge an additional premium to those deferring private health insurance until they are more likely to need it.

The public–private boundary is a difficult one to negotiate for those who do not qualify for special (income-tested) health care concessions, but find even the subsidised premiums difficult to meet. And others, regardless of their ability to afford private insurance, will prefer to rely on the public system alone. Consequently, the proportion of the population covered by private insurance remains fixed at about 40 per cent. For ministers at the state and territory levels in charge of public health budgets, the political problems of this kind of publicness are demanding. Make the public system too good, and no one will use the private sector. But make it too exiguous, and bad press inevitably results.

If we compare the way the United States, the UK and Australia define publicness, we see a spectrum, from the high universality (and high publicness) of the UK through to the low universality (and low publicness) of the United States. Australia and the Netherlands occupy a midpoint between the two: each is arguably less universal in its approach than the UK, but more public than the United States. Australia has greater choice than the Netherlands on key points – for example, private health insurance is not compulsory. But while many US-based commentators may look at the Australian health care system as an acceptable balance between public care and private responsibility, the two values are almost unrecognisable once filtered through the noise of federal duplication and cost-shifting, and the complex requirements of a private sector traditionally dominated by not-for-profits, but which is increasingly attracting the profit-seeking private sector, particularly in day surgery and 'round-the-clock' health clinics.

The impact of the profit motive on the values of those working within the health sector is difficult to assess. A profit-driven system may inspire innovation and the highest standards of care, or it may undermine commitment to meeting the needs of patients. Where the profit motive is more constrained, as in the British NHS, professionalism must be its own reward. The Australian system seeks the best of both worlds, but it suffers from unregulated costs (in the private sector) and disincentives for the public sector to compete too strongly. The complexities of federalism mean that administrative forms dominate (and distort) the value orientations they are meant to support. The values of universality and choice interact with a multiplicity of individual and corporate interests to produce a constantly changing kaleidoscope of outcomes. Moreover, there is a deep ambiguity at the heart of the system, because there is a reluctance to address the nature of its publicness. Are public hospitals for those who cannot afford private treatment? If choice is to be the province of those who can afford it, how are costs to be contained in a private sector, where health insurance premiums are rebated? Better trade-offs between universality and choice may be available, if choice is seen within a public context, rather than outside it.

Education

Universality, choice and publicness are equally as important in education as they are in health. For societies with an unstable interface between the public and private sectors, the same risks are evident: moving the balance too far in the direction of choice may rob the public sector of its all-important middle-class clients. On the other hand, a uniform, universal system may meet the needs of very few children or their parents. Moreover, these value conflicts are intertwined within a complex historical reality. Originally, the conflict between public and private in education manifested itself as a confrontation between state and religious schools. This conflict occurred in both the continental and Anglo-American democracies, beginning in the middle to the later parts of the nineteenth century and extending in some cases well into the twentieth (Manzer, 2003). In every system a modus vivendi was ultimately developed. But in the Anglo-American democracies, the public system that had seemed so all-embracing in the period before and after World War II ultimately came under attack – and not just from those who had long been its foes.

Public education, the great support of equity, was being challenged from the right on the basis that it was failing those for whom it was intended. For the left this was a hard argument to ignore, because it was difficult to deny that many public schools appeared to be failing. Supporters of public education argued that public schools lacked adequate funding for the increasingly difficult tasks they were required to perform. Opponents argued that there was insufficient competition to keep them on their toes. For public policy, these political waves created tensions and counter-tensions that drove further change. We follow this pattern in four systems, noting those factors that seemed to exacerbate the tension and those that appear to ameliorate it.

In the UK, the 1902 Education Act integrated denominational schools with the state system, establishing what was effectively a universal system with only a small number of elite, privately funded and maintained schools outside the public system. Universalism was, however, meritocratic rather than comprehensive. From the mid-1960s, Labour governments at the national level began to dismantle the grammar school system, which, up until that point, had been seen as the best hope for advancement for the bright sons and daughters of working class parents. Comprehensive schools educated everyone in the same institution, with each school representing diversity within itself, rather than differentiating schools on the basis of the academic ability of those attending them. Local education authorities determined the character and composition of schools within their jurisdiction, and most opted for comprehensive schooling.

Mrs Thatcher's government began major reform of the system by allowing schools to opt out of local authority control. This was a mechanism for wresting political control away from Labour-controlled authorities and for reducing the role of teachers' unions in school decision-making. But it would also allow schools to voice the values of choice that Mrs Thatcher had placed at the centre of her political philosophy. The 1988 Education Reform Act and those that followed it remodelled the governance and financing of schools (Fitz and Beers, 2002). The 1996 Act required that 'funding authorities shall have regard to the general principle that pupils are to be educated in accordance with the wishes of their parents, so far as that is compatible with the provision of efficient instruction and training and the avoidance of unreasonable public expenditure'. The Act also stated that the secretary of state should devote his efforts to the improvement of standards, diversity and choice.

Blair and Thatcher policies are both usually identified as 'neo-liberal' (see, for example, Thomson, 2005). But there were differences between them in the way that choice was conceptualised. The Blair government elected in 1997 did not alter the emphasis on choice. Indeed in many ways, it went further than Mrs Thatcher's governments had done. But the language of reform was not to construct choice as the active agent of a competitive education market, rather, choice was the marker of diversity. The Blair government directed taxpayer-derived funds towards schools of widely differing character. Schools of faith were encouraged to establish themselves. Charter schools opened up the prospect of new forms of ownership outside the public sector. And leagues tables (subsequently substantially abandoned in Scotland and in Wales following devolution) remained paramount in England.

Public policy values can never be assumed to carry over from one sector to another. In the United States, in most people's minds the land of private enterprise, the Constitutional restriction on public support of religious schools keeps the private sector relatively small. While 24 per cent of all schools are private, only 10 per cent of elementary and secondary school pupils in the United States attend private schools, reflecting the relatively small size of many of these establishments (NCES, 2006). But as with its health system, traditions of localism are strong. And the Constitution reserves to the states the primary authority over education. The US school education system represents, therefore, an enormous number of local practices and priorities, and choice operates at this level. Within the public system, newer and freer versions of choice are also being tried. Charter schools are operated in many states, and leagues tables are also (to varying degrees) available (Le Grand, 2003). Assumptions are dangerous in the case of Australia, too. Curiously for a country in which public power has been so significant in many ways, the private sector has always been strong in Australian education, largely because of the importance of Catholic schools which, despite efforts to force them to do so, were never integrated into the public system. The values balance between the two systems is 'hardwired' by history (Stewart, 2005).

There is a further, significant difference between Australia on the one hand, and the United States and the UK on the other. In the United States and the UK, public funds do not go directly to private schools, so that, unless other mechanisms of support are devised, those wishing to have a private education for their children pay the full cost of doing so. (In all three systems, on the other hand, private schools enjoy tax exempt status). But it is only in the Australian case that public funds are channelled directly to privately owned and operated schools. In the Australian case, a split between state and federal funding allows federal funds to be channelled to private schools in a way that bypasses state-level decision-making.

Under the Australian Constitution, responsibility for school education is in the hands of state and territory governments. Had they wished to do so, state and territory governments could have implemented British-style New Labour policies in relation to public schools (for example, opening up the delivery of public schooling to private interests as a mechanism for improving performance). Yet no Australian public school system followed the example of New Labour, despite the dominance of Labor in the governments of the Australian states and territories through much of the 1990s and into the twenty-first century. The power of teachers' unions in the public sector had much to do with this reluctance. At the same time, this conservatism created a political opportunity to use the fiscal resources of the federal government (which are not constitutionally constrained in their application) in the field of education. The federal Coalition government led by John Howard (1996–2007) made the most of this opportunity by steadily increasing the real value of payments to non-government schools throughout its term in office.

The Howard government in Australia justified its support for private schooling on the basis that doing so increased the choices available to Australian parents. In reducing tuition fees below what they would otherwise be, this claim is (at the margin) undoubtedly true, although the extent to which parents on average incomes could send their children to the most expensive private schools was undoubtedly minimal. Of course, the policy increased votes going to the government as well, but this in turn reflected a pronounced (and growing) trend for parents (many of whom had been to public schools themselves) to choose private education for their children.

What do these schools offer that the public system does not? Ball suggests that the basis for choice is driven, less by ideology, than by a mixture of factors, including family traditions, parents' sense of what their children need and a desire to ensure suitable companions for their children (Ball, 1997). In Australia at least, the sense that private schools teach 'values' to children and public schools do not is strongly entrenched. The public sector has not done well in promoting its values of equity, universality and inclusiveness, and as a result, the 'publicness' of the system has declined. But as we have seen in relation to health, the publicness of a system does not necessarily rest on public provision. The contrast between Australia and the Netherlands, both of which have a high proportion of religious schools, is instructive here. The Dutch education system is characterised by two principles: firstly, freedom of education (that is freedom to establish schools, to organise them and to determine the religion or other ideology on which they are based); and secondly, equal state support for public and private schools.

In terms of the debate in the Anglo-American democracies, then, the Dutch system is neoliberal. Indeed in comparing the Dutch with the Scottish, Welsh and English systems, Teelken observed that the Netherlands most closely approximated the market mechanism (Teelken, 1999). Historical factors were clearly important here: the deal which brought denominational schools into the public sphere materialised in 1917, reflecting a need to effect broadly based compromises within a consociational democracy. But this historically contingent liberalism is also highly egalitarian. While the Dutch system allows competition between schools, the extent of the competition is strictly managed. All schools, whether publicly owned or not, are funded on an equal, relatively generous basis. Each school's allocation is weighted according to the socio-economic background of its pupils (Justesen, 2002), and parental topping-up is not allowed. While schools vary in terms of their governance and the values they endorse, all must deliver a prescribed curriculum, in a prescribed way. To a significant degree, then, the domain of choice is publicly constructed. In this context, choice and universality are not mutually in conflict to the same degree as in polities (such as Australia) where choice is construed outside the domain of publicness.

Health, education and the sustainability of the public realm

We are now in a position to review the public–private relationship through the lens of values analysis. We have seen that, while systems that value equity also tend to value publicness, different mixes of public and private provision may be used to achieve this result. Many types of choice are possible within public systems – for example, permitting parents to enrol their children in any school in a given jurisdiction, or allowing patients to access any hospital of their choice. But there is a risk that the resulting competition may be destabilising, if it leads to overstretched facilities in one area and under-used facilities in another.

It is possible to bring private providers into public systems, for example, by paying providers on the basis of the children they educate or the people they treat. The degree to which the 'publicness' of the system is thereby altered varies between nations. In Australia, there has been a long tradition of federal funding for private schools, which has tended to privatise significant aspects of education (Stewart, 2005). In the Netherlands, on the other hand, there is a principle of equal state support for public and private schools (Teelken, 1999). In health care, the difficulties of managing choice become greater because of the much stronger profit-making possibilities in the sector. In the United States, choice in health tends to mean market-based choice. The more choice is valued the greater the involvement of the private sector. The example of the UK suggests that the more universality is valued the lesser tends to be the involvement of the private sector. But by bringing a country like the Netherlands into the comparison, we see that choice (between public and private) can itself be part of publicness, provided that resource allocation is carefully controlled.

The example of the Netherlands suggests that choice can never be separated from social responsibility. In practical terms, this is a necessary step to take because of the social importance of both health and education. If the wealthy are able to opt out, this choice has implications for society as a whole because the non-wealthy, lacking the capacity to choose, receive inadequate health care and education in a depleted public system. What of the moral argument that people are the best judges of their own interests? As soon as individual choice implies action in the public realm (and in any politically based policy system, this point is reached virtually instantaneously) the value of choice starts to become clouded. As Evans puts it, 'it's not obvious that the patient's special knowledge about what is best for him in practical terms can in any sense entitle him to require specific provision at society's expense' (Evans, 1999). To some degree all choices, of necessity, become public choices.

Setting moral arguments aside, choice in the real world has the effect of constraining its own exercise. The unconstrained exercise of market-based choice eventually proves counterproductive, and steps must be taken (for example through the mandating of managed health care) to limit costs. But limiting costs, for example, through collective purchasing arrangements, restricts choice to those providers prepared to enter contracts with the programme. For those wishing to enhance choice, even within an overall ethos of publicness, the freedom to move is limited.

It is possible to allow some choice, but not too much. Otherwise, those who can, will remove themselves from institutions designed to cater to everyone. Reform in health and education is supremely difficult, not only because of the strength of the interests involved, but also because of the demanding nature of these constraints.

Conclusion

The values perspective highlights the nature of 'publicness', not in the sense of 'how much does government own or even control', but in the sense of 'how far, and in what ways, do health and education systems give practical form to ideas of mutual obligation among citizens?' A comparative perspective shows us that 'publicness' may take many forms. In the United States, for example, while public funding may be meagre and market imperatives paramount, there are long traditions of publicness in the provision of hospital-based care at the local level.

The example of the Netherlands (in both health and education) shows us that publicness does not necessarily preclude choice. It seems to do so if we focus solely on the English-speaking democracies and if we equate choice with the operation of markets. But if we cast the net a little wider, we see that the titanic struggle between 'neoliberalism' and more collectivist ideologies, construed as a fight between public and private, is itself an artefact of the way particular values have been transmitted into policy in the English-speaking democracies. European traditions (the German health care system provides a further example), give more space to choice (particularly provider choice), while enforcing work-related contributions to health insurance.

It is true that economics, as a science of choice, acknowledges many shortcomings of markets. The free play of preference will often require evening up the capacity of consumers to pay, perhaps through vouchers, perhaps by intervening actively in schools and hospitals (often those in poorer areas) that are seen to be failing their clients. It could also be argued that the value of choice is facilitated by forcing providers to give more information about the quality of their service (for example through publicly available leagues tables). But the comparative analysis suggests that it is possible (at least up to a point) to achieve choice within publicness, rather than equating choice only with the operation of markets. In this way, what might otherwise be a trenchant conflict between universality (providing equally for everyone) and choice (allowing parents/patients to choose and giving them something to choose between), becomes less difficult to manage.

Where universality is seen as a badge of the left, and choice of the right, the value conflict seems intractable because it is bound up with very long-standing debates about the legitimate role of the government. But from a policy values perspective, we have seen that choice need not be a trademark of the right alone. Social democratic parties may make extensive use of choice, as New Labour showed in the UK. What matters in determining the shape of the trade-off is the overall publicness of the system. So, should policy reformers see the problem as one of enhancing publicness? To do so would be one way of smoothing the conflict between liberalism and more collective forms of thinking in these fields. At the very least, searching for ways of transcending value conflict might at least force interests to fight more productively than in the past.

10
Conclusion

Most political scientists would agree that values matter in public policy. But it is how they matter that is contentious. If policy is what governments do, explaining these choices has traditionally been done in terms of the operation of interests (usually economically based) within structures (institutions) that represent the outcomes of previous interest struggles. Values are clearly present in the mix, but they are viewed, essentially, ideologically; that is, as constructions in the service of interests. So (according to mainstream political science) values are just a façade – we don't need them analytically.

In contrast to this view, I have argued that if we take values seriously, we can develop a perspective on public policy that is both distinctive and useful. It is distinctive because it highlights neglected aspects of the lived reality of public policymaking: both the contestation of values that swirls around and through it and the values choices that must be made in policy design. It is useful, because it helps us to see how deeply the process we call public policy is structured by the goals it is intended to serve. Further, this 'deep structure' of public policy – a dynamic interplay of objectives, instruments and interactions with past policies – is itself a significant driver of policy change.

This concluding chapter will show how each of the constituent chapters has contributed to this view, consolidating the case for the addition of values analysis to the methodological toolkit of political science. The key insight, developed throughout the book, is that all public policies hold important values in tension, either directly, through compromises and trade-offs, or indirectly, by excluding or marginalising other approaches. By using value pairs to illuminate this tension, it is possible to gain a greater understanding of patterns of stability and change across a diverse range of policy fields and policy contexts.

Each chapter suggested some substantive conclusions: the relative stability of welfare states with high levels of both obligation and entitlement (Chapter 3); the paradigmatic role of efficiency (Chapter 4); the importance of 'publicness' in health and education (Chapter 9) and perhaps most importantly, the enormous significance of values in structuring administrative action (Chapters 5–8). These findings are not, in themselves, surprising and complement work undertaken from other perspectives. What matters is that a previously almost residual category has been brought out into the open.

It is true that the policies that demonstrate these points are drawn from a relatively limited set of nations, principally the English-speaking nations. However, the method can be used to extend and deepen the analysis of policy in other national settings, particularly at the elusive 'meso', or mid-level of analysis. Scholars will find that the method of looking for values tensions, particularly at the agency level, will yield rich dividends in a variety of regional and national situations. For example, research into relationships between political control and policy impact has often found that clear-cut answers are difficult to achieve because of the power of agency values, and the capacity of agencies to hold values in tension (see, for example, Ringquist, 1995). Indeed pre-existing values or organisational cultures are frequently cited as reasons for the success or failure of new administrative policies in both developed and developing countries (see, for example, Lancaster and Brierley, 2001; Analoui, 1998). By using values to illuminate the operations of process and structure, further illumination may be gained of the often-troubling intersection between policy and its organisational expression.

There are, in addition, some broader implications of the research, not directly addressed in preceding chapters, which are drawn out here. I suggest a number of possibilities for further work:

- Using values analysis in comparative public policy
- Exploring value conflict and policy change
- Identifying the role of values in policy paradigms
- Tracing relationships between value conflict and policy implementation
- Elucidating the role of the media as 'values-brokers'

Finally, I suggest that the approach developed here has important lessons for the achievement of broad, generally accepted values – peace, human rights and environmental protection – through public policy.

In particular, the challenge posed by climate change has a significant values dimension that links it with earlier theories about the values basis of capitalism itself. I also suggest, at a more abstract level, how values analysis might be used to link the 'inside' and the 'outside' of policy, simplifying certain aspects of the 'argumentative turn' in policy analysis.

Using values in comparative policy analysis

The best policy analysis is always implicitly comparative, in the sense that distinctive factors are rarely self-evident, but are brought out by the activity of contrast and comparison. Value differences serve as a useful armature for this work, as demonstrated by comparative studies that are explicitly normative in character (see, for example, Kildal and Kuhnle's (2006) study of the normative foundations of the Nordic welfare state). But comparison is also a way of using difference for explicit analytical purposes. We may (for example) compare the welfare states of a set of countries in order to discover the key variables that seem to be important in shaping outcomes. Or we may compare one policy type (such as agricultural policy) across a number of countries, in order better to understand the operation of policy networks. These small-number comparative case studies produce very rich accounts of agency and structure. In relation to networks, for example, we see differences in the kinds of networks that are evident, each dependent upon institutional traditions that have been established for facilitating communication and for brokering deals.

Values analysis tends to take our purview broader still. Indeed we can properly 'see' our own country's values only by comparing ourselves with societies that behave very differently. In Chapters 3, 5 and 9 values analysis was used to produce wide-ranging descriptions of policy settings and policy change in a number of different contexts. The method – using values to discern the shape of deep-seated balances or trade-offs – can be used to make cross-national comparisons, as well as tracking policy change within nations over time. In Chapter 3, we saw how welfare states can be compared and contrasted in terms of the way in which they balance obligation and entitlement in achieving fairness. While equality is the outcomes-based measure usually associated with welfare state comparisons, it turns out that concepts of 'fairness' are just as important as those of equality in explaining recent political developments in welfare states. 'Fairness' is the politics of equality. While equality can be measured, and equity has a certain philosophical grandeur, fairness is more immediate, more personal and more upfront. It is the way we see our entitlements in relation to those of others. The balance between obligation and entitlement, and the way that balance is perceived (itself related to the way the relationship is structured by policy institutions), is an important factor in producing reactions that create political opportunity and precipitate change. More inclusive values balances, on the other hand, have supported more stable patterns, as in the Scandinavian welfare states during the 1990s.

Some kinds of tensions are more implicit than they are explicit. They may surface in daily policymaking in various ways, but it is only by searching for these meta-problems across a broader policy frame (including using insights from comparative study of other countries) that we become aware of their pervasiveness. As shown in Chapter 9, the balance between universalism and choice describes key tensions in health and education policy. In investigating how this balance plays itself out in different systems, it is possible to discern the possibilities of more favourable trade-offs between design values. For example, in the case of the Dutch education system, a broader, structuring value – the value of publicness – enables the universality-choice dilemma to be played out in ways that play down, rather than exacerbate, tension.

From a values perspective, policy instruments are not simply a means to an end – they construct and reflect a relationship between the bearers of policy and those who are its clients, consumers or subjects. In Chapter 5 we saw that by using values 'pairs', such as 'tough and tender', it is possible to construct analytical frameworks that illuminate policy fields as diverse as unemployment policy, drugs policy, criminal justice, business regulation and policy towards asylum seekers. These values pairs, more fully described in Chapter 1, have considerable potential as heuristics. For example, it is possible to view a variety of industry development policies from the point of view of the extent to which they enhance cooperation on the one hand, or competition on the other. Development policies might be constructed as balances, altering over time, between centralisation and devolution. These dynamics help to explain not only patterns of stability and change, they also constitute useful ways of comparing states across space, as well as states across time.

Comparison may bring out commonality as well as difference. It has long been realised that norms and values provide the basis for understanding choice, and the context of choice, in comparative policy analysis (Dierkes, Wiler and Antal, 1987, p. 19). But unless we maximise variance, and bring values out into the open, we may unconsciously be operating within unproblematised value constructs of our own. This may mean that, as policy analysts, we lack sensitivity to points of change or that we exaggerate apparent differences because we have lost sight of the possibility that different states may have equivalent values – it is just that their public policies achieve these values in different ways.

Values and policy change

Values are integral to the discussion of policy change at the 'meso' or programmatic, level. The perspective highlights the importance of conflict between bearers of different values, the capacity of institutions to 'soak up' this kind of conflict, and the significance of public opinion in reflecting, transmitting and, often, generating the momentum for change. We have long known that institutions (that is the patterns of rules that characterise political life) structure policy in various ways, and that policy, in turn, influences institutions. One of the important ways in which policy influences these institutions is through repeated bouts of value conflict and intermediation.

At the same time, policy change is difficult to explain in institutionalist terms. If actors operate within a framework of rules, how is it that the rules themselves change? Gaining a vantage point from outside the system (either by employing long-run time horizons, or shifting the level of analysis) may blur the change itself. By focusing deliberately at the level of public policy, and on the nature of values within policy, we gain an additional purchase on the problem of change. As I argued in Chapter 2, value conflict is of prime importance in this explanation, because points of value conflict describe axes around which change can occur.

There are many fields where key values are directly opposed to each other, and where we see outright conflict as a result: think of religious versus secular values in relation to the regulation of abortion, for example, or the continuing controversy in many societies about gay marriage. Think, too, of the many ways in which economic growth (particularly property development) comes into conflict, not only with those espousing green values but also with those who want to preserve the amenity of their area as it is. At other times, often in response to external (and internal) threats, the values balance swings sharply from one side to the other, as when many Western countries restricted civil liberties in order to grapple with the threat posed by Islamist-inspired terrorism. Other conflicts may be submerged (although certainly not extinguished) by economic developments. In regulating labour markets in an age of global competition, for example, it is difficult to think of ways of increasing efficiency, without compromising other important values, such as equity.

As they implement public policies, public agencies become themselves subject to value conflicts, a situation that administrative techniques strive to avoid. Many of these techniques are described in Chapter 2: they include methods for displacing, hybridising and technicising values. At the higher levels, departments and agencies may be created to 'carry' new values, or elaborate restructurings may be undertaken in order to emphasise changed priorities. These arrangements are necessary in order to prevent confusion in decision-making, but they also permit considerable flexibility at the policy level. To attain true policy consistency would be both costly and time-consuming. It is far easier simply to add new layers to the policy sediments – another piece of legislation, a regulatory fix (see, for example, Kay, 2007).

Chapter 6 examined a number of areas of very high value conflict – including abortion and euthanasia. This discussion showed how many governments avoid direct value conflict by displacement: pushing (or keeping) key decisions out of the public policy arena and relying on legal stand-offs or casuistic practices to do the work for them. So we have something of a paradox: where public policy enters these areas, it does so as indirectly as possible. Roe *v* Wade hinged on the right of privacy, but had the effect of legalising abortion in the United States. The fact that difficult choices must be expressed administratively is a saving grace for public policy in that the underlying dilemma can be pushed to one side.

Of course, this kind of displacement is not always possible. When (for example) law and policy must make judgments about cultural practices such as female genital mutilation, the relativist assumptions of multi-culturalism collide head-on with basic human rights. But even this kind of dilemma does not necessarily prove overwhelming, as various forms of values hybrid are created. For example, a stance for secular values in the form of firm legal proscription in practice may be softened by an educational approach at the level of implementation (Guine and Fuentes, 2007). Values hybrids may be confusing for clients, but they are convenient for policy-makers, as they enable partially inconsistent objectives to be maintained simultaneously. Attempting to deal with values directly is high-risk policy-making (Stewart, 2006).

But value conflict cannot always be avoided or contained. It 'breaks out' in various ways – administrative agencies can no longer do their jobs properly; or the media seizes upon an unfortunate event that highlights the consequences of past decisions. Pressures for change can be immense and overwhelming. As the social movements of the 1960s and 1970s demonstrated, value conflict that 'breaks out' can be energising, leading to new solutions and new forms of governance. In day-to-day policy contexts, deliberate attempts to enlarge existing networks, or to involve communities more deeply in the implementation of policy can enhance learning. But in states that are already weak, value conflict can be deeply destabilising, particularly where religious or ethnic divisions are involved.

The role of values within paradigms

It is usual to see paradigms as primarily cognitive structures. In the words of the British sociologist Stephen Cotgrove, paradigms 'provide maps of what the world is believed to be like. . . . They constitute guidelines for . . . identifying and solving problems. Above all, paradigms provide the framework of meaning within which "facts" and experiences acquire significance and can be interpreted' (Cotgrove, 1982, p. 26). Since the path-breaking work of Peter Hall (Hall, 1993), the importance of paradigms in both marking and explaining policy change has been accorded a prominent place. Paradigms are seen as indicators of profound change (for example the replacement of Keynesianism by monetarism in the 1970s). But they also help to explain change, because they give due weight to the importance of ideas in the making of policy.

Frameworks of meaning also encompass values, and in fact, values and ideas co-mingle in the production of paradigms. When they are fully functional, paradigms reduce conflict by creating particular policy agendas (usually by ruling other approaches out of contention). On the other hand, they can also be used directly as agents of change – the politics of reform, of betterment, are built around this attribute. In fact, paradigms are powerful agents of change precisely because they offer value change in the form of critique. The old values are discredited, the new privileged. We saw this with the examination of economic rationalism in Chapter 4 and new public management in Chapter 7. New public management offered a critique of more traditional approaches to public administration by endorsing new value positions (such as responsiveness and efficiency) in contrast to older values such as due process.

Economic rationalism combined the analytical cachet of neoclassical economics with a powerful commitment to markets and the value of efficiency. In Australia, as shown in Chapter 4, the efficiency value transmitted in this way demolished an earlier era based on the protection of industry. Decisions to reduce tariffs, to open the manufacturing sector to global trade and to even float the dollar were taken because the basic theorems of competition and of free trade prescribed this course of action. In seeing efficiency as a value, we become aware of the choices that are involved in basing policy upon it. A paradigm of this type, which excludes other kinds of discourse, is powerful precisely because of its 'value-free' packaging. But as critics of economic rationalism have long maintained, economic analysis is about ends as well as means. Assuming the primacy of the marketplace is a values-based choice.

Of course, paradigms do not enter public policy in disembodied form. They must be espoused by a particular group or interest in order to exercise influence. Political science often depicts professional groups as interests, but their role as bearers of paradigms (or more broadly, as epistemological communities) helps to explain some types of policy change that would appear to run counter to material interests. When a knowledgeable group espouses a particular policy (such as economists the cause of free trade; doctors the cause of tobacco control; dentists the addition of fluoride to the water supply; climate scientists the need to cut carbon emissions), these pronouncements have much greater impact than those from business or industry (certainly when business interests oppose scientifically endorsed policy), because these groups, when they speak *ex cathedra*, do not have an obvious interest to push. The public may not understand all that they are saying, but they are prepared to trust these groups, because of the values they are believed to represent. While professionals most certainly have material interests and fight obsessively to protect them, their sense of service to a calling, when translated into a policy stance, has power precisely because it is seen to be disinterested.

Values, public organisations and the implementation of policy

The values perspective draws our attention to the role of organisation in policy. It does so in quite precise ways. Public organisations operate in a world of interests, and they undoubtedly have interests of their own. But their existence is premised upon the implementation of public policies – an activity that, far from being machine-like in character, always involves a sense of values, both in the way those in the organisation see themselves, and the way they define, operationally, the tasks they perform. Organisation is the mobilisation of bias, so we should not be surprised. But while this observation is often cited, the connections it implies between policy and organisation and in particular, between implementation and organisation, have not been well-appreciated. As work on organisational culture shows, the need to build public agencies around the values they serve is a powerful structuring force.

Where agencies are established to implement the new value (or to give greater emphasis to one that has been around for a while), they are able to organise around a clear agenda, even if effectiveness is often constrained by competing interests. As shown in Chapter 8, the new Environmental Protection Agencies set up in the 1970s and 1980s were in this category. But just as often, new values are given to existing agencies to implement, or the balance between existing values is altered, often without a commensurate increase in resources. In the 1990s, for example, child protection policies in many countries emphasised the importance of keeping families intact, rather than taking children into care. Yet as successive reports into the Queensland child protection system demonstrated, resources for family support remained scant, while at the same time, inadequate institutional and foster care posed additional risks to children (Tilbury, 2005). Where indigenous children were involved, a desire to promote culturally appropriate child protection practices complicated the picture still further because many indigenous communities suffered from violence, alcoholism and child sexual abuse (Elarde and Tilbury, 2007). The results, as a particular case widely reported in late 2007, could be horrendous (Elks, 2007).

In some cases, practical policy implementation may go from one extreme to the other (the 'flip-flops' described in Chapter 1). Common sense flies out the window when organisational group-think has its way. There are many examples of well-intentioned people doing pointless or, sometimes, dangerous things in public management. Gregory's analysis of New Zealand's Cave Creek disaster, when employees of a 'can do' public agency exercised less care in erecting a viewing platform for tourists than they would have done in extending the back deck at home, points to a large and under-acknowledged problem (Gregory, 1998). The common sense of public agencies may be compromised when they are in the grip of crude management priorities. Policy-makers tend to forget that their policies will be carried out by human beings whose decisions are shaped by the values they believe they are serving. These values are, in turn, incorporated in the culture of implementing agencies. When the values of one era are discredited, the result may be that the organisation forgets its own past, and moves too rapidly into the new way of working, without fully understanding what it is doing. While the practical 'change-management' literature emphasises organisational recalcitrance in the face of reform, the risks of overly rapid change may be equally great (see Stewart and Kringas, 2003).

The media as values brokers

There have been many studies highlighting the impact of the mass media on policy agendas, particularly in relation to terrorism, foreign policy and crime (see, for example, Entman, 2004; Hess and Kalb, 2003; Roberts, 2003). The media help to frame or form policy issues by concentrating on some issues at the expense of others (agenda formation), and by 'priming' audiences to make particular kinds of connections (for example, linking terrorism with relaxed gun control laws) (Callaghan and Schnell, 2005; Gilliam and Iyengar, 2005). Although I have not expressly identified media activity in the accounts of policy in this book, it seems appropriate at this point to ask: in what ways might media-influenced agenda formation and 'priming' exhibit a values-based dimension?

I believe it is helpful to see the media as significant 'values-brokers' of public policy. Indeed in highlighting this role we see more clearly the interaction between the personal and the political that all journalists convey through their work. The media construct policy agendas when journalists present political decisions and stances to the public, mediated by judgements about what the public wants. In choosing which items to prioritise (out of thousands of possibilities), editors must have an understanding of what will interest the public (while not causing discomfort to sponsors); and in choosing the 'angle' from which the story is to be written, journalists will seek a value orientation or stance that will appeal to readers. Most journalists obviously have their own orientations towards the news: indeed as 'facts' are transmitted instantly through the electronic media and the Internet, newspapers rely increasingly on the power of opinion to remain viable. In turn, media-savvy politicians in search of votes are finely tuned to the possibilities and the challenges of these equations. It is often said that the Internet, as a kind of electronic commons, reduces the gatekeeping power of the conventional media. This may be true, but it does not alter the fact that if policy is to be influenced, a concentration of political opinion must somehow occur.

In assisting this concentration, the serious media forms part of the communication network of policy communities, dampening some concerns, igniting others. The popular media seize upon the controversial, the personal and the particular. Populist radio commentators (or shock-jocks as they are called in Australia) trade in outrage, compassion for the underdogs (provided they are reasonably appealing) and triumphalism, sometimes in *schadenfreude*. The power of emotion, linked to the view that 'they' should do something about it, serves as a kind of policy 'trigger'. Something happens, often a 'something' that reflects a deeper problem. A child is killed crossing the road to get to school – why is there no overbridge? Someone dies in the emergency room of a hospital waiting for treatment. Why was he overlooked? In briefing their ministers, officials try to explain that the overbridge will cost hundreds of thousands of dollars, and there are many worse 'black spots' that need attention. They defend the hard-worked nurses and doctors who treat thousands of cases correctly and promptly, for every one that slips through the net. But ministers must act (or at least, be seen to act), and the overbridge is accelerated up the list. An inquiry is ordered into the operations of the emergency room.

Public servants, wedded to their routines and their rationalisations, view journalists much as they would carriers of the plague. Journalists are seen as searching (unfairly) for the weak spot, playing, where they can, to the unlovely public image of the bureaucrat. On the other hand, the instinct of the good journalist for the 'story' behind the policy has the potential to convey both correction and connection. The beauty of media-driven politics is its ability to channel public sentiment into allocation processes (such as budgets) where the human implications may have been lost. Policy does not necessarily improve as a result, but it is a reminder that decisions that have been handled in certain ways to make them manageable may be desensitising their implementers. On occasion, the whistle-blowing powers of the media may bring about more fundamental change, as occurred in the Australian state of Queensland in the 1980s, when the extent of official corruption was exposed by a journalist working for the Australian Broadcasting Commission (Hede, Prasser and Neylan, 1992).

When politicians communicate with the public, they trade in the language of values, in many ways the lingua franca of political communication. Powerful interests are at play as well. But those who see politicians as simply the mouthpieces of interests overlook the fact they are human: they need values to orientate their activity in a confusing world. The values they are promulgating may actually be ones they believe in. George Bush, when advised in June 2004 of the transfer of Iraqi sovereignty from the US Administrator to Prime Minister Ayad

Allawi, scrawled across the message advising him of what he then thought was the successful outcome of the invasion, 'let freedom reign' (Bush, 2004). We can argue that Bush was simply a front for more calculating interests. The truth – that he really believed he was bringing 'freedom' to Iraq – may be even more unsettling.

Of course, governments use the techniques of values-based communication for more calculating purposes. Spin doctors trade in values when they put a particular interpretation on a policy or action. Political parties use marketing to devise policies and advertising to sell them. And policy professionals are increasingly learning the value of 'road-testing' the names they give to particular initiatives. The Australian Department of Health and Ageing, for example, trialled a number of names for its policy to encourage take-up of private health insurance before settling on 'Lifetime cover'. The point is that the power of the media links with the power of values in public policy. This may be one reason why in democratic states, the impact of the media on public policy is so hard to pin down and so difficult to fit into any one explanatory model of policy-making.

Public policy, values and the environment

If there is a basic incompatibility between economic growth and the environment, what is the likely future of attempts to 'rebalance' our societies in the direction of environmental values? In Chapter 8, I showed how institutions, in a number of settings, have dealt with these problems in the past, and discussed the extent to which existing paradigms and processes have been able to absorb 'green-ness' within the institutions of growth. From the perspective of values analysis, what capacity might there be for the reverse to occur?

For those hoping for a more transformative approach, climate change represents something of a mixed blessing. On the plus side, climate change has started to bring home to those otherwise impervious to nature the fact that 'the environment', insufficiently understood or ignored, may cause real damage to humanity's material interests. On the negative side, the fact that climate change policy is being constructed within the envelope of growth (we can have growth *and* we can save the planet by capping and trading emissions) obscures the more fundamental dilemma – the relationship between our systems of production and our needs as human beings. While clearly a problem that goes much deeper than public policy, it remains a shaping force for the future of policy practice and thinking.

Of course, there is a vast interpretative literature on this question, but thinking about it from a values perspective helps to bring the analysis full circle. For the relationship between capitalism and human values is a debate as old as capitalism itself. While a materialist in his view of change, the earlier Marx, in particular, saw a significant value conflict at the heart of capitalism. Capitalism, he believed, deeply alienated the worker who, enmeshed in ever-larger systems of production, was deprived of any personal association with the product of his own labour. In important ways, Marx was ambivalent about the system he saw emerging around him. He saw how its productive power was changing social relations around him, and dreamed of a time when the working class would, through revolution, control and use that power for the collective good.

Marx did not foresee the ways in which politics and public policy would eventually tame the rampant unequalising forces of capitalism, at least within those states which were the first to industrialise. In these countries, the history of the latter part of the twentieth century showed that it was possible to have both capitalism and a much more equal society than would have been thought possible in the nineteenth. But there was a sense in which Marx was right: as he clearly saw, capitalism displaces local allegiances. Global markets concentrate people and production in cities and industrialise the countryside in a relentless drive to produce raw materials and food for the urban multitudes. The environment clearly suffers as a result, even as living standards improve.

For many people, however, there remains an attachment to, even a hunger for, the natural world we despoil. It is a sensitivity that has always been present to some degree – we know of nineteenth-century farmers, for example who saw themselves as stewards, rather than as exploiters of the land. The early conservationists, who agitated to set aside areas of natural beauty, were responding to this same sentiment. As the scale of the destruction has grown, so has the sense of loss. The environmental movement that began to grow in the 1960s represented many strands of opinion, but at its core, was a desire to live more harmoniously with nature, or at least to do less damage to the natural world. This fundamentally 'green' value would apply, whether or not environmental damage was also damaging to human interests.

If we have to overcome our addiction to growth in order to make peace with our planet, how might the necessary change in values come about? Structuralist forms of analysis propose contradiction as an engine of change. The perspective developed here sees policy systems as sentient and reflexive. Value conflict, as we have seen, can be managed in many ways. When they are at their best, states can learn through these conflicts by changing their own institutions, if they have the motivation to do so. The key question, then, becomes that of the generation of political will. My analysis suggests that green-ness will outreach growth in a transformative way, using the full resources of the democratic state, only as and when the institutions of growth are perceived to be losing their legitimacy. Historically, changes of this kind have taken centuries to occur. The broad-scale networks of the global village may speed the process: it remains to be seen whether our planet gives us sufficient time to make the change.

Implications for connecting theory and practice

It is now time to return to the question raised in the Introduction to this volume – the use of values analysis as a way of connecting theory and practice in public policy. How, specifically, might this be done? One of the key theoretical problems in policy analysis concerns the relationship between actors, processes and structures on the one hand, and the role of ideas on the other. Sabatier's celebrated work on policy analysis excluded constructivist approaches because (with some exceptions) Sabatier considered that there was no attempt in this work to attach ideas to the activities of actors or to connect them to socio-economic conditions or institutions (Sabatier, 1999, p. 11). At the same time, the Sabatier approach appeared to downplay the work of the policy analyst.

My suggestion is that an emphasis on values may provide a way through this hall of mirrors. The 'inside' of policy (the work of analysis with which practitioners are familiar) involves values. The 'outside' sees them elided because the values can no longer be attached to the structures in whose production they were involved even though, as Hudson and Lowe point out, the 'assumptive values' of individuals play a key role in shaping the value systems of institutions (Hudson and Lowe, 2004, p. 197). If, however, values could be imagined as providing a kind of 'wormhole' between the world of thought and the world of action, it might be possible to sketch a way forward.

Post-empiricist policy analysis, in rejecting simplistic forms of positivism, proposes (for the engaged policy analyst) the task of formulating reflexive discourses. These discourses are seen as '[e]xtending from concrete questions concerning the efficiency of a programme up through its situational context and the societal system to the abstract normative questions concerning the impact of a policy on a particular way of life' (Fischer, 2003, p. 192). These interconnected discourses (following

Habermasian theory) are considered to engage with deliberative activity in a way that empowers both ordinary citizens and professionals.

The approach advocated here takes a simpler route between fact and value. If scholars wish to influence the world of action, they need to engage in a form of reflexive prescription. As defined here this means, firstly, defining one's own values in relation to the project under consideration, then establishing how values are allocated and, finally, advocating a change in the way the system operates so as to produce a shift or rebalancing in the desired direction. In theoretical terms, we might think of this as a way of 'stepping into' the system under consideration, in a way that allows for the importance of meaning creation, while avoiding the relativism implied by deconstruction.

In terms of the life-world, reflexive prescription might most fruitfully take place wherever evaluative activity is mandated or is possible. Indeed, it gives a sharper edge to evaluation as the decisive activity in the theory–practice link. We know that the quest for evidence-based policy, particularly where the evidence derives from evaluative research, is almost invariably qualified by the politics of a given situation (see, for example, Doherty, 2000). While realist forms of evaluation confront this inevitability head-on (see Pawson and Tilley, 1997), a more straightforward evaluative interrogation may, paradoxically, prove more fruitful, precisely because the analyst lays bare what is normally occluded or assumed. (Interestingly, in surveying voters about policy and political issues, Kinder and Nelson advocate just such an 'up front' approach) (Kinder and Nelson, 2005).

How might reflexive prescription work in relation to an actual policy problem? Let us say we are interested in reducing recidivism rates among criminals. Obviously, a vast amount of work has been done on this question and many values stances are potentially involved. Approaching the problem from the point of view developed in Chapter 5 might involve the researcher investigating (within himself or herself) how tough or tender am I? Then one would examine how the existing system, in all its complexity, allocated these values. This would involve investigating structure, process and culture (or using studies that already provided this data). We would in all probability find that toughness and tenderness are enacted in specific ways, by specific processes, that may have more to do with bureaucratic tradition (mediated by political panic) than with individual need. Reflexive prescription would, therefore, involve some clarification of the process, together with a clear intersection between the values of the academic or policy analyst and the system under review. Such prescription is not more likely to be taken up than prescription deriving from other sources – that will always be a political task. But it does have an important 'argumentative' advantage in that it leaves those who wish to take issue with it, much less room to hide. The burying of values may be administratively convenient, but frustrate potentially productive dialogue (or even conflict).

In addition to its prescriptive advantages, values analysis has some implications or, at least, some messages for the ways in which political scientists construe public policy in the descriptive sense – that is, when we produce accounts of the development of policy in a particular field. When we write about policy, whatever the ostensible analytic frame employed, it is the savour and tang of value conflict, the political dimension of public policy that we observe, that we are drawn to (Dunn, 1983: 40–41). The story of 'social policy' in the latter part of the 20th century, for example, could scarcely be told without reference to the movement to the right in politics. Constant references to the advent and reach of 'neo-liberal' policies during this period, testify to the importance of values in the way we all think about policy – without them, it would be difficult even to begin to discuss the subject.

The values perspective makes explicit what is implicit in these accounts in several ways. Firstly, even when writing descriptively, we need to be more open about our own values. No social scientist worth the name believes there is such a thing as 'value-free' social science. But we tend to take our acknowledgment for granted when it comes to writing up the work that we do. Many policy commentators are attracted to social policy, because they care about social inequality. Many others work on environmental policies because they want to see a better environment. These are admirable impulses – we should make more of them. We should not make assumptions either, that interests care only about material values. The attitudes of political science to business are a good example of this. It is assumed that business cares only about 'the bottom line'. Sometimes, we may grant business its 'triple bottom line', but that is about it. If a business group argues for a particular policy on the basis of a certain value position, we tend to discount both the argument and the value – 'they would say that, wouldn't they'?

Our accounts should more freely acknowledge complex value positions, not only in business but also in public agencies and not-for-profits. There is a tendency, for example, to begin the analysis of not-for-profits from the perspective that these are uniquely values-driven organisations. They generally try to make the world a better place, but self-interest must necessarily be present, as well. When confronting the values territory of the state (for example through implementation partnerships), virtue is not always on the side of the not-for-profit provider. There are questions of emphasis, too. Scholars of public policy have produced a huge body of knowledge about social policy (construed as policies designed to alleviate inequality). Far less is done on science, technology, transport, education, regional development, employment, taxation, immigration, criminal justice and so on. These policies deal with significant values, too. Yet we know far less about them than we do about social policy.

We need to acknowledge that we are not outside the systems we write about, but within them. 'How I came to do this research' should be a more common excursus in the academic paper, and not just in the seminar room. We not only analyse policy agendas, we are influenced by them – there are more environmental conference papers now than 10 years ago, not because it has become more analytically interesting, but because it has become so much more important in the world of activism and of government. This being so, a more reflexive, albeit still empirical, engagement with our subject matter would appear to be in order.

Achieving values through policy

It is through public policies that societies aim to give practical form to their collectively held values. But the question remains – if public policies are so shot-full of ambiguities, how can we achieve anything coherent through them at all? More to the point, what does the analysis of public policy values mean for the resolution of the most difficult policy questions of our time, such as the prevention of war, safeguarding of human rights, and the management of climate change? What of the future of public policy in a world where technology is transforming, not only the ways in which we communicate, but (perhaps) our very modes of being?

As we have seen, policy values are themselves complex, ever-changing and not always clear-cut. Some of the most sensitive public policy debates are not about an abstract entity called 'the economy' but about the sort of society we are (or want to be). Should gays be allowed to marry? Should every spare piece of land be looked at from the point of view of its development potential? Should universities be run as businesses? What place do we give in our school curricula to the teaching of subjects such as history (as a specialised subject), and if history has a place, what kind of history should it be? Should the citizens of the UK apologise for slavery? Having (in February 2008) apologised for their treatment of Aborigines, should Australians pay them compensation?

Public policy creates successive compromises in relation to these issues. Sometimes it hides them, sometimes it switches debate to areas that seem more comfortable, or more technical. For those on one side or the other of these debates, the compromises that are struck will seem disappointing. For the majority in the middle, the outcome may be more acceptable. But there will be many times when public policy disappoints, when promised outcomes disappear under the weight of pressure politics, or are simply buried within bureaucratic complexities. As many community groups have discovered, the original impetus for change becomes part of broader value-setting processes.

Consider the Australian novelist Ruth Park, whose novel, *Harp in the South*, set in the inner-city slums of Sydney, was taken up after the war by an ambitious housing minister interested in slum clearance. When, later, she visited the places she had lived in and written about, she found they had been replaced by soulless piles of flats that alienated families from each other, and from the street. The new flats were bright and airy, they had plumbing that worked, and there were lots of them, easing overcrowding. But much had been lost, as well.[1] When social improvement meets the budget, the interests of the poor are apt to be interpreted in ways that are convenient to decision-makers, rather than the people themselves. These days, it is likely that people will be 'consulted' before their neighbourhoods are swept away, but no more likely than in the past that their wishes will be taken into account.

When they become policy values, our personal values are 'captured' in particular ways through the structure and intent of programs of action. The ways in which public agencies actually carry out these policies means that the overall result is a palimpsest of values, with new ones piled on top of the old ones. In part, this messiness is desirable because, as with the mutually conflicting personal values we all harbour, governments could not survive if they were forced to impose a coherent values-ordering on all that they do. True coordination would mean death. On the other hand, in this setting of constant compromise, it is easy to be pessimistic about progress.

If policy oscillates between values, it is difficult to see how learning can occur. When (particularly within organisations) we believe we have 'seen it all before' (as for example, when an administrative configuration is exactly the same as it was a decade before), it is easy to feel cynical. What have we learned if we end up in the same place? Perhaps the lesson is that change may have been oversold, when our repertoires of organisational action remain relatively limited. But there is reassurance here, too, because many dilemmas that may appear unprecedented have been confronted before. Many policy-making dilemmas are restatements of old problems. As the saying has it, 'history is past politics, and politics is present history'.

Moreover, the record is more cheering in relation to the achievement of broader, more consensual values than it is for those that command only small-scale allegiances. Most of us want (or say we want) more just, peaceful, prosperous and environmentally sustainable societies. The governments of advanced industrial societies have, on the whole, improved their performance in relation to the first three goals: their record on the fourth is more equivocal. They have done this through practical, commonsense action, moving incrementally most of the time, but on occasion, essaying much more ambitious reforms. 'Big picture' policy learning has occurred. The Allies understood that Germany should be rebuilt after World War II, not crushed by reparations as had been the case following World War I. Public financial managers understand that in times of financial crisis it is more important to maintain liquidity than it is to punish greedy lenders.

Increasingly, taking action on the problems that confront us takes us beyond the world of the nation-state. The international realm of public policy parallels the national-level one, with one significant difference – in the international realm nation states are themselves parties to many kinds of supra-national institutions (the United Nations, the World Trade Organisation) whose guiding values may be strong, but whose implementation capacity is often weak. Where conflicting interests cannot be reconciled through negotiation (such as those of the developed and developing worlds in relation to climate change), there is no overarching 'values-allocator' to make the call. With its often strife-torn foundations and uncertain budgets, international governance struggles to create the power that is needed for the deployment of authoritative public policy.

Would public policy work more effectively if means were found to confront more openly the conflicting values underpinning these issues? As Schön and Rein argued persuasively, we lack good ways of bridging these divides (Schön and Rein, 1994). We have many good techniques for mediating conflict, but too often they are not used in the hard-edged contexts we often construct for the consideration of policy. For policy analysts (as I have previously suggested) there could be a case for bringing out the values implications of the work that they do, highlighting trade-offs as a way of focusing attention on the deficiencies of current policy. The realpolitik of international diplomacy and negotiation may be more open than we suppose to the moral suasion of countries that practise what they preach.

Often, though, it seems that values are most likely to be achieved when we are not aiming directly for them. This is because institutions are built very slowly, and when we attempt to re-order their values ambiguities, they often become quite unstable. When we go looking for evidence of the successful pursuit of particular values, with a few exceptions (such as the abolition of the British slave trade) it is hard to pinpoint a particular time, context or campaign as having been decisive. Although welfare states do mitigate social inequality, their actual origins were complex and contested, as detailed work on the United States, European countries and the advanced industrial countries of Asia has shown. Even for William Wilberforce, it was an oblique assault – prohibiting the use of flags of convenience by British slavers – that made the first decisive attack on the pro-slaving interests.

So, finally, what is the future of public policy?

In a notable definition, Davis, Wanna, Warhurst and Weller described public policy as 'the interaction of values, interests and resources, guided through institutions and mediated by politics' (Davis et al., 1993, p. 15). In bringing the values aspect out of the shadows, what do we gain? We do not gain a new theory of public policy, in the sense of a new mode of explanation, because there is much that we do not see (for example, the operation of interests). What we do perceive more freshly than before is a sense of structure and of change, and of the capacity of policy systems to deal with conflict – their ingenuity and resilience amidst all the chaos. We gain an appreciation that regardless of their origins, public policies do, indeed, allocate values. More than this: public policies balance values.

Policy structures, however contingent, always carry with them elements of values choice. And as with any choice, it is not possible to optimise every value. Although we are dealing with sentient systems, rather than with mechanisms, the values of the past are our starting point, whether we are aware of them or not. If we want to understand the policies of tomorrow the best predictors are those of today. This incrementalism need not be too disheartening: there are many activities that citizens will continue to expect their governments to do. Governments must defend the nation; require citizens to be educated, while continuing to undertake a large part of the job themselves; regulate business, and (to varying degrees and in different ways) support people when they are unemployed, sick and old. It is to the government that we turn to fix the environment and to protect us from the side effects of new technologies.

The politics of these activities remain trenchant, at least among the interested groups that cluster around politicians in power and the bureaucracies they lead. But increasingly, it seems, this traditional world of public policy is divorced from the more informal world of the Internet, where increasingly, connections are made, business is done and opinions formed. Many people are no longer paying attention to the contests of the past. The postmodern world seems to require a different mindset. As Australian futurologist Hugh Mackay put it in 1999, change is endemic, and it is difficult to form a clear picture of what the future might bring, except to hope that, in all the uncertainty, 'our reaction to present insecurities and discontinuities will be a move towards reconnection' (Mackay, 1999).

But the role of public policy in a postmodern world remains unclear, because policy tends to reflect current (and past) perceptions of reality – governments are not postmodern. For the foreseeable future, politics will continue to be driven by an intricate interaction between private and public emotion. Graham Little, in *The Public Emotions*, wrote that '[t]he biggest paradox of the emotions is that they link us to other people while making us the individuals we are' (Little, 1999, p. 49). He might have said the same of values. At this broader, societal level, the key to understanding what happens and why it happens may, increasingly, lie in appreciating the values that drive political action, as much as the operations of institutions. Our paths will be structured by these emotionally shaped orientations, and value conflict will continue to provide a motive force for change. Where we end up will depend upon the evolution of our capacity to make these discussions more productive than in the past: the policy values of the future will be what we make of them.

Notes

Introduction

1. For a good short account of the issues, see Thalia Anthony 'Equal pay but no jobs', Online Opinion, 1 September 2006, http://www.onlineopinion.com.au/view.asp?article=4839, date accessed 20 February 2008.

3 Implementing Fairness

1. See Japan Access 'Women's Issues: changing roles in a changing society', http://www.sg.emb-japan.go.jp/JapanAccess/women.htm, date accessed 1 March 2008.

4 The Impact of Efficiency

1. 'Sarkozy pledges new era of change', BBC News 16 May 2007, http://news.bbc.co.uk/2/hi/europe, date accessed 15 December 2007.

5 Values and Policy Instruments

1. Material from http://www.liberation.fr/actualite/societe/284788.FR.php, date accessed 29 November 2007.

7 Values and Public Management

1. This discussion derives from material on the National School of Government website (http://www.nationalschool.gov.uk) and the Civil Service website (http://www.civilservice.gov.uk), date accessed 10 March 2008.

8 Greenness and Growth

1. Council of Australian Governments (1992) *National strategy for ecologically sustainable development*, http://www.environment.gov.au/esd/national/nsesd/strategy/index.html; Australian Government (1992) *Intergovernmental agreement on the environment*, www.environment.gov.au/esd/national/igae/index.html, date accessed 22 June 2007.

10 Conclusion

1. Recounted in Ruth Park's autobiography *Fishing in the Styx*, Penguin Books, 1994.

References

Aaron, H., Mann, T. and T. Taylor (1994) *Values and Public Policy*, Washington: The Brookings Institution.

ABC [Australian Broadcasting Corporation] (2004) 'PM unfurls flags and fitness for schools', ABC News Online, http://www.abc.net.au/news/newsitems/200406/s1137645.htm, date accessed 17 February 2008.

ABC [Australian Broadcasting Corporation] (2007) Stott Despoja slams abortion counselling decision, ABC News Online 2 January 2007, http://www.abc.net.au/news/newsitems/200701/s1820358.htm, date accessed 10 June 2007.

Abelson, P. (1987) 'Fairness in the real world: rules, choices, expectations and policies', *Australian Economic Papers*, 26(48): 1–19.

ABS [Australian Bureau of Statistics] (2006) *Australian social trends*, Cat 4102.0, http://www.abs.gov.au.

ABS [Australian Bureau of Statistics] (2007) *4390.0 – Private hospitals, Australia 2005—2006*, http://www.abs.gov.au.

ACCC [Australian Competition and Consumer Commission] (2005) 'ACCC immunity policy for cartel conduct', Canberra: Commonwealth of Australia, http://www.accc.gov.au, date accessed 15 May 2007.

Alcock, P. and G. Craig (2001) 'The United Kingdom: rolling back the welfare state?' in P. Alcock and G. Craig (eds), *International Social Policy: Welfare Regimes in the Developed World*, Houndmills, Basingstoke: Palgrave Macmillan.

Alexander, M., Baxter, J., Hughes, J. and J. Renda (2005) 'Australians working together: evaluation of the impact of activity requirement for parenting payment customers on their children aged 13–15 years', Canberra: Australian Institute of Family Studies, http://www.workplace.gov.au. Accessed 7 March 2008.

Aljazeera (2003) Chirac backs hijab ban, Aljazeera News Archive, 17 December 2003. http://www.english.aljazeera.net, date accessed 9 March 2008.

Analoui, F. (1998) Behavioural and causal influences on individual managerial effectiveness in the Ghanaian public sector, *The International Journal of Public Sector Management*, 11(4): 300–13.

APSC [Australian Public Service Commission] (2004) *State of the Service Report 2003–04*. Canberra: Commonwealth of Australia.

APSC [Australian Public Service Commission] (2006) *Supporting Ministers, Upholding the Values* Canberra: Commonwealth of Australia.

Argy, F. (2003) 'Beware of economic fundamentalism (or what makes a good policy adviser)', *Australian Review of Public Affairs*, http://www.australianreview.net/digest/2003/03/argy.html. Accessed 2 March 2008.

Aspalter, C. (2006) 'The east Asian welfare model', *International Journal of Social Welfare*, 15: 290–301.

ATO [Australian Taxation Office] (2006) *Compliance Program 2006-07*, http://www.ato.gov.au. Accessed 27 October 2007.

Aucoin, P. (1990) Administrative reform in public management: paradigms, principles, paradoxes and pendulums, *Governance* 3(2): 115–37.
Australian Government (2006) *Income support programmes*, http://www.workplace.gov.au, date accessed 24 August 2006.
Australian Government (2006a) *Rethinking regulation: report of the taskforce on reducing regulatory burdens on business*, Canberra: Commonwealth of Australia, http://www.regulationtaskforce.gov.au, date accessed 3 March 2008.
Australian Government (2007) *Best Practice Regulation Handbook*, Canberra: Office of Best Practice Regulation, http://www.obpr.gov.au, date accessed 3 March 2008.
Ayres, I. and J. Braithwaite (1992) *Responsive Regulation: Transcending the Regulation Debate*, New York: Oxford University Press.
Bachrach, P. and M. Baratz (1962) 'The two faces of power', *American Political Science Review*, 56, 947–52.
Baggini, J. (2006) 'The rise, fall and rise again of secularism'. *Public Policy Research* December 2005–February 2006.
Bainbridge, J. (1985) 'The return of retribution', *ABA Journal*, May, 61–63.
Baldwin, P. (1997) State and citizenship in an age of globalisation' in P. Koslowski and A. Follesdal (eds), *Restructuring the Welfare State: Theory and Reform of Social Policy*, Springer: New York.
Bale, T. and N. Roberts (2002) 'Plus ca change? Anti-party sentiment and electoral system change: A New Zealand case study', *Commonwealth and Comparative Politics* 60(2): 1–20.
Ball, S. (1997) 'On the cusp: parents choosing between state and private schools in the UK: action within an economy of symbolic goods', International Journal of Inclusive Education, 1(1): 1–17.
Bank, R. (2000) 'Reception conditions for asylum seekers in Europe: an analysis of provisions in Austria, Belgium, France, Germany and the United Kingdom', *Nordic Journal of International Law*, 69: 257–88.
Bardach, E. (2006) 'Policy dynamics' in M. Moran, M. Rein, and R. Goodin (eds), *The Oxford Handbook of Public Policy*, Oxford: Oxford University Press.
Bartlett, R. (1986) 'Rationality and the logic of the National Environmental Policy Act', *The Environmental Professional* 8: 105–11.
Baumgartner, F. and Jones, B. (1993) Agendas and instabilities in American politics, Chicago: University of Chicago Press.
Bell, D. (1973) *The Coming of Post-industrial Society: Venture into Social Forecasting*, New York: Basic Books.
Bell, S. (1993) Australian Manufacturing and the State, Melbourne: Cambridge University Press.
Bell, S. (2002) *Economic Governance and Institutional Dynamics*, South Melbourne: Oxford University Press.
Bennett, J. (1991) 'Environmental values and water policy', Australian Geographical Studies 41(3): 237–50.
Berlin, I. (1998) *The Proper Study of Mankind: an Anthology of Essays*, London: Pimlico.
Beveridge, W. (1942) 'Social insurance and allied services' [report], New York: Macmillan.
Blowers, A. (1997) 'Environmental policy: ecological modernisation or the risk society?' *Urban studies* 34(5–6): 845–71.

BOPCRIS [British Official Publications Collaborative Reader Information Service] Sessional Papers 1983–84, http://www.bopcris.ac.uk, date accessed 9 March 2008.

Borghi, V. and R. van Berkel (2007) 'Contextualising new modes of governance in activation policies', *International Journal of Sociology and Social Policy*, 27(9–10): 353–63.

Boston, J., Martin, J., Pallot, J. and Walsh, P. (1996) *Public Management: the New Zealand Model*, Auckland: Oxford University Press.

Braithwaite, J. and P. Drahos (2000) *Global Business Regulation*, Cambridge and Melbourne: Cambridge University Press.

Braithwaite, J., Healy, J. and K. Dwan (2005) *The Governance of Health, Safety and Quality*, Canberra: Commonwealth of Australia.

Brand, J. (1976) 'Local government' in R. Rose (ed.) *The Dynamics of Public Policy: a Comparative Analysis*, London: Sage.

Bremner, C. (2007) 'Anger as rock star Bertrand Cantat who murdered girlfriend is freed after four years', *Times Online* 17 October 2007, http://www.timesonline.co.uk, date accessed 29 November 2007.

Briggs, L. (2005) 'A passion for policy', ANZSOG/ANU Public Lecture Series, Canberra, June 2005, http://www.apsc.gov.au, date accessed 16 August 2007.

Brookfield, D. (2001) 'The effect of rules, habits and bureaucracies on costing in the UK National Health Service', *International Journal of Public Sector Management*, 14(7): 530–39.

Brown, A. J. (2001) 'Beyond public native forest logging: national forest policy and Regional Forest Agreements after South East Queensland', *Environmental and Planning Law Journal*, 18(2): 189–208.

Brumby, J. (2007) 'Victoria's contribution to the stem-cell debate', *ATSE Focus* 144, Melbourne: Australian Academy of Technological Sciences and Engineering.

Burstein, P. and M. Bricher (1997) 'Problem definition and public policy: Congressional committees confront work, family and gender', 1945–1990, *Social Forces*, 75(4): 135–69.

Bush, G. (2004) 'President Bush discusses early transfer of Iraqi sovereignty', White House, Office of the Press Secretary, 28 June 2004, http://www.whitehousse.gov/news/releases/2004/06, date accessed 28 December 2007.

Caiden, G. (1965) *Career Service: an Introduction to the History of Personnel Administration in the Commonwealth Public Service of Australia 1901–1961*, Melbourne: Melbourne University Press.

Callaghan, K. and F. Schnell (2005) 'Introduction: framing political issues in American politics', in K. Callaghan, and F. Schnell (eds), *Framing American Politics*, Pittsburgh: University of Pittsburgh Press.

Calloni, M. (2001) 'Debates and controversies on abortion in Italy' in M. Stetson (ed.), *Abortion Politics, Women's Movements, and the Democratic State – A Comparative Study of State Feminism*, Oxford: Oxford University Press.

Carter, N. (2001) *The Politics of the Environment: Ideas, Activism, Policy*, Cambridge: Cambridge University Press.

Carvel, J. (2004) 'Opposition to immigrants hardens under Blair', *Guardian*, 7 December. Parliamentary Library [Australia] online text 1182710, http://www.aph.gov.au, date accessed 7 March 2008.

CASA [Civil Aviation Safety Authority – Australia](2004), 'CASA's priorities for aviation safety', http: //www.casa.gov.au/corporat/safety.htm, date accessed 2 March 2008.

Casciani, D. (2003) 'Asylum questions: are we being swamped?', BBC News 16 July 2003. http://news.bbc.co.uk/1/hi/uk/3067869.stm, date accessed 7 March 2008.
Castles, F., ed. (1982) *The Impact of Parties: Politics and Policies in Democratic Capitalist States*, London and Beverly Hills: Sage Publications.
Castles, F., ed. (1989) *The Comparative History of Public Policy*, Cambridge: Polity Press.
Castles, F. and D. Mitchell (1993) 'Worlds of welfare and families of nations' in F. Castles (ed.), *Families of Nations: Patterns of Public Policy in Western Democracies*, Aldershot: Dartmouth.
Caulcutt, C. (2007) 'No change in the banlieues since 2005', http://www.france24.com/france24/public/en/special-reports, 28 November, 2007, date accessed 26 February 2008.
Chanley, S. A. and N. Alozie (2001). 'Policy for the "deserving", but politically weak: the 1996 welfare reform act and battered women' *Policy Studies Review* 18:2 (Summer).
Childers, K. (2006) 'The evolution of the welfare state: social rights and the nationalization of welfare in France, 1880–1947'[review], *French Politics, Culture and Society*, 24(2): 135–36.
Christensen, T., Laegreid, P. and L. Wise (2002) 'Transforming administrative policy', *Public Administration* 80(1): 153–78.
Christoff, P. (1996) 'Ecological modernisation, ecological modernities', *Environmental Politics* 5(3): 476–500.
Clarke, C. (2005) 'Controlling our borders: making immigration work for Britain' [press release 7 February 2005], London: Home Office Press Office, http://press.homeoffice.gov.ul, date accessed 7 March 2008.
Clarke, J. and F. Fox Piven (2001) 'United States: an American welfare state?' in P. Alcock and G. Craig (eds), *International Social Policy: Welfare Regimes in the Developed World*, Houndmills, Basingstoke: Palgrave Macmillan.
Claver, E., Llopis, J., Gasco, J., Molina, H. and F. Conca (1999) 'Public administration: from bureaucratic culture to citizen-oriented culture', *International Journal of Public Sector Management* 12(5): 455–64.
Cobb, R. and J. Coughlin (1998) 'Are elderly drivers a road hazard? Problem definition and political impact', *Journal of Aging Studies* 12(4): 411–27.
Cobb, R. and M. Ross (1997) 'Conclusion; Agenda denial: the power of competing cultural definitions' in R. Cobb and M. Ross (eds), *Cultural Strategies of Agenda Denial: Avoidance, Attack and Redefinition*, Lawrence: University of Kansas Press.
Colebatch, H. (2002) *Policy* (2nd edn), Buckingham: Open University Press.
Connelly, J. and G. Smith (2003) *Politics and the Environment: from Theory to Practice* (2nd edn), London: Routledge.
Considine, M. (2003) 'The impact of competition on non-profit organisations', *Australian Journal of Political Science*. 38 (1): 63–77.
Cook, R., Dickens, B. and L. Bliss (1999) 'International developments in abortion law from 1988 to 1998. *American Journal of Public Health* 89(4): 579–86.
Costa, D. (1998) *The Evolution of Retirement: an American Economic History 1880–1990*, Chicago: University of Chicago Press.
Cotgrove, S. (1982) *Catastrophe or Cornucopia: the Environmental Politics of the Future*, London: John Wiley.

CSA [Child Support Agency Australia] (2006) *Strategic Plan 2006–2008*, Canberra: Child Support Agency.
Curl, A. and M. Hokenstad (2006) Reshaping retirement policies in post-industrial nations: the need for flexibility, *Journal of Sociology and Social Welfare*, 33(2): 85–99.
Curran, G. and R. Hollander (2002) 'Changing policy mindsets: ESD and NCP compared' *Australian Journal of Environmental Management*, 9(3): 158–69.
Cyert, R. and J. March (1963) *A Behavioural Theory of the Firm*. Englewood Cliffs, NJ: Prentice Hall.
Dahl, R. (1997) *Toward Democracy: a Journey. Reflections 1942–1997* (vol. 1), Berkeley: University of California Press.
Davies, J. (2005) 'The social exclusion debate: strategies, controversies and dilemmas', *Policy Studies* 26(1): 1–27.
Davis, G., Wanna, J., Warhurst, J. and P. Weller (1993) *Public Policy in Australia* (2nd edn), Sydney: Allen & Unwin.
den Exter, A. (2005) Access to health care in the Netherlands: the influence of (European) treaty law, *Journal of Law, Medicine and Ethics*, Winter: 698–707.
Devos, K. (2004) 'Penalties and sanctions for taxation oin selected Anglo-Saxon countries: Implications for taxpayer compliance and tax policy' *Revenue Law Journal* 14: 32–101.
DEWR [Australian Department of Employment and Workplace Relations] (1999) *Evaluation of the Work for the Dole Pilot Program*, EMB report 1/99, Canberra: Evaluation and Monitoring Branch.
Dierkes, M., Wiler, H. and A. Antal (1987) *Comparative Policy Research: Learning from Experience*, London: Gower.
Dixon, G. (2003) 'Sir Reginald Ansett Memorial Lecture', September 2003, http://www.qantas.com.au/regions.
Dobson, A. (1995) *Green Political Thought*, London: Routledge.
Doherty, J. (2000) 'Housing: linking theory and practice' in H. T. O. Davies, S. M. Nutley and P. C. Smith (eds), *What Works? Evidence-based Policy and Practice in Public Services*, Bristol: Polity Press.
Dolin, B. (2001) 'National drug policy: the Netherlands'. Canada: Library of Parliament. http: //www.parl.gc.ca, date accessed 26 October 2007.
Domanick, J. (2004) *Cruel Justice: Three Strikes and the Politics of Crime in America's Golden State*, Berkeley: University of California Press.
Dowding, K. (1995) The Civil Service, London: Routledge.
Downs, A. (1972) Up and down with ecology: the 'issue-attention' cycle. *The Public Interest*, 28: 38–50.
Doyle, T. (1990) 'Environmental movement power brokers', *Philosophy and Social Action* 16(8): 37–52.
Drabsch, T. (2005) *Abortion and the Law in New South Wales*, Sydney: NSW Parliamentary Library Research Service.
Dror, Y. (1971) *Design for Policy Sciences*, New York: American Elsevier Publishing Co.
Dror, Y. (2006) 'Training for policy makers' in Mora et al.
Dryzek, J. (1987) *Rational Ecology: Environment and Political Economy*, Oxford and New York: Blackwell.
Dryzek, J. (2000) Deliberative Democracy and Beyond, Oxford: Oxford University Press.

Dryzek, J., Downes, D., and C. Hunold (2003) *Green States and Social Movements: Environmentalism in the United States, United Kingdom, Germany and Norway*, Oxford: Oxford University Press.
Dunn, W., ed. (1983) *Values, Ethics and the Practice of Policy Analysis*, Lexington, MA: Lexington Books.
Durr, R. (1993) 'What moves policy sentiment?' *American Political Science Review* 87: 158–70.
Dye, T. (2005) *Understanding Public Policy* (11th edn), Upper Saddle River, NJ: Pearson Prentice Hall.
Eardley, T. (2002) 'Mutual obligation and the job network: the effect of competition on the role of non-profit employment services'. *Australian Journal of Social Issues*, 37(3): 301–14.
Easton, B. (1999) *The Whimpering State: Policy After MMP*, Auckland: Auckland University Press.
Easton, D. (1965) *A Framework for Political Analysis*, Englewood Cliffs, NJ: Prentice-Hall.
ESDSC [Ecologically Sustainable Development Steering Committee Australia] (1992) 'Draft national strategy for ecologically sustainable development' [discussion paper], Canberra: AGPS.
Economou, N. (1993) 'Accordism and the environment: The Resource Assessment Commission and national environmental policy-making' *Australian Journal of Political Science* 28(3): 399–412.
Edwards, L. (2002) *How to Talk to an Economist: Reopening Political Debate in Australia*, Cambridge: Cambridge University Press.
Elarde, P. and C. Tilbury (2007) 'The experiences of Aboriginal and Torres Strait Islander children in the child protection system', *Children Australia* 32(2): 8–14.
Elks, S. (2007) 'Gang rape was "childish experiment"', *The Australian*, 11 December, 2007, http:// www.theaustralian.news.com.au/story, date accessed 18 March 2008.
Entman, R. (2004) *Projections of Power: Framing News, Public Opinion, and US Foreign Policy*, Chicago: University of Chicago Press.
EPA [Environmental Protection Agency United States] (2007) *Taking to the Air*, http://www.epa.gov/history/publications/formative5.htm.
Esping-Andersen, G. (1990) *Three Worlds of Welfare Capitalism*, Cambridge: Polity Press.
Esping-Andersen, G. (1996) 'Welfare states without work: the impasse of labour shedding and familialism in continental European social policy' in G. Esping-Andersen (ed.), *Welfare States in Transition: National Adaptations in Global Economies*, London: Sage Publications.
Evans, B., Richmond, T. and J. Shields (2005) 'Structuring neoliberal governance: the nonprofit sector, emerging new modes of control and the marketisation of service delivery', *Policy and Society*, 24(1): 74–97.
Evans, M. (1999) 'Reconciling conflicting values in health policy', *Policy Futures for UK Health Technical Series No 9*. London: The Nuffield Trust.
Feldman, S. (2003) 'Values, ideology and the structure of political attitudes', in D. Sears, Huddy, L. and R. Jervis (eds), *Oxford Handbook of Political Psychology*, Oxford: Oxford University Press..
Fenna, A. (2004) *Australian Public Policy* (2nd ed), French's Forest (NSW): Pearson Education.

Fischer, F. (2003) *Reframing Public Policy*, Oxford: Oxford University Press.
Fischer, F. and J. Forester (1993) 'Introduction' in F. Fischer and J. Forester (eds), *The Argumentative Turn in Policy Analysis and Planning*, Durham: Duke University Press, pp. 1–17.
Fitz, J. and B. Beers (2002) 'Education management organisations and the privatisation of public education: a cross-national comparison of the USA and Britain' *Comparative Education* 38(2): 137–154.
Franklin, M., Mackie, T. and H. Valen (1992) *Electoral Change: Responses to Evolving Social and Attitudinal Structures in Western Countries*, Cambridge: Cambridge University Press.
Fukuyama, F. (1992) *The End of History and the Last Man*, New York: Maxwell Macmillan International.
Fushimi, Y. (1997) 'The social security system in Japan', in P. Koslowski and A. Follesdal (eds), *Restructuring the Welfare State: Theory and Reform of Social Policy*.
Galasso, V. (2006) *The Political Future of Social Security in Aging Societies*, Cambridge, MA: MIT Press.
GAO [Government Accounting Office] (1999) 'Airline deregulation: changes in airfares and service at Buffalo, New York, Testimony before the Subcommittee on Aviation, Committee on Transportation and Infrastructure. Washington: GAO, http://www.gao.gov/archive/1999/rc99286t.pdf, date accessed 2 March 2008.
Gilliam, F. and S. Iyengar (2005) 'Social predators or victims of societal neglect? Framing effects in juvenile crime coverage', in K. Callaghan and F. Schnell (eds) *Framing American Politics*.
Gillespie, J. (1991) *The Price of Health: Australian Governments and Medical Politics 1910–1960*, Melbourne: Cambridge University Press.
Gilroy, B., Lukas, E. and T. Volpert (2005) 'The European "no-frills" aviation market: current and future developments', in P. Forsyth (ed), *Competition versus Predation in Aviation Markets: a Survey of Experience in North America, Europe and Australia*, Burlington VT: Ashgate.
Goldberg, J. (1996) 'Environmental impact assessment: why reform is needed', *Prometheus*, 14(1): 90–9.
Good, D. (2003) *The Politics of Public Management: the HRDC Audit of Grants and Contributions*, Toronto: University of Toronto Press.
Goodin, R. (1988) *Reasons for Welfare: the Political Theory of the Welfare State*, Princeton, NJ: Princeton University Press.
Goodin, R. (2002) 'Structures of mutual obligation' *Journal of Social Policy*, 31(4): 579–96.
Goodin, R., Rein, M. and M. Moran (2006) 'The public and its policies' in M. Moran, M. Rein and R. Goodin (eds) *The Oxford Handbook of Public Policy*.
Goodin, R., Headey, B., Muffels, R. and H-J. Dirven (1999) *The Real Worlds of Welfare Capitalism*, Cambridge: Cambridge University Press.
Goodman, R. and I. Peng (1996) 'The East-Asian welfare states: peripatetic learning, adaptive change and nation-building', in G. Esping-Andersen (ed.), *Welfare States in Transition: National Adaptations in Global Economies*.
Gottinger, H. and M. Takashima (2000) 'Japanese telecommunications and NTT Corporation: a case in deregulation', *International Journal of Management and Decision Making* 1(1): 68–102.
Gow, J. and C. Dufour (2000) 'Is the new public management a paradigm? Does it matter?', *International Review of Administrative Sciences*, 66: 573–97.

Gregory, R (1998) 'Political responsibility for bureaucratic incompetence: tragedy at Cave Creek', *Public Administration* 76(3): 519–38.
Grin, J. and A. Loeber (2007) 'Theories of policy learning: agency, structure and change', in F. Fischer, G. Miller and M. Sidney (eds), *Handbook of Public Policy Analysis: Theories, Politics and Methods*, London: Taylor and Francis.
Gross, M. (2002) 'Abortion and neonaticide: ethics, practice and policy in four nations, *Bioethics* 16(2): 202–31.
Guine, A. and M. Fuentes (2007) 'Engendering redistribution, recognition, and representation: the case of female genital mutilation (FGM) in the United Kingdom and France', *Politics and Society* 35(3): 477–519.
Hajer, M. (1993) 'Discourse coalitions and the institutionalization of practice: the case of acid rain in Britain'in F. Fischer and J. Forester (eds). *The Argumentative Turn in Policy Analysis and Planning*.
Hall, P. (1993) 'Policy paradigms, social learning and the state: the case of economic policy-making in Britain', *Comparative Politics* 25(3): 275–96.
Halligan, J. (2001) 'Politicians, bureaucrats and public sector reform in Australian and New Zealand' in B. Peters and J. Pierre (eds), *Politicians, Bureaucrats and Administrative Reform*, London: Routledge.
Halligan, J. (2003) 'The reassertion of the center in a first generation NPM system', in T. Christensen and P. Laegreid (eds), *Autonomy and Regulation: Coping with Agencies in the Modern State*, Cheltenham: Edward Elgar.
Harris, T. (2006) Submission to the Australian Senate Finance and Public Administration References Committee *Inquiry into the transparency and accountability of Commonwealth public funding and expenditure*, http://www.aph.gov.au/Senate/committee/fapa_ctte, date accessed 14 February 2007.
Heclo, H. and A. Wildavsky (1981) *The Private Government of Public Money: Community and Policy Inside British Politics* (2nd edn), London: Macmillan.
Hede, A., Prasser, S. and M. Neylan (1992) *Keeping Them Honest: Democratic Reform in Queensland*. St Lucia: University of Queensland Press.
Heidenheimer, A., Heclo, H. and C. Adams (1975) *Comparative Public Policy: the Politics of Social Choice in Europe and America*. New York: St Martin's Press.
Helderman, J-K., Schut, F., van der Grinten, T. and W. van de Ven (2005) 'Market-oriented health care reforms and policy learning in the Netherlands', *Journal of Health Politics, Policy and Law*, 30(1–2): 189–209.
Henderson, K. (2004) Characterizing American public administration: the concept of administrative culture, *International Journal of Public Sector Management* 17(3): 234–50.
Herman, R. (2003). 'Image theory and strategic interaction in international relations' in D. Sears, Huddy, L. and R. Jervis (eds), *Oxford Handbook of Political Psychology*.
Hess, S. and M. Kalb, eds (2003) *The Media and the War on Terrorism*, Washington: Brookings Institution Press.
HFEA [Human Fertilization and Embryology Authority] (2007) *Annual Report and Accounts 2006–07*. London: HFEA.
HMRC [HM Revenue and Customs] (2007) 'HM revenue and customs and the taxpayer: modernizing powers, deterrents and safeguards, a new approach to compliance checks', London: HMRC.
Hodge, G. (2000) *Privatization: an International Review of Performance*, Boulder, CO: Westview.

Hort, S. (1997) 'Sweden: 21st century post-modern people's home?' in P. Koslowski and A. Follesdal (eds), *Restructuring the Welfare State: Theory and Reform of Social Policy*.

House of Lords (2002) *Select Committee on Stem Cell Research Report*. London: Stationery Office, http://www.parliament.the-stationery-office.co.uk.

Howe, B. (2007) *Weighing Up Australian Values*, Sydney: UNSW Press.

Howlett, M. (1994) 'Policy paradigms and policy change: Lessons from the old and new Canadian policies towards Aboriginal peoples'. *Policy Studies Journal*, 22(4): 631–649.

Hudson, J. and S. Lowe (2004) *Understanding the Policy Process: Analyzing Welfare Policy and Practice*, Bristol: Policy Press.

Hummel, R. (2000) *The Bureaucratic Experience*, New York: St Martin's Press.

Humphry, R. (2000), *Review of the Whole of Government Information Technology Outsourcing Initiative*, Canberra: Department of Finance and Administration.

ICAR [Information Centre about Asylum and Refugees] (2005) 'Public opinion and policy', http://www.icar.org.uk/?lid=5019, Date accessed 28 October 2007.

Inglehart, R. (1977) *The Silent Revolution: Changing Values and Political Styles among Western Publics*, Princeton, NJ: Princeton University Press.

Jacobs, D. and J. Carmichael (2001) 'The politics of punishment across time and space: a pooled time-series analysis of imprisonment rates', *Social Forces*, 80(1): 61–91.

James, S., Murphy, K. and M. Reinhart (2005) 'Taxpayer beliefs and views: two new surveys', *Australian Tax Forum* 20(2): 157–88.

Janicke, M. (2004) 'Industrial transformation between ecological modernisation and structural change', in Jacob, K., Binder, M. and Wieczorek (eds), Governance for Industrial Transformation: Proceedings of the 2003 Berlin Conference on the Human Dimensions of Global Environmental Change, Berlin: Environmental Policy Research Centre.

JANIS [Joint ANZECC/MCFAA National Forest Policy Statement Implementation Sub-committee] (1997). *Nationally Agreed Criteria for the Establishment of a Comprehensive, Adequate and Representative Reserve System for Forests in Australia*, Canberra: ANZECC.

Job, J. and D. Honaker (2003) 'Short-term experience with responsive regulation in the Australian Taxation Office', in V. Braithwaite (ed.), *Taxing Democracy: Understanding Tax Avoidance and Evasion*, London: Ashgate.

John, P. (2003) 'Is there life after policy streams, advocacy coalitions, and punctuations: using evolutionary theory to explain policy change?' *Policy Studies Journal*, 31(4): 481–98.

Johnson, C. (1982) *MITI and the Japanese Miracle: the Growth of Industrial Policy 1925–1975*, Stanford: Stanford University Press.

Johnson, J. and E. Williams (2004) *Stem Cell Research*, Washington DC: Library of Congress Congressional Research Service.

Jones, B. D. (1994) *Reconceiving Decision-making in Democratic Politics: Attention Choice and Public Policy*. Chicago: University of Chicago Press.

Jones, B. D. (2001) *Politics and the Architecture of Choice: Bounded Rationality and Governance*, Chicago: University of Chicago Press.

Jones, M. (1996) *The Australian Welfare State: Evaluating Social Policy* (4th edn), St Leonard's (NSW): Allen & Unwin.

Jones, M. (1997) *Reforming New Zealand Welfare: International Perspectives*, Sydney: Centre for Independent Studies.

Justesen, M. (2002) *Learning from Europe: the Dutch and Danish School Systems*, London: Adam Smith Institute.
Kain, J. and R. Webb (2003) 'Turbulent times: Australian airline issues 2003', Parliamentary Library Research Paper No 10 2002–2003, Canberra: Department of the Parliamentary Library.
Kamieniecki, S. (2000) 'Testing alternative theories of agenda setting: forest policy change in British Columbia', Canada. *Policy Studies Journal* 28(1): 176–89.
Kay, A. (2007) 'Tense layering and synthetic policy paradigms: the politics of health insurance in Australia', *Australian Journal of Political Science*, 42(4): 579–91.
Keating, M. (1990) 'Managing for results in the public interest', *Australian Journal of Public Administration*, 49(4): 387–89.
Kelly, A. (1989) 'An end to incrementalism? The impact of expenditure restraint on social services budgets 1979–1986', *Journal of Social Policy*, 18(2): 187–211.
Kelsey, J. (1997) *The New Zealand Experiment: a World Model for Structural Adjustment?* Auckland: Auckland University Press.
Keman, H. (1998) `The waning of solidarity?' in Cavanna, H.(ed), Challenges to the Welfare State: Internal and External Dynamics for Change, Aldershot: Edward Elgar, pp. 21–48.
Kemp, D. (1978) *Society and Electoral Behaviour in Australia: a Study of Three Decades*, St Lucia: University of Queensland Press.
Kenny, S. (2000) 'Third sector and state partnerships: unpacking the discourses and practices', in S. Kenny, R. Melville and M. Wilkins (eds), *Third Sector and State Partnerships*. Geelong: Deakin University.
Kernaghan, K. (2003) 'Integrating values into public service: the values statement as centrepiece', *Public Administration Review*, 63(6): 711–19.
Kettl, D. (2006) 'Public bureaucracies' in R. Rhodes, S. Binder. and B. Rockman (eds), *The Oxford Handbook of Political Institutions*, Oxford: Oxford University Press.
Khadem, N. (2006) 'RU486 bill finds support', *The Age* (Melbourne) 8 February 2006, http://www.theage.com.au/news/national/ru486-bill-finds-support, Date accessed 10 August 2007.
Kildal, N. and S. Kuhnle, eds (2006) *Normative Foundations of the Welfare State: the Nordic Experience*, London: Routledge.
Kinder, D. and T. Nelson (2005) 'Democratic debate and real opinions' in K. Callaghan and F. Schnell (eds), *Framing American Politics*.
Kingdon, J. (1984) Agendas, alternatives and public policies, Boston: Little, Brown.
Klyza, C. (2002) 'The United States army, natural resources, and political development in the nineteenth century', *Polity* 35(1): 1–29.
Koslowski, P. and A. Follesdal (eds) *Restructuring the welfare state: theory and reform of social policy*, Springer: New York.
Kubler, D. (1999) 'Ideas as catalytic elements for policy change: advocacy coalitions and drug policy in Switzerland', in D. Braun and A. Busch (eds), *Public Policy and Political Ideas*, Cheltenham: Edward Elgar.
Kukutau, T. (2004) `The problem of defining an ethnic group for public policy: who is Maori and why does it matter?' Social Policy Journal of New Zealand, 23, December. Available online at http://www.msd.govt.nz/about-msd-and-our-work/publications-resources/journals-and-magazines/social-policy-journal/index.html.

Lafreniere, G. (2001) 'National drug policy: United Kingdom', Canada: Library of Parliament, http://www.parl.gc.ca, date accessed 26 October 2007.
Lafreniere, G. (2002) 'National drug policy: Sweden', Canada: Library of Parliament, http://www.parl.gc.ca, date accessed 26 October 2007.
Laham, N. (1993) *Why the United States Lacks a National Health Insurance Program*, Westport,CT.: Greenwood Press.
Lancaster, G. and G. Brierley (2001) 'A comparative study of the emergence of marketing culture within three formerly nationalised companies', *The International Journal of Public Sector Management*, 14(4–5): 341–71.
Langford, J. (2004) 'Acting on values: an ethical dead-end for public servants', *Canadian Public Administration*, 47(4): 429–51.
Lasswell, H. (1948) *The Analysis of Political Behaviour: an Empirical Approach*, London: Kegan Paul.
Laurance, J. (2008) 'Millions unable to find NHS dentist', *The Independent* 16 January 2008, http://www.independent.co.uk, date accessed 15 March 2008.
Le Grand, J. (2003) Motivation, agency and public policy: of knights and knaves, pawns and queens, Oxford: Oxford University Press.
Le Grand, J. (2007) *The Other Invisible Hand: Delivering Public Services Through Choice and Competition*, Oxford and Princeton: Princeton University Press.
Leisering, L. (2001) 'Germany: reform from within', in P. Alcock and G. Craig (eds), *International Social Policy: Welfare Regimes in the Developed World*.
Levy, J. (2003) 'Political psychology and foreign policy' in D. Sears, Huddy, L. and R. Jervis (eds), *Oxford Handbook of Political Psychology*.
Levy, M. (1993) 'European acid rain: the power of tote-board diplomacy', in P. Haas, Keohane, R. and M. Levy (eds), *Institutions for the Earth: Sources of Effective International Environmental Protection*. Cambridge, MA: MIT Press.
Lewis, C. (2007) 'The Howard government: the extent to which public attitudes influenced Australia's federal policy mix', *Australian Journal of Public Administration*, 66(1): 83–95.
Lewis, E., Grimes, A., Wilkinson, B. and D. Teece (1996) 'Economic reform in New Zealand 1984–1995: the pursuit of efficiency', *Journal of Economic Literature*, 34 (December): 1856–902.
Lin, C., Pervan, G. and D. McDermid (2007) 'Issues and recommendations in evaluating and managing the benefits of public sector IS/IT outsourcing', *Information Technology and People*, 20(2): 161–83.
Lindblom, C. (1995) 'The science of muddling through' in D. McCool (ed.), *Public Policy Theories, Models, and Concepts*. Englewood Cliffs, NJ: Prentice Hall.
Linder, S. and B. Peters (1984) 'From social theory to policy design', *Journal of Public Policy*, 4: 237–59.
Linder, S. and B. Peters (1987) 'A design perspective on policy implementation: the fallacies of misplaced prescription', *Policy Studies Review*, 6(2): 459–76.
Linder, S. and B. Peters (1989) 'Instruments of government: perceptions and contexts', *Journal of Public Policy*, 9(1): 35–58.
Little, G. (1999) *The Public Emotions: from Mourning to Hope*, Sydney: ABC Books.
Lomborg, B. (2001) *The Sceptical Environmentalist: Measuring the Real State of the World*. New York: Cambridge University Press.
Lord, W. and B. Kenny. (1995) 'Evaluation of two institutional arrangements for resolving interstate water disputes' in Water management and conflict

resolution, in Dinar, A. and Loehman, E. (eds), *Water Quantity and Quality Disputes and Their Resolution*, Westport, CT: Praeger.
Lynn, L. (2003) 'Public management' in B. Peters and J. Pierre (eds), *Handbook of Public Administration*, London: Sage.
Mackay, H. (1999) *Turning Point: Australians Choosing Their Future*, Sydney: Pan Macmillan.
Maley, M. (2000) 'Too many or too few? The increase in Federal Ministerial Advisers 1972–1999' *Australian Journal of Public Administration*, 59(4): 48–53.
Manzer, R. (2003) *Educational Regimes and Anglo-American Democracy*, Toronto: University of Toronto Press.
March, J. and J. Olsen (1984) 'The new institutionalism: organisational factors in political life' *American Political Science Review*, 78: 734–37.
March, J. and J. Olsen (2006) 'The logic of appropriateness', in M. Moran, M. Rein and R. Goodin (eds) *The Oxford Handbook of Public Policy*.
Marginson, S. and M. Considine (2000) *The Enterprise University: Power, Governance and Reinvention in Australia*, Melbourne: Cambridge University Press.
May, P. (2003) 'Policy design and implementation', in B. Peters and J. Pierre (eds), *Handbook of Public Administration*.
Memon, A. (2002) 'Reinstating the purpose of planning within New Zealand's Resource Management Act', *Urban Policy and Research* 20(3): 299–308.
Michael, E. (2006) *Public Policy: the Competitive Framework*, South Melbourne: Oxford University Press.
Ministerial Task Force on Child Support [Australia] (2005) *In the Best Interests of Children: Reforming the Child Support Scheme*, Canberra: Commonwealth of Australia.
Molle, F. (2001) 'Water pricing in Thailand: theory and practice', Kasetsart University, Doras Center, Research report 7, http://www.iwmi.cgiar.org/assessment/Reseach_Projects, date accessed 14 June 2007.
Morrell, K. (2006) 'Policy as narrative: new Labour's reform of the National Health Service', *Public Administration*, 84(2): 367–85.
NCES [National Center for Education Statistics] (2006) *Characteristics of Private Schools in the United States: results from the 2003–2004 Private School Universe Survey*, Washington: US Department of Education.
Niestroy, I. (2007) 'Sustainable development governance structures in the European Union', in *Institutionalising Sustainable Development*. Paris: OECD.
Nord, E., Richardson, J. and Kuhse, H. and P. Singer (1995) 'Who cares about cost? Does economic analysis impose or reflect social values?', Melbourne: Monash University Centre for Health Program Evaluation, http://www.buseco.monash.edu.au/centres/che/pubs/wp46.pdf, date accessed 15 May 2007.
Norman, R. and R. Gregory, R. (2003) 'Paradoxes and pendulum swings: performance management in New Zealand's public sector', *Australian Journal of Public Administration*, 62(4): 35–49.
Nozick, R. (1974) *Anarchy, State and Utopia*, Oxford: Blackwell.
OECD (2006) *OECD Health Data: How Does the US Compare?*, http://www.oecd.org, date accessed 16 March 2008.
Olsen, G. (2007) 'Towards global welfare state convergence? Family policy and health care in Sweden, Canada and the United States', *Journal of Sociology and Social Welfare*, 34(2): 143–64.
Olsson, S. (1990) *Social Policy and Welfare State in Sweden*, Lund: Archiv forlag.

Paehlke, R. (2003) *Democracy's Dilemma: Environment, Social Equity and the Global Economy*, London: MIT Press.
Pakes, F. (2005) 'Under siege: the global fate of euthanasia and assisted-suicide legislation', *European Journal of Crime, Criminal Law and Criminal Justice* 13(2): 119–138.
Palier, B. (2000) '"Defrosting" the French welfare state' in M. Ferrara and M. Rhodes (eds) *Recasting European Welfare States*, London: Routledge.
Palley, H. (2006) 'Canadian abortion policy: national policy and the impact of federalism and political implementation on access to services', *Publius: The Journal of Federalism*, 36(4): 565–586.
Palmer, E. and E. Wadensjo (2004) 'Public pension reform and contractual agreements in Sweden – future directions' in M. Rein. and W. Schmall (eds), *The Political Economy of Pension Reform*, London: Edward Elgar.
Palmer, M. (2005) *Inquiry into the Circumstances of the Immigration Detention of Cornelia Rau*, Canberra: Commonwealth of Australia.
Parry, R., and N. Deakin (2003) 'Control through negotiated agreements: the changing role of the Treasury in controlling public expenditure in Britain', in J. Wanna, L. Jensen, L. and J. de Vries (eds), *Controlling Public Expenditure: the Changing Roles of Central Budget Agencies – Better Guardians?*, Northampton, MA: Edward Elgar.
Parsons, W. (1995) *Public Policy: an Introduction to the Theory and Practice of Policy Analysis*. Cheltenham, UK: Edward Elgar.
Pawson, R. and Tilley, N. (2003) Realistic evaluation, London: Sage.
Pearson, N. (2007) 'Noel Pearson discusses the issues faced by indigenous communities', ABC *Lateline* 26 June 2007, http://www.abc.net.au/latelinehttp://www.abc.net.au/lateline/content/2007/s1962844.htm, date accessed 20 October 2007.
Peele, G. (2005) 'Electoral politics, ideology and American social policy', *Social Policy and Administration*, 39(2):150–65.
Peng, I. (2000) 'A fresh look at the Japanese welfare state', *Social Policy and Administration*, 34(1): 87–114.
Peters, B. (1991) *The Politics of Taxation: a Comparative Perspective*, Cambridge, MA: Blackwell.
Phillips, J. and A. Millbank (2005) 'The detention and removal of asylum seekers' [e-brief], Canberra: Parliament of Australia, Parliamentary Library, http://www.aph.gov.au/library, date accessed 14 February 2008.
Pierson, P. (1994) *Dismantling the Welfare State? Reagan, Thatcher and the Politics of Retrenchment*, Cambridge: Cambridge University Press.
Pierson, P. (2000) 'Increasing returns, path dependence and the study of politics', *American Political Science Review*, 94(2): 251–67.
Pilkington, C. (1998) *Issues in British politics*. Basingstoke: Macmillan.
Pocock, B. (2006) *The Labour Market Ate My Babies: Work, Children and a Sustainable Future*, Sydney: Federation Press.
Pollitt, C. and G. Bouckaert (2000) *Public Management Reform: a Comparative Analysis*, Oxford: Oxford University Press.
Pratchett, L. and M. Wingfield (1996) 'Petty bureaucracy and woolly-minded liberalism? The changing ethos of local government officers', *Public Administration* Winter, 74: 639–56.

Pratt, A. (2005) 'Public versus private? An overview of the debate on private health insurance and pressure on public hospitals', Research note no. 54 2004–2005. Canberra: Parliamentary Library (Australia).
Productivity Commission (1997) 'Data envelopment analysis: a technique for measuring the efficiency of government service delivery', Canberra: Commonwealth of Australia, http://www.pc.gov.au/gsp/reports/research/dea/index.html, date accessed 8 May 2007.
Productivity Commission (1999) 'Implementation of ecologically sustainable development by Commonwealth departments and agencies', Inquiry report no 5, Canberra: Ausinfo.
Pugh, D. (1991) 'The origins of ethical frameworks in public administration' in Bowman, J. (ed) Ethical frontiers in public management: seeking new strategies for resolving ethical dilemmas, San Francisco: Jossey-Bass.
Pusey, M. (1991) *Economic Rationalism in Canberra: a Nation-building State Changes Its Mind*, Cambridge and Melbourne: Cambridge University Press.
Reference Group on Welfare Reform (2000) 'Participation support for a more equitable society' [final report], Canberra: Department of Family and Community Services.
Reich, B. and C. Adcock (1976) *Values, Attitudes and Behaviour Change*, London: Methuen.
Rezsohazy, R. (2001) 'Values: psychological perspectives' in N. Smelser and P. Baltes (eds) *International Encyclopedia of the Social and Behavioral Sciences*, Amsterdam and New York: Elsevier.
Richardson, H. (1997) *Practical Reasoning about Final Ends*, Cambridge: Cambridge University Press.
Ringquist, E. (1995) Political control and policy impact in EPA's Office of Water Quality, *American Journal of Political Science*, 39(2): 336–63.
Roberts, J. (2003) *Penal Populism and Public Opinion: Lessons from Five Countries*, Oxford: Oxford University Press.
Robinson, B. (2004) 'France: attacks on the freedom of religious expression'. Ontario: Ontario Consultants on Religious Freedom, http://www.religioustolerance.org/rt_franc2.htm, date accessed 7 March 2008.
Robinson, M. (2001) 'Accrual accounting and the public sector', *Economic Papers* June: 57–66.
Rochefort, D. and R. Cobb, eds (1994) *The Politics of Problem Definition*, Lawrence: University of Kansas Press.
Rokeach, M. (1973) *The Nature of Human Values*, New York: Free Press.
Rokeach, M. (1979) *Understanding Human Values: Individual and Societal*, New York: Free Press.
Romzek, B. (2000) 'Dynamics of public sector accountability in an era of reform', *International Review of Administrative Sciences*, 66: 21–44.
Rose, R. (1990) 'Inheritance before choice in public policy', *Journal of Theoretical Politics*, 2: 263–91.
Rose, R. and P. Davies (1994) *Inheritance in Public Policy: Change Without Choice in Britain*, New Haven, CT: Yale University Press.
Sabatier, P., ed. (1999) *Theories of the Policy Process*, Boulder, CO: Westview Press.
Sabatier, P and H. Jenkins-Smith (1993) *Policy Change and Learning: an Advocacy Coalition Approach*, Boulder, CO: Westview Press.

Sagoff, M. (1991) 'The limits of cost-benefit analysis', in C. Mills (ed.), *Values and Public Policy*, San Diego: Harcourt Brace Jovanovich.

Savoie, D. (1990) *The Politics of Public Spending in Canada*, Toronto: University of Toronto Press.

Sawer, M. (1990) *Sisters in Suits: Women and Public Policy in Australia*, St Leonard's: Allen & Unwin.

Schattschneider, E. (1960) *The Semisovereign People: a Realist's View of Democracy in America*. New York: Holt, Rinehart and Winston.

Schneider, A. and H. Ingram (1990) 'Behavioural assumptions of policy tools', *Journal of Politics*, 52, 2: 510–30.

Schneider, A. and H. Ingram (1993) 'Social construction of target populations: implications for politics and policy', *American Political Science Review* 87(4): 334–38.

Schneider, A. and H. Ingram, eds (2005) *Deserving and Entitled: Social Constructions and Public Policy*, Albany, NY: State University of New York.

Schön, D. and M. Rein (1994) *Frame Reflection: Toward the Resolution of Intractable Policy Controversies*, New York: Basic Books.

Scott, G. (2001) *Public Sector Management in New Zealand: Lessons and Challenges*, Canberra: Centre for Law and Economics, Australian National University.

Self, P. (1993) *Government by the Market? The Politics of Public Choice*. Basingstoke: Macmillan.

Sen, A. (1973) *On Economic Inequality*, Oxford: Clarendon Press.

Shepherd, E. (2007) Human Fertilisation and Embryology Bill [HL], House of Lords Library Library Note 2007/007, http://www.parliament.uk/documents/upload/HLHumFertEmbrBill.pdf, date accessed 2 May 2009.

Shergold, P. (2003) A foundation of ruined hopes? Delivering government policy. Public Service Commission SES Breakfast Briefing October 2003.

Shergold, P. (2007) 'What really happens in the Australian Public Service: an alternative view' *Australian Journal of Public Administration*, 66(3): 367–70.

Simonsen, B., Johnston, N. and R. Barnett (1996) 'Attempting non-incremental budget change in Oregon: an exercise in policy sharing', *American Review of Public Administration*, 26(2): 231–51.

Smith, G. (1996) 'The role of assessment of environmental effects under the Resource Management Act 1991', *Environmental and Planning Law Journal*, 13(2): 82–102.

Smolowe, J. (1993) 'New, improved and ready for battle the abortion pill is finally coming to the US' *Time Magazine*, 14 June 1993, http://www.time.com/time/magazine, date accessed 11 August 2007.

Soss, J. (1999) Lessons of welfare: policy design, political learning and political action, *American Political Science Review*, 93, 2: 363–96.

SSC [State Services Commission, New Zealand] (2005) 'Development goals for the State Services', http://www.ssc.govt.nz, dateaccessed 22 November 2007.

Steinberger, P. (1980) 'Typologies of public policy: meaning construction and the policy process', *Social Science Quarterly*, 61(2), 195–97.

Steiner, C. (2007) 'Vive la difference'. *Forbes Asia*, 3(13): 162–63.

Stetson, M., ed. (2001) *Abortion Politics, Women's Movements, and the Democratic State: A Comparative Study of StateFeminism*, Oxford: Oxford University Press.

Stewart, A., Brice, P., Burton, H., Pharoah, P., Sanderson, S. and R. Zimmerman (2007) *Genetics, Health Care and Public Policy: an Introduction to Public Health Genetics*, Cambridge: Cambridge University Press.

Stewart, J. (1994) *The Lie of the Level Playing Field: industry Policy and Australia's Future*, Melbourne: Text Publishing.
Stewart, J. (1997) Australian water management: towards the ecological bureaucracy? *Environmental and Planning Law Journal*, 14(4): 259–67.
Stewart, J. (2005) 'Educational policy: politics, markets and the decline of "publicness"', *Policy and Politics*, 33(3): 475–87.
Stewart, J. (2006) 'Value conflict and policy change', *Review of Policy Research*, 23(1): 183–96.
Stewart, J. (2007) 'Managing across boundaries: the problem of conflicting values' *Third Sector Review*, 13(2): 71–86.
Stewart, J. and G. Jones (2003) *Renegotiating the Environment: the Power of Politics*. Sydney: Federation Press.
Stewart, J. and M. Maley (2007) 'The Howard government and political management: the challenge of policy activism', *Australian Journal of Political Science*, 42(2): 277–94.
Stewart, J. and P. Kringas (2003) 'Change management strategy and values in six agencies from the Australian Public Service', *Public Administration Review*, 63(6): 662–74.
Stilwell, F. (1975) *Normative Economics: an Introduction to Microeconomic Theory and Radical Critiques*, Sydney: Pergamon Press.
Stone, D. (1997) *Policy Paradox: the Art of Political Decision Making*, New York: WW Norton.
Taber, C. (2003) 'Information processing and public opinion', in D. Sears, Huddy, L. and R. Jervis (eds), *Oxford Handbook of Political Psychology*.
Tait, J. (1997) 'A strong foundation: report of the task force on public service values and ethics', Summary provided to members by CAPAM, February 1997.
Talbot, C. (2005) 'Professionalism: a matter of choice and context'. *PA Times International Supplement*, February: 7–8.
Talbot, C. and C. Johnson (2007) *Seasonal Cycles in Public Management: Disaggregation and Re-aggregation*, 27(1): 53–60.
Teelken, C. (1999) 'Market mechanisms in education: school choice in the Netherlands, England and Scotland in comparative perspective', *Comparative Education*, 35(3): 283–302.
Tews, K., Busch, P-O. and H. Jörgens (2003) 'The diffusion of new environmental policy instruments', *European Journal of Political Research*, 42(2): 569–600.
Thacher, D. and M. Rein (2004) 'Managing value conflict in public policy', *Governance*, 17(4): 457–486.
Thatcher, M. (1993) *The Downing Street Years*, London: HarperCollins.
Thelen, K. and I. Kume (2006) 'Coordination as a political problem in coordinated market economies', *Governance*, 19(1): 11–42.
Thomson, P. (2005) 'Bringing Bourdieu to policy sociology: codification, misrecognition and exchange value in the UK context', *Journal of Education Policy* 20(6): 741–58.
Tilbury, C. (2005) 'Child protection services in Queensland post-Forde inquiry' *Children Australia*, 30(3): 10–16.
Trouille, H. (2000) 'Holiday camp or boot camp? Where does France stand in the prison reform debate?', *The Justice Professional*, 13: 391–403.
Turner, L. (2006) 'Learning from accounting history: will we get it right this time?' *Issues in Accounting Education*, 21(4): 383–407.

Uehling, G. (2004) 'Irregular and illegal migration through Ukraine', *International Migration*, 42(3): 77–107.

UNECE [United Nations Economic Commission for Europe] (2007) 'The 1979 Geneva Convention on long-range transboundary air pollution', http://www.unece.org/env/lrtap/lrtap_h1.htm, date accessed 7 June 2007.

Ure, J. (2003) 'Telecommunications privatisation: evidence and some lessons', *Asia Forum on ICT Strategies and e-Strategies*, Bangkok: UNDP/APDIP, http://www.trp.hku.hk/papers/2003.

US Census Bureau (2006) *American Factfinder* 2002 economic census: sector 62, http://factfinder.census.gov.

US Census Bureau (2007) *Income, Poverty and Health Insurance Coverage in the United States: 2006*, Washington: US Census Bureau.

Uzubashi, T. (2001) 'Japan: bidding farewell to the welfare society', in P. Alcock and G. Craig (eds), *International Social Policy: Welfare Regimes in the Developed World*.

Vanderheiden, S. (2004) 'Justice in the greenhouse: climate change and the idea of fairness', *Social Philosophy Today*, vol. 19.

van Wart, M. (1998) *Changing Public Sector Values*, New York: Garland Publishing.

Vickers, G. (1965) *The Art of Judgement: a Study of Policy Making*, London: Chapman and Hall.

Vitiello, M. (1997) 'Three strikes: can we return to rationality?' *The Journal of Criminal Law and Criminology*, 87(2): 395–482.

Vowles, J., Aimer, P., Karp, J., Banducci, S., Miller, R. and A. Sullivan (2002) *Proportional Representation on Trial: the 1999 Election in New Zealand and the Fate of MMP*, Auckland: Auckland University Press.

Wallis, J. and B. Dollery (2001) 'Understanding cultural change in an economic control agency: the New Zealand Treasury', *Journal of Public Policy*, 21(2): 191–212.

Wanna, J., Kelly, J. and J. Forster (2000) *Managing Public Expenditure in Australia*, Sydney: Allen & Unwin.

Warnock, M. (1984) 'Report of the committee of inquiry into human fertilisation and embryology', Cmnd 9314, London: Stationery Office.

Warnock, M. (2005) 'Public policy in bioethics and inviolable principles', *Studies in Christian Ethics*, 18(1): 33–41.

Weber, L. (2002) 'The detention of asylum seekers: 20 reasons why criminologists should care', *Current Issues in Criminal Justice*, 14(1): 9–30.

Weissert, C. and M. Goggin (2002) 'Nonincremental policy change: lessons from Michigan's Medicaid managed care initiative', *Public Administration Review*, 62(2): 206–17.

Weller, P. (2002) *Don't Tell the Prime Minister*, Sydney: Scribe Publications.

Wiering, M. and B. Arts (2006) Discursive shifts in Dutch river management: 'Deep' institutional change or adaptation strategy, *Hydrobiologia*, 565: 327–338.

Wildavsky, A. (1984) *The Politics of the Budgetary Process*. (4th edn), Boston: Little Brown.

Wilenski, P. (1986) *Public Power and Public Administration*, Sydney: Hale and Iremonger.

Wilson, J. (1975) *Thinking about Crime*, New York: Basic Books.

Wison, C. (2000) 'Policy regimes and policy change'. *Journal of Public Policy*, 20(3): 247–74.

Wu, J. (2000) *Unemployment-related Benefits System in the United Kingdom*, Hong Kong: Research and Library Services Division, Legislative Council Secretariat, http://www.legco.gov.hk, date accessed 26 February 2008.

Yanow, D. (1996) *How Does a Policy Mean? Interpreting Policy and Organizational Actions*, Washington DC: Georgetown University Press.

Yanow, D. (2002) *Conducting Interpretive Policy Analysis*, Thousand Oaks, CA: Sage.

Yeend, P. (2000) 'Mutual obligation/Work for the dole' [e-brief], Canberra: Parliament of Australia, Parliamentary Library, http://www.aph.gov.au/library, date accessed 27 October 2007.

Zahariadis, N. (1995) 'Policy change and learning: an advocacy coalition approach' [review article] *Policy Studies Journal*, Summer 23(2): 378–83.

Zysman, J. (1983) *Governments, Markets and Growth: Financial Systems and the Politics of Industrial Change*, Ithaca, NY: Cornell University Press.

Index

Abbott, Tony, 111
Abelson, P, 20
Aboriginal affairs, 5
abortion law and policy, 108, 109–12
accountability
  as design value, 28
  and new public management, 134–5, 136, 141, 143
acid rain, 166
Adams, C, 45
administrative values, 29
Adorno, T, 107
advocacy coalition framework (ACF), 16
  and parliamentary systems, 36
  and policy change, 35, 36–7
  and presidential systems, 36
  and value conflict, 36
  and values, 36
agenda management, 4
  and efficiency, 70–2
  and media as values brokers, 195–7
  and policy change, 35
airline industry, and deregulatory policies, 73–4
Allawai, Ayad, 196–7
Ansett (airline), 74
argumentative turn, 3, 16
Argy, F, 69
Asian countries, and public management, 128
asylum seekers, and tough/tender policies, 103–4
  Australia, 105–6
  United Kingdom, 104–5
attention allocation, 35
Aucoin, P, 138
Australia
  and abortion law and policy, 111–12
  and business regulation, 99, 102
  and child support policy, 119–20
  and deregulation, airline industry, 73–4
  and drug policy, 97–8
  and ecologically sustainable development (ESD), 157–8
  and education, 180; private schools, 180–2, 183
  and efficiency value, 77
  and environmental impact assessments, 159
  and environmental policy, 149; role of citizens, 162
  and health sector, 176–7; hospital provision, 176
  and immigration policy, asylum seekers, 103, 105–6
  and integrated resource management, 160
  and Job Network, 82
  and labour market reform, 84
  and national parks, 156
  and new public management: financial management, 135–6; politico-bureaucratic relationships, 131, 132–3; public interest, 141; special advisers, 132–3
  and outsourcing, 77
  and public service as profession, 141–2
  and religious values, 122
  and reproductive technologies, 117–18
  and stem cell research, 117
  and trade liberalisation, 76–7
  and unemployment policies, 91–3
  and voluntary euthanasia, 112–13
  and welfare policy, 53–5
  and working hours, 81
Australian Industry Commission, 77
Australian National Council on Drugs, 98

Australian Productivity
  Commission, 158
Australian Public Service, 138, 139
Australian Public Service Act (1999),
  138, 139
Australian Public Service Commission,
  132–3, 138, 141
Australian Tax Office (ATO), 102
Australians Working Together, 93
authoritarian personality, 107
autonomy, 11

backlashes, and policy change, 45–6
Baggini, Julian, 123
Bartlett, R, 154
Baumgartner, F, 35
behavioural change
  and policy instruments, 88–90
  and public policy, 87
  and tough/tender policies, 90–1,
    106–7; asylum seekers, 103–6;
    business regulation, 98–102;
    criminal justice, 93–5; drug
    policy, 95–8; unemployment,
    91–3
Belgium, and voluntary euthanasia,
  112, 121
Bell, Daniel, 21
benchmarking, 71
Berlin, Isaiah, 9–10, 14
Beveridge Report, 27
bias, and value conflict, 41–4
Blair, Tony, 58, 180
Blunkett, David, 105
Bouckaert, G, 128–9
bounded rationality, and policy
  change, 34–5, 36
Brand, J, 44
Briggs, Lynelle, 141
British Telecom, 74
Brookfield, D, 137
Brundtland, Gro Harlem, 165–6
budgetary process, 25
  and casuistry, 40
budgetary rationing, and health
  sector, 78
bureaucracies, 20
  and incrementalism, 41
  and policy change, 35

and policy paradigms, 42–3
and resistance to change, 41
and technicisation, 43
see also public management
Bush, George W, 4, 196–7
business regulation, and tough/tender
  policies, 98–102

Canada
  and abortion law and policy, 110
  and politico-bureaucratic
    relationship, 133–4
Canadian Task Force on Public Service
  Values and Ethics, 133–4
Cantat, Bertrand, 93–4
capitalism, and values, 198
Carter, Jimmy, 73
Castles, F, 52
casuistry
  and policy change, 37
  and value conflict, 30, 37, 40–1
  and voluntary euthanasia, 112
centralisation, as design value, 28
Child Support Agency (Australia),
  119–20
child support policy, 118–21
'children overboard affair', and
  asylum seekers, 106
Chirac, Jacques, 123
choice, 11, 170
  and counterproductivity of, 183
  as design value, 28
  and education, 170, 178; Australia,
    181; Netherlands, 182;
    United Kingdom, 179–80;
    United States, 180
  and health sector, 170; Netherlands,
    175–6; United Kingdom, 174;
    United States, 174–5, 183
  and limits on, 183–4
  as outcomes value, 28
  and policy change, 171
  and policy design, 170–1
  and policy values, 24–5
  and social responsibility, 183
civil service, *see* public management
class, and declining influence of, 24
climate change, 22, 188, 197
  and fairness, 47

climate change (*Continued*)
  and international environmental governance, 166
  see also environmental policy
Clinton, Bill, 45, 59
cloning, 115, 117
coalition formation, 16
Cobb, R, 16
codes of conduct, 138
Colebatch, H, 7
communities of practice, and health and education, 172
comparative methodology, and policy values, 30–1
comparative policy analysis, and values analysis, 188–90
competition
  as design value, 28
  and efficiency, 70–1
competition watchdogs, 100–1
consistency, and administrative values, 29
constructivism, 199
control, as design value, 28
cooperation, as design value, 28
coordination, as design value, 28
Costa, D, 59
Cotgrove, Stephen, 192
Council of Australian Governments (COAG), 117
criminal justice, and tough/tender policies, 93–5
culture wars, 5
Curran, G, 158
customer service, and administrative values, 29
cycling
  and policy change, 37; backlashes, 45–6; flip-flops, 44
  and value conflict, 30, 37, 44–6
Cyert, R, 120

Davies, J, 58
Davies, P, 39
Davis, G, 205
decentralisation, as design value, 28
deregulation, 72–3
  and airline industry, 73–4
  and equity, 80

  and free trade, 75–7
  and labour market reform, 84
  and telecommunications industry, 74–5
  see also efficiency
design values, 28
discourse analysis, 16
  and post-empiricist policy analysis, 199–200
distribution, and fairness, 50
diversity, as outcomes value, 27
divorce policy, 108, 118
Dolin, B, 96
dominant values, and policy paradigms, 42–3
Dowding, K, 131–2
Downs, A, 148
Doyle, Tim, 43
Dror, Yehezkel, 19, 22
drug policy, and tough/tender policies, 95–8
Dryzek, J, 18, 154
Dye, Thomas, and public policy, 1
Dylan, Bob, 22

Easton, David, 14, 25
ecological modernisation, 167
ecologically sustainable development (ESD), 157–8
economic growth, 11
  and environmental impact, 147–8
  and environmental values, 149, 168, 197
  as governance paradigm, 149
  as outcomes value, 27
economic nationalism, 21
economic rationalism
  and environmental policy, 150–1
  as paradigm, 71
  and role of, 85
education policy, 11
  and Australia, 180; private schools, 180–2, 183
  and choice, 170, 178; Australia, 181; Netherlands, 182; United Kingdom, 179–80; United States, 180
  and communities of practice, 172
  and Netherlands, 182

and organised interests, 171
and public-private relationship, 178–9, 182–3
and publicness, 178, 182, 183, 184–5
and restriction of competition, 79
and social responsibility, 183
and structural separation, 38
and United Kingdom, 179–80
and United States, 180
and universality, 170, 178; allocation of resources, 172; Netherlands, 182; United Kingdom, 179–80
Education Reform Acts (UK, 1980, 1996), 179–80
efficiency, 10
and administrative values, 29
and agenda setting, 70–2
and allocative efficiency, 70; improving, 71
as asymmetric value, 69
and backlashes against: Australia, 84; New Zealand's institutional reforms, 83–4
and cost efficiency, 70
and costs of, 68, 80–1; equity, 80; implications of cost-cutting, 81; organisational values, 82; public values, 80; work-life balance, 81–2; working hours, 81
and deregulatory policies, 72–3; free trade, 75–7; telecommunications industry, 74–5; transport industry, 73–4
and implementation of, 72, 83
and labour market reform: Australia, 84; France, 84–5; Germany, 84
and measurement of: benchmarking, 71; competition surrogates, 70–1
as outcomes value, 27
and outsourcing, 77–8
as policy value, 68–9
and productive efficiency, 70; improving, 70–1
and public sector, 70–1
and restrictions on, 79–80; education, 79; health, 78–9

emotions, 206
Endangered Species Act (USA, 1973), 162
energy policy, 167–8
Enron, 99
entitlement
as design value, 28
and public policy, 47–8
and social policy, 67
and welfare policy, 53
see also welfare policy
environmental concern ('greenness'), 11, 146
and business cycle, 148
and conservative political sentiment, 148–9
and contingent nature of, 148
and contrast with environmental values, 147
and economic growth, 147–8
and environment as source of value conflict, 147–8
as outcomes value, 27
Environmental Defender's Office (Australia), 162
environmental impact assessments (EIAs), 153, 159
environmental policy, 146
and ecological modernisation, 167
and economic rationalism, 150–1
and giving the environment a 'voice', 161–3; conservationists, 162–3; returning resources, 162; role of citizens, 162; role of the state, 161–2; water management, 162
and integrating mechanisms, 157; environmental impact assessments (EIAs), 159; integrated resource management, 160–1; strategic planning, 157, 158–9; structural coordination, 157–8
and international environmental governance, 165–7
and law, 153–4
and planning, 152–3
and resolving value conflicts, 163; Regional Forest Agreements (Australia), 163–5

environmental policy (*Continued*)
and science, 151–2
and structural separation, 38, 155; national parks, 155–6; pollution control, 156–7
and sustainable development, 154
and technicisation, 43
Environmental Protection Agency (EPA) (USA), 156–7
environmental values, 147
and economic growth, 149, 168, 197
and the policy agenda, 148–9
and public policy, 169
and values analysis, 197–9
epistemic communities, and paradigms, 71
equity, 10
and economic analysis, 86
and efficiency, 80
and fairness, 49
as outcomes value, 27
Esping-Andersen, G, 30, 52
ethical values, and public policy, 108–9
European Union, and deregulation of airline industry, 73
euthanasia, voluntary, 108, 112–13, 121
evaluation, 200
Evans, M, 183
evidence-based policy, 200

fairness, 10
and comparative approach, 31
and complexity of, 50
and concept of, 48–9
and equity, 49
and obligation/entitlement relationship, 47–8, 51
as outcomes value, 27
in policy world, 49–51
and public policy, 47
and social construction of, 51
and social policy, 47, 66
and taxation, 64–5
and value analysis, 52–3
and welfare policy, 52, 64–5; Australia, 53–5; France, 61–2; Germany, 60–1; Japan, 62–3;
New Zealand, 55–7; Sweden, 60; United Kingdom, 57–8; United States, 58–9
and welfare states, 52
family law, 11
family policy
and child support, 118–21
and divorce, 118
federalism
and abortion law and policy, 110–11
and stem cell research, 116
feminism, 19
finance capitalism, 21, 22
firewalls
and policy change, 37, 38
and value conflict, 30, 37
Fischer, F, 3
flip-flops, and policy change, 44
forest management, and Australia, 163–5
Forester, J, 3
Forster, J, 40
framing, 19
France
and abortion law and policy, 121
and criminal justice, 93–4, 95
and labour market reform, 84–5
and religious dress, 123
and welfare policy, 61–2
free trade, and deregulation, 75–7

gay marriage, 108
General Agreement on Tariffs and Trade (GATT), 76
Geneva Convention (1951), 103
Germany
and labour market reform, 84
and welfare policy, 60–1
Gillespie, James, 171
globalisation, 21
globalism, 21
Goggin, M, 41
Gomery Royal Commission (Canada, 2005), 134
Good, D, 130
Goodin, R, 17–18, 22
governance, as values-based activity, 1
government
and casuistry, 40

criticism of, 1
expectations of, 1
and hybridisation, 39
and structural separation, 38–9
and value conflict, management of, 37
greenness, *see* environmental concern ('greenness'); environmental policy; environmental values
green taxes, 151
green values, 22
Greenpeace, 157
Gregory, G, 137
Gross, Michael L, 110

Hall, Peter, 192
Hanson, Pauline, 45
health, 11
health sector policy, 176
and budgetary rationing, 78
and choice, 170; Netherlands, 175–6; United Kingdom, 174; United States, 174–5, 183
and communities of practice, 172
and financing of: Australia, 176–7; Netherlands, 175; United Kingdom, 173; United States, 174–5
and hospital provision: Australia, 176–7; United Kingdom, 174; United States, 174
and organised interests, 171
and profit motive, 178
and public-private relationship, 182–3
and publicness, 173, 176, 177, 178, 183, 184–5
and restrictions on efficiency, 78–9
and social responsibility, 183
and universality, 170; allocation of resources, 172; National Health Service (UK), 173–4; Netherlands, 175, 176; United Kingdom, 183
Heclo, H, 40, 45
Heidenheimer, A, 45
heritage effect, 10
Hollander, R, 158
Honaker, D, 102

hospital provision
and Australia, 176–7
and United Kingdom, 174
and United States, 174
Howard, John, 45, 55, 97–8, 111, 181
and symbolic politics, 4–5
Hudson, J, 199
Human Fertilisation and Embryology Act (UK, 1990), 113
Human Fertilisation and Embryology Authority (UK), 114–15, 116, 117
human relations, and public policy, 10–11
Hummel, R, 129
hybridisation, and value conflict, 30, 39

idealism, and public policy, 5
identity politics, 21
ideology
and political sociology, 18
and values, 13, 23–4
Immigration Act (UK, 1971), 104
immigration policy, and asylum seekers, 103–4; Australia, 105–6; United Kingdom, 104–5
implementation, 3
and behavioural change, 87
and nature of, 8
and policy values, 32
and public organisations, 193–5
in vitro fertilisation (IVF), 113–15
incentives
and instrument-related values, 29
and policy instruments, 88–9
incrementalism
and public policy, 205
and value conflict, 41
independence, 11
industrial policy, 5–6
Infertility Treatment Act (Australia, 1995), 117
Infertility Treatment Authority (Australia), 117
information technology, and public policy, 206
Inglehart, R, 18
Ingram, H, 8, 28, 88–9

institutionalism
  and policy change, 33–4, 190;
    bounded rationality, 34–5
  and public policy, 8
instrument-related values, 28–9
instrumental rationality, 43
integrated resource management, 160–1
interest-based theories, 2
interests
  and political sociology, 18
  and public policy, 15
internal markets
  and National Health Service (UK), 174
  and new public management, 136–7
international organisations
  and environmental governance, 165–7
  and public policy, 204
international trade, and liberalisation of, 75–7
Internet, and public policy, 206
interpretivism, and public policy, 7
Islam, 122
  and religious dress, 123
issue construction, 16
issue definition, 36
Italy, and abortion law and policy, 110

Japan
  and business regulation, 101
  and privatisation, telecommunications industry, 74, 75
  and public management, 128
  and welfare policy, 62–3
Jenkins-Smith, H, 16, 35, 36
Job, J, 102
Job Network (Australia), 82
John, Peter, 34
Jones, B, 35

Keating, Paul, 45
Kelly, J, 40
Kemp, D, 24
Kernaghan, Kenneth, 29
Kettl, D, 134
Kyoto Protocol, 166

labour markets
  and efficiency, 81
  and working hours, 81
Laham, Nicholas, 171
Langford, J, 137–8
Lasswell, Harold, and values, 7, 19
law, and environmental policy, 153–4
leadership, and new public management, 139
learning, and public policy, 203–4
legislatures, and policy change, 35
liberalism, and secularism, 122–3
Lindblom, C, 20
Linder, S, 170
Little, Graham, 206
local government, and policy cycling, 44
Lomborg, Bjorn, 150
Long-Range Trans-boundary Air Pollution, Convention on (LRTAP), 166
Lowe, S, 199
Lowi, Theodore, 52

McClure, Patrick, 55
Mackay, Hugh, 206
Major, John, 58
managerialism, and public management, 126–7; new public management, 131, 132
manufacturing, 6
March, J, 31, 120, 125
markets, and role of, 6
marriage, 11, 118
Marx, Karl, 198
May, Peter, 87
meaning, and public policy, 7, 16
media, as values brokers, 195–7
Medicare (Australia), 176–7
Memon, A, 161
Michael, E, 68
mission statements, 138
Moran, M, 22
motivation, and policy values, 23–4
multiculturalism, 45
multiple streams approach
  and issue definition, 36
  and policy change, 35, 36

mutual obligation, 26
  and Australian unemployment policy, 92–3
National Competition Policy (Australia), 158
National Environmental Policy Act (USA), 159
National Environmental Policy Plans (Netherlands), 157, 158–9
National Health and Medical Research Council (Australia), 117
National Health Service (UK), 173–4
National Park Service (USA), 156
national parks, 155–6
National Parks Commission (UK), 156
National Parks Services (Australia), 156
neo-liberalism, 18
  and welfare policy, 65
neoconservatism, 20
Netherlands
  and drug policy, 95–6
  and education, 182, 183
  and environmental policy, 158–9
  and health sector, 175–6
  and voluntary euthanasia, 112
  and water management, 162
neutrality
  and administrative values, 29
  and public management, 125, 130, 131, 132, 134, 138
new public management, 125
  as academic construct, 129
  and accountability, 134–5, 136, 141, 143
  and contradictions within, 129
  and delegitimating old order, 129
  and diversity in expression, 127
  and financial management, 135–7
  and flexibility, 135
  and hybridisation, 39
  and leadership, 139
  and nature of, 144
  and organisational culture, 129–30
  and origins of, 126–7
  and performance management, 135
  and politico-bureaucratic relationships, 130–4; Australia, 131, 132–3; Canada, 133–4;

New Zealand, 131, 133; politicisation, 143–4; special advisers, 132; United Kingdom, 131–2, 133
  and quasi-markets, 136–7
  and technicisation, 137
  and value conflicts, 130, 137–9, 143
New Zealand
  and efficiency-oriented reforms, 83
  and electoral reform, 83–4
  and integrated resource management, 160–1
  and new public management: financial management, 135; politico-bureaucratic relationships, 131, 133; public interest, 141–2
  and public service as profession, 141
  and welfare policy, 55–7
Nippon Telegraph and Telephone (NTT), 75
non-profit organisations, and organisational values, 82
Norman, R, 137
Northcote-Trevelyan report (UK), 126
Norway, and environmental policy, 165–6
Nozick, R, 18
nuclear power, 168

obligation
  as design value, 28
  and public policy, 47–8
  and social policy, 67
  and welfare policy, 53
  see also welfare policy
Olsen, J, 31, 125
Organisation for Economic Cooperation and Development (OECD), 155
organisational change, and policy cycling, 44
organisational culture, and new public management, 129–30
organisational values
  and public management, 124–5
  and regulatory change, 82
outcomes values, 27–8
outsourcing, and efficiency, 77–8

Paehlke, R, 147, 148, 166
Pakes, Francis, 113
Palley, Howard, 110
paradigms
  and commonality, 71
  and efficiency, 70
  and exclusion of alternatives, 150
  as governance mechanisms, 150
  and power, 71
  and public policy, 42–3
  and role of values within, 192–3
Pareto optimality, 48
Park, Ruth, 203
parliamentary systems, and advocacy coalition framework (ACF), 36
Parsons, W, 26
participation, as design value, 28
Pearson, Noel, 90
Pendleton Act (USA, 1883), 126
pension policy
  and Australia, 54
  and France, 62
  and Germany, 61
  and Japan, 63
  and New Zealand, 56
  and Sweden, 60
  and United Kingdom, 57
performance management, and new public management, 135
personal values, 5, 6
Peters, B, 170
Pfaff, William, 85
planning, and environmental policy, 152–3
policy change, 9–10
  and advocacy coalition framework (ACF), 35, 36–7
  and agenda, 35
  and bias, 41–4
  and bureaucracies, 35
  and casuistry, 37, 40–1
  and choice and universality, 171
  and cycling, 37, 44–6; backlashes, 45–6; flip-flops, 44
  and exclusion of alternatives: policy paradigms, 42–3; technicisation, 43–4
  and firewalls, 37, 38
  and hybridisation, 39
  and incrementalism, 41
  and legislatures, 35
  and multiple streams approach, 35, 36
  and rational choice models, 34–5, 36
  and structural separation, 38–9
  and theories of, 34–7
  and value conflicts, 33–4, 190–2
  and values analysis, 190–2
policy design, 26
  and choice and universality, 170–1
  and context, 87–8
  and policy instruments, 87–90
  and values-based component, 88
policy implementation, see implementation
policy instruments, 10
  and authority-based tools, 88
  and behavioural change, 88–90
  and capacity-based tools, 88
  and choice of, 28–9
  and hortatory tools, 88
  and incentives, 88–9
  and policy design, 87–90
  and regulatory theory, 90
  and sanctions, 88–9
  and symbolic tools, 88
  and tough/tender mindedness, 90–1, 106–7; asylum seekers, 103–6; business regulation, 98–102; criminal justice, 93–5; drug policy, 95–8; unemployment, 91–3
policy learning, 203–4
policy paradigms, 42–3
policy sciences, 19–21, 22
policy studies, and dual features of, 7
policy values
  and allocation of, 25–6
  and capture of personal values, 203
  and changes in, 21–2
  and classification of: administrative values, 29; design values, 28; instrument-related values, 28–9; outcomes values, 27–8
  and comparative approach, 30–1
  and contrasting pairs, 9

and definition of, 14
and functions of, 23; basis for choice, 24–5; motivation, 23–4
and identification of, 25–6
and importance of, 14
and incompatibility, 29–30
and management of, 30
and nature of, 13, 14, 202
and policy sciences, 19–21, 22
and political philosophy, 17–18
and political sociology, 18–19
and political values, 14
and role in policy analysis, 15–16
and tensions between, 31
and value of perspective, 30
see also value conflicts; values; values analysis
political philosophy, 17–18
political psychology, 23
political sociology, 18–19
political values, and policy values, 14, 23–4
politicisation, and public management, 143–4
politics
and public policy, 52
and symbolic politics, 4–5
and values, 4
Pollitt, C, 128–9
pollution control, 156–7
positivism, and policy studies, 7
post-empiricist policy analysis, 199–200
postmodern world, and public policy, 206
power, and paradigms, 71
Pratchett, L, 39
pre-implantation genetic diagnosis (PGD), 116–17
presidential systems, and advocacy coalition framework (ACF), 36
price-based instruments, and environmental policy, 150–1
Primary Care Trusts (UK), 174
principled decision-making
and abortion law and policy, 109–12
and child support policy, 118–21
and public policy, 108–9

and reproductive technologies, 113–18
and voluntary euthanasia, 112–13, 121
privatisation, and telecommunications industry, 74–5
see also efficiency
public administration
and public policy, 8
and values, 11
see also public management
public agencies, and policy implementation, 193–5
public choice theory, 2, 6, 85
and deregulation of trade, 76
and efficiency, 72
and public management, 126
public interest, and public management, 141–3
public management
and accountability, 141, 143
and Anglo-American tradition, 127; diversity among, 128
and future of, 144–5
and managerial theory, 126–7
and neutrality, 125, 130, 131, 132, 134, 138
and organisational values, 124–5
and political context, 125
and politico-bureaucratic relationships, 127–8, 130–4; Australia, 131, 132; Canada, 133–4; New Zealand, 131, 133; politicisation, 143–4; special advisers, 132; United Kingdom, 131–2, 133
and public administration tradition, 126
and public choice theory, 126
and public interest, 141–3
and public policy, 124
and public service as profession, 139–42; accountability, 140; Australia, 141–2; institutional relationships, 140; New Zealand, 141; professional identity, 139–40; United Kingdom, 140–1; United States, 140

public management (*Continued*)
  and *Rechsstaat* tradition, 127
  see also new public management
public opinion
  and abortion law and policy, 111
  and asylum seekers, 103, 105, 106
  and criminal justice, 94
  and drug policy, 96, 98
  and environmental policy, 167
  and voluntary euthanasia, 113
public organisations, and policy implementation, 193–5
public ownership, and values-balancing capacity of, 75
public policy
  and aims of, 3
  and allocation of values, 25–6
  and analytical approaches to, 16–17
  and behavioural change, 87
  and compromises over, 203
  and deep structure of, 186
  and design of, 26
  and ethical values, 108–9
  and future of, 205–6
  and idealism, 5
  and incrementalism, 205
  and institutionalist perspective, 8
  and international realm, 204
  and interpretivist perspective, 7
  and learning, 203–4
  and nature of, 7, 205
  and obligation/entitlement relationship, 67
  and ordering reality, 32
  and personal values, 5, 6
  and policy values, 14
  and political process, 3
  and politics, 52
  in postmodern world, 206
  as process, 24
  and public administration, 8
  and religious values, 122–3
  and social change, 121
  and symbolic politics, 4–5
  and traditional explanation of, 186
  and values, 1–2, 186, 187, 202
public sector
  and efficiency, 70–1
  and outsourcing, 77–8

Public Service Act (Australia, 1999), 132
publicness
  and education, 178, 182, 183, 184–5
  and health sector, 173, 176, 177, 178, 183, 184–5
Pusey, M, 18

rational choice theory, 2
  and policy change, 34–5, 36
Reagan, Ronald, 59
Rechsstaat tradition, and public management, 127
redistribution
  and fairness, 50
  and social policy, 66
  see also welfare policy
Reference Group on Welfare Reform, 55
reflexive prescription, 200–1
Regional Forest Agreements (Australia), 163–5
regulation, and business regulation, 98–102
regulatory agencies, 125
  and environmental policy: national parks, 155–6; pollution control, 156–7
regulatory theory, 90, 99
Rein, M, 19–20, 22, 30, 33, 37
religion
  and abortion law and policy, 109, 110, 112
  and reproductive technologies, 113–14
  and resurgence of religious values, 122–3
  and voluntary euthanasia, 113
  and weakening hold of, 121
rent-seekers, 6
reproductive technologies, 113–15
  and pre-implantation genetic diagnosis (PGD), 116–17
  and stem cell research, 115–16
  and *in vitro* fertilisation, 113–15
Resource Assessment Commission (Australia), 160
Resource Management Act (New Zealand, 1991), 160–1
responsibility, as outcomes value, 28

responsiveness, 11
  and administrative values, 29
  as design value, 28
Rezsohazy, R, 14
Richardson, H, 30
Rochefort, D, 16
Rokeach, M, 23, 27
Romzek, B, 140
Rose, R, 39
  and the heritage effect, 10
Roussel Uclaf, 121

Sabatier, P, 16, 35, 36, 199
Sagoff, Mark, 108, 123
sanctions
  and instrument-related values, 29
  and policy instruments, 88–9
Sarbanes-Oxley Act (USA), 99
Sarkozy, Nicolas, 84–5
Savoie, D, 40
Sax, Sydney, 171
Schattschneider, E, 41
Schneider, A, 8, 28, 88–9
science
  and environmental policy, 151–2
  and regulation of, 109;
    pre-implantation genetic
    diagnosis (PGD), 116–17;
    reproductive technologies,
    113–15; stem cell research,
    115–16
secularism, and liberalism, 122–3
security, as outcomes value, 28
self-determination, as outcomes
  value, 28
self-interest, 1
Sen, Amartya, 20
Singapore, and public
  management, 128
Singapore Public Service, 128
single parents, 11
social change, and public policy, 121
social constructivism
  and fairness, 51
  and policy interventions, 89
  and public policy, 16
social movements, 19
social policy, 26
  and fairness, 47, 66

  and obligation/entitlement
    relationship, 67
  and redistribution, 66
social responsibility, and choice and
  universality, 183
special advisers, 132–3
spin, 20–1, 197
stem cell research, 115, 116–18
Stern report, 150
Stone, Deborah, 20, 50, 70
structural separation
  and environmental policy, 155;
    national parks, 155–6; pollution
    control, 156–7
  and value conflict, 30, 38–9
structuralism, 18
sustainable development, 154
  and giving the environment a
    'voice', 161–3; conservationists,
    162–3; returning resources, 162;
    role of citizens, 162; role of the
    state, 161–2; water management,
    162
  and integrating mechanisms,
    157; environmental impact
    assessments (EIAs), 159; integrated
    resource management, 160–1;
    strategic planning, 157, 158–9;
    structural coordination, 157–8
  and international environmental
    governance, 165–7
  and resolving value conflicts, 163;
    Regional Forest Agreements
    (Australia), 163–5
  and structural separation: national
    parks, 155–6; pollution control,
    156–7
Sweden
  and drug policy, 95–6
  and environmental policy, 162
  and welfare policy, 60
Swedish Commission on Narcotic
  Drugs, 96
symbolic politics, 4–5

Tampa incident, and asylum seekers,
  105–6
tax-collecting agencies, and business
  regulation, 100, 101, 102

taxation, and welfare policy, 64–5
technicisation, 43–4
   and new public management, 137
   and professional paradigms, 150
   and value conflict, 30
Teelken, C, 182
telecommunications industry, and privatisation, 74–5
tenderness, 10
   and instrument-related values, 29
Thacher, D, 19–20, 30, 33, 37
Thatcher, Margaret, 57, 179, 180
Therapeutic Goods Administration (Australia), 111–12
toughness, 10
   and instrument-related values, 29
transport industry, and deregulation, 73–4
Trintingant, Marie, 93–4
trust, as design value, 28

Uehling, Greta, 103
unemployment, and tough/tender policies, 91–3
unemployment benefits
   and Australia, 54–5
   and France, 62
   and New Zealand, 56
   and United Kingdom, 58
   and United States, 59
United Kingdom
   and business regulation, 100
   and child support policy, 119
   and drug policy, 97
   and education, 179–80
   and health sector, 183; hospital provision, 174; National Health Service (UK), 173–4
   and immigration policy, asylum seekers, 103, 104–5
   and national parks, 156
   and new public management: financial management, 135; politico-bureaucratic relationships, 131–2, 133
   and pre-implantation genetic diagnosis (PGD), 116–17
   and privatisation, telecommunications industry, 75
   and public service as profession, 140–1
   and stem cell research, 115, 116
   and *in vitro* fertilisation policy, 113, 114–15
   and welfare policy, 57–8
United Nations, 204
   Framework Convention on Climate Change, 166
United States
   and abortion law and policy, 110–11
   and business regulation, 99
   and criminal justice, 94, 107
   and deregulation, airline industry, 73
   and education, 180
   and environmental impact assessments, 159
   and health sector, 174–5, 183; hospital provision, 174
   and national parks, 156
   and new public management, 127, 129
   and pollution control, 156–7
   and public service as profession, 140
   and religious values, 122
   and stem cell research, 116
   and voluntary euthanasia, 112
   and welfare policy, 58–9
United States Supreme Court, and *Roe v Wade*, 110–11
universality, 11, 170
   and allocation of resources, 172
   as design value, 28
   and education, 170, 178; Netherlands, 182, 183; United Kingdom, 179–80
   and health sector, 170; National Health Service (UK), 173–4; Netherlands, 175, 176; United Kingdom, 183
   and policy change, 171
   and policy design, 170–1
   and social responsibility, 183
   and welfare policy, 67
universities, and impact of efficiency, 82
urban planning, and environmental policy, 152–3

value conflicts, 2, 10
  and advocacy coalition framework (ACF), 36
  and capitalism, 198
  and choice and universality, 171
  and the environment, 147–8
  and environmental policy, resolution of, 163
  and exclusion of alternatives: policy paradigms, 42–3; technicisation, 43–4
  and firewalls, 38
  and incompatibility of values, 29–30
  and institutional structures, 33
  and management of, 30, 37; bias, 41–4; casuistry, 37, 40–1; cycling, 37, 44–6; firewalls, 37; hybridisation, 39; incrementalism, 41; structural separation, 38–9
  and new public management, 137–9
  and policy change, 33–4, 190–2
  and public management, 125, 143
  and sources of, 36–7
values
  and analytical use of, 3–4
  and capitalism, 198
  and capture of, 203
  and changes in, 21–2
  and compromises over, 2
  and functional nature of, 14
  and identification of, 8–9
  and ideology, 13, 23–4
  and incommensurability of, 9–10
  and interests, 15
  and media as values brokers, 195–7
  and nature of, 14
  and paradigms, 192–3
  and personal values, 5, 6
  and political process, 3
  and public policy, 1–2, 186, 187, 202
  and symbolic politics, 4–5
  see also policy values
values analysis, 3–4, 8
  and applicability of, 187–8
  and comparative policy analysis, 188–90
  and connecting theory and practice, 199–202; avoiding assumptions about values, 201–2; descriptive accounts, 201; evaluation, 200; reflexive prescription, 200–1
  and environmental values, 197–9
  and fairness, 52–3
  and identifying values, 8–9
  and media as values brokers, 195–7
  and policy change, 190–2
  and policy implementation and public organisations, 193–5
  and role of values in paradigms, 192–3
  and utility of, 12
  and welfare policy, 64, 66
vectors, and advancing new values, 72
Vickers, G, 42
Virgin Blue Airlines, 74
voluntary euthanasia, *see* euthanasia, voluntary
voting behaviour, 24

Wanna, J, 40
Warnock, Dame Mary, 114, 123
Warnock Report (UK, 1984), 114
water allocation
  and efficiency, 81
  and environmental policy, 162
Weber, Max, 43
Weissert, C, 41
welfare economics, 20
welfare policy, 10
  and Australia, 53–5
  and classification of welfare states, 52
  and fairness, 52, 64–5
  and France, 61–2
  and Germany, 60–1
  and Japan, 62–3
  and 'movement to the right', 65–6
  and neo-liberalism, 65
  and New Zealand, 55–7
  and policy cycling, 44
  and Sweden, 60
  and taxation, 64–5
  and United Kingdom, 57–8
  and United States, 58–9
  and universalism, 67
  and values analysis, 64, 66

Welfare to Work (Australia), 93
whaling, 166
whistleblowers, 196
Wilberforce, William, 205
Wildavsky, A, 40
Wilderness Society, 157
Wilenski, Peter, 144
Wilson, James Q, 97
Wingfield, M, 39
women's movement, and abortion law and policy, 110

Work for the Dole (Australia), 92–3
workfare, and United States, 59
working class politics, 18
working hours, 81
World Trade Organisation (WTO), 76, 204
WorldCom, 99

Yanow, D, 7

Zahariadis, N, 34